GREATEST GAMES
EVERTON

GREATEST GAMES
EVERTON

THE TOFFEES
FIFTY FINEST MATCHES

JIM KEOGHAN

First published by Pitch Publishing, 2017

Pitch Publishing
A2 Yeoman Gate
Yeoman Way
Worthing
Sussex
BN13 3QZ
www.pitchpublishing.co.uk
info@pitchpublishing.co.uk

ISBN 978-1-78531-314-1

Typesetting and origination by Pitch Publishing

Printed and bound in India by Replika Press Pvt. Ltd.

Contents

Dedication

To Nicky

For Everything

Foreword

By Kevin Ratcliffe

WHEN you look back over the history of our club, it's amazing to think just how many great moments there have been. Titles won, FA Cups brought home, European adventures. We might moan our lot now and then, but we are lucky as Evertonians to follow a club that has experienced so much. There are fans of other teams whose idea of 'greatness' can't reach the levels enjoyed by Everton since the club was founded back in 1878.

Take a glance at Everton's history, and it's clear that every decade has given the fans something to cherish. Sometimes it's been silverware, other times it's been a hero to lionise, and then there have been those occasions when we have produced performances of dazzling brilliance just for the simple joy of it.

I've been fortunate to experience Everton's greatness as both a player and a fan. I know what it feels like to be out there on the pitch living it and out in the terraces or the stands watching on.

When I was a player, I was very lucky to not just be part of some of the great moments included in this book but also to represent the club at the time as captain too. To lift silverware as Everton captain was a huge honour for me and something I never failed to appreciate.

I played at a time when we had so many great games, it's probably hard to sort which ones go in and which ones don't make it. Moments like destroying Manchester United 5–0, winning the FA Cup against Watford or the night that so many of us remember: the semi-final victory over the mighty Bayern Munich – arguably the greatest game to have ever taken place at Goodison.

Back then, we had a side that was capable of winning anything. We used to go into games thinking, not would we win – that was a given – but rather how many would we win by. It was a great time to be a Blue.

But nothing lasts forever, and, as the history of the club has illustrated, great moments and great periods can be fleeting.

We've had times, like the era of Dixie Dean in the 1920s and 1930s, the era of Catterick in the 1960s and the era of Kendall in the 1980s, that have been magnificent. But we have also had the dry spells, the difficult eras, the times when nothing seems to be going right.

Times like the 1950s, when the club was relegated and then struggled when promoted; the 1970s, when promise turned to frustration and we had to suffer in Liverpool's shadow; and the 1990s, when it felt like relegation was constantly at the back of our minds.

But we've tended to bounce back. There is a sense of resilience about Everton that always gives the fans hope. And that in itself is something great, something to celebrate.

When you look all the way back to 1888, when the Football League first kicked off, and run your eyes over those chosen to join that first elite, it's amazing how few have enjoyed the kind of lasting success that Everton have managed. Most have endured more than a century of frustration. By contrast, Everton have managed to punctuate that long stretch with times of unadulterated joy and undeniable class.

And even when times have been dark, maddening or mediocre, the club has always managed to rustle up a little bit of magic here and there. That's what this book proves. Whether it be knocking Manchester United out of the FA Cup while in the Second Division, winning the FA Cup in the grim 1990s or qualifying for the Champions League against all the odds under David Moyes, Everton have always been capable of finding that bit of sunshine when skies are grey.

Ours is a grand old team to play for and a grand old team to support. And, if you don't know your history: then here it is. This is the story of Everton, told through the prism of 50 wonderful moments. It's the club's story delivered by those who were there at the time: the players, the writers, the fans. The story of how a small church team from Liverpool became one of the greats of the English game.

Introduction

I N late March 2014, on an overcast, yet clammy spring afternoon, my four-year-old son and I navigated our way past the delicatessens, the fusion cuisine restaurants, the pop-up Iberian cheese markets of south-west London and headed towards Craven Cottage.

This was not the first game I had planned for Jamie. That should have been at Goodison. But cost, ticket availability and an unwillingness to take a four-year-old on a 600-mile round trip meant that, like many an offspring from our club's wide diaspora, he would first see the Blues on foreign soil.

It was the business end of the first Martinez season (or, as it's otherwise known, the 'good Martinez season'). Flying high in the league, winning with ease and playing attractive, attack-minded football, this was an Everton side that seemed to promise so much.

After making our way through the unerringly polite Fulham fans (all of whom appeared to be eating hot dogs), we took our seats amongst our own, savouring the sights and sounds of the only part of the ground that appeared to contain any atmosphere.

As a jaded Blue, who in 35 years of following the club thought he had experienced pretty much everything football had to offer, I had sort of accepted that defining experiences were a thing of the past (or *my* past at least). But I was wrong.

On that unremarkable afternoon, one on which an accomplished Everton side easily dealt with relegation-threatened Fulham, emerging 3–1 victors, I got to see the game through my son's eyes: the excitement of the players coming out, the joy of being able to sing and shout amongst other fans, the delight of seeing your team score and win.

It felt new, novel *and* defining. It was, in short, a magical experience.

At the end of the 90, as we made our way once again through their fans, who remained happy and polite despite an anaemic performance and the prospect of almost certain relegation (perhaps those hot dogs had a palliative quality?), I felt happy in a way that was almost unrecognisable to me as an Evertonian – a sense of untarnished joy, with no undercurrent of anxiety.

But, as wonderful as I felt, I am almost certain that no other Blue felt the same (unless they'd also been on the hot dogs). For them, it was simply an away win. Unquestionably a good one – but nothing to write home about.

And that's the problem when it comes to defining a great game. So much of what we consider 'great' is wrapped up in how we experience a match. I loved that Fulham match, and to me it is my happiest moment as a Blue. But I doubt it would make the list of the top 500 Everton matches of all time.

The idea of what makes a 'Great Game' is something that has consumed me over the course of writing this book. The knee-jerk answer is one that yields tangible success. It's the matches when titles were won, FA Cups lifted, when a European trophy was brought home. And that is true. There is something undeniably special about opening the trophy cabinet and adding another trinket to the collection.

Because so few clubs, certainly in modern football, ever get to bring home silverware, it's important to recognise Everton's achievements. To win the league nine times, to hold aloft five FA Cups and to win a European trophy are markers of success that need to be celebrated. In football's long history, we are amongst the lucky few to have periodically enjoyed success at the highest level.

So you can put a big tick next to silverware.

But what happens if silverware isn't on the agenda? In recent years, as football has changed, tangible success has become considerably harder to come by. Since the inauguration of the Premier League, English football has become a closed shop to a degree never previously seen. With the exception of the Leicester City aberration and Blackburn Rovers' cash-fuelled tilt at the top, just a handful of clubs have claimed the title since 1992.

In the FA Cup, the modern elite has enjoyed just as tight a dominance, with, again, only two clubs – Portsmouth and Wigan Athletic – breaking the stranglehold that the likes of Chelsea, Manchester United and Arsenal have had on the trophy.

Only the League Cup (generally unloved by the elite of late) has offered any chance of silverware to lesser lights. But even here, although the competition has enjoyed a much more diverse number of winners, with clubs such as Swansea City, Birmingham City and Middlesbrough claiming the cup over the past 25 years, they are still outnumbered by the big guns.

Everton, long an elite club themselves, by accident and design forwent membership of the crème de la crème during the 1990s and never got it back. As such, they joined the swollen ranks of those for whom tangible success is consistently out of reach.

Because of this, the definition of 'success' alters in the closing stages of the book. It embraces different kinds of achievements, ones thought beyond the modern capabilities of the club, such as qualifying for the Champions League, reaching the FA Cup Final and actually beating Liverpool. These matches might not seem great by historic standards – but, in a modern context, and for the modern Evertonian, they have still mattered.

But 'success' isn't everything. Games can be great for other reasons too.

Sometimes a game is simply magnificent on its own merit. There have been several occasions in the club's history when, without warning, a match of outstanding quality has taken place (usually against Sunderland for some reason).

The need to win sometimes robs fans of the simple enjoyment that football played well can provide. Luckily for us Evertonians, because we follow a club so well versed in the need to play the game 'well', instances of such quality have been relatively commonplace.

Other times, a game can be 'great' because of its emotional intensity. As an Evertonian who followed the club avidly in the 1990s, I remember the narrow escapes from the jaws of death against Wimbledon in 1994 and Coventry City in 1998 as being great occasions. They weren't matches you'd want to go through again: they weren't enjoyable, and had the results gone differently, they would unquestionably have been awful games to attend. But the results went Everton's way, and so those attending got to sit through matches of incredible emotional intensity, where the future of the club was balanced on a knife edge. There was no trophy at stake, no title to claim, no terrace hero to lionise. But at the final whistle you knew you'd witnessed something momentous.

In putting these games together, it struck me that what you also have is something more than just a succession of snapshots (as illuminating as they can be). The story of Everton is revealed too.

The vast span of Evertonia is on show: from humble beginnings (when the St Domingo's church team first started kicking a ball around a park) to today, when Everton stand on the precipice of an historic move away from Goodison and the club's possible re-entry into the elite of English football. Through the games looked at, each one momentous in its own right, Everton's grand narrative is illustrated: the ups and downs, the highs and lows, the good times and the Mike Walker times.

We all have our favourites from this long history, and unquestionably some of yours might not be here. Notions of what constitutes a 'great' game are too subjective for a complete consensus to be achieved. Some of those I have loved and enjoyed didn't make the cut.

But these are my 50. You might not agree with all of them. But you can't deny they (mostly) show our club at its best.

UTFT

v Bolton Wanderers 2–1

19 November 1887
FA Cup First Round (Third Replay)
Anfield. Attendance: 8,000

Everton: Smalley, Dick, Dobson, Higgins, Gibson, Weir, Izatt, Farmer, Goudie, Watson, Briscoe

Bolton Wanderers: Unsworth, McKernan, Parkinson, Bullough, Steel, Roberts, Davenport, Brogan, Parkinson, Owen, Howarth

Referee: W. Stacey

In The Beginning

I N the winter of 1878, the parishioners of St Domingo's Methodist Church, a chapel in the district of Everton, first began kicking a ball around the local park, unaware of the momentous step they had just taken.

Back then, football was on the rise in England, particularly in Liverpool, which quickly became the epicentre of the late-Victorian football boom.

Links to local churches were not uncommon at the time. Of the 112 football clubs in the city, 25 had similar religious origins.

In its early days, this church team largely confined itself to exhibition matches against local parishes, which were described by Thomas Keates, an early biographer of Everton FC, as being played in 'a very crude character'. Think low-rent Sunday league, but with better moustaches and bigger shorts.

But, quickly, the team began to develop a reputation as one of the better footballing sides, and as local appetite for the sport grew, which it did exponentially in the 1870s and 1880s, more and more people were drawn to watch their games.

In an effort to extend inclusivity and capture this growing interest, a decision was made to change the club's name, and, in November 1879, Everton Football Club came into the world.

In the 1880s, this new club expanded rapidly. With a forward-thinking management committee, Everton understood the way in which football was changing. As the decade progressed, it was clear that amateurism, which had been the dominant model since the sport's emergence, was less able to yield success. What clubs who aimed high needed was paid professionals, and the best way to achieve the necessary income to provide this was to develop stadiums and bring in investment.

After a few years playing on Stanley Park and a financially unproductive season at Priory Road, in 1884 Everton were able to engineer a move to a field on Anfield Road, just outside the city's boundaries.

The move was hugely advantageous for the club. In return for unencum- bered use, Everton merely had to keep the existing walls in good repair, pay the taxes, and either pay a small amount of rent or make a donation each year to the Stanley Hospital in the name of the owner, Mr Orrell.

Once they were ensconced in Anfield, the facilities were improved, capacity increased and Everton began to blossom financially – benefitting from rising attendances and gate receipts. They could now afford to compete at a higher level by bringing in those paid professionals.

Illustrative proof of how this benefitted the club was Everton's dominance of the Liverpool District Cup, which the club won three times in the mid-1880s. Everton were rapidly outpacing former peers, such as Earlestown and St Peter's.

But, as good as they were locally, the club still lacked national recognition. That was to change in the latter half of the 1880s. Everton's proto-professionalism and local dominance led them to compete in the FA Cup for the first time in 1886.

Disappointingly, the club's first taste of the competition was not a roaring success. They were drawn against Glasgow Rangers in the first round, and when the Scots arrived at Anfield the home side discovered that they had an ineligible player in their ranks and were compelled to forfeit the tie and play a friendly instead (which Everton lost 1–0).

After that inglorious beginning, Everton got a second bite the following year, when they were drawn against Bolton Wanderers in the opening round.

Bolton's relationship with Everton was an interesting one, representing a useful measure of the Anfield club's progress. Everton had played them a few times over the preceding decade and, after some hefty beatings early on, had gradually improved (for the most part) against what had traditionally been a better-organised and stronger club.

But, regardless of the improvement, Bolton were still widely seen as the favourites, and viewed their county compatriots as a lesser entity. Despite the fixtures that the two clubs had played against each other, Bolton had never deigned to invite Everton to their ground at Pikes Lane. It took the FA to make that happen.

The match captured the imagination of the local fans, and over 700 of them made the journey to Bolton on what was the first recorded football special excursion train ever to leave the city. It was a travelling mass that helped swell the attendance to around 5,000 people.

Frustratingly for those who had journeyed to support Everton, the game ended in defeat for the away side, a narrow 1–0 loss.

But salvation was at hand! The FA committee, having checked the home side's line-up, discovered that the Bolton executive had neglected to register one of their players in time for the contest, and therefore he was not eligible to play. The committee declared the game void and ordered it to be replayed at Anfield two weeks later.

The return match, which was watched by a crowd of over 8,000 people, ended 2–2, with Everton's goals coming from Farmer and Watson. This draw meant a third game back at Pikes Lane a fortnight later. The closely fought encounter was now attracting the attention of the FA executive in London, who dispatched their president, Francis Marindin, to officiate.

Another draw, this time 1–1, meant a third replay back at Anfield. Cumulatively, nearly 20,000 people had witnessed these matches by this point. It was raising Everton's profile, not just for how long it was taking to settle the tie but also for how well they had played against opponents who were expected to comfortably beat them.

On a bright, sunny afternoon, 3,000 people (8,000 by half-time) lined up to watch this epic cup tie conclude.

Everton got quickly into their stride and were rewarded almost instantly. 'Izatt centred,' reported the *Liverpool Daily Post,* 'and to the increased delight of the Evertonians, Goudie drew first blood by a rattling shot. Great cheering resulted, as two minutes had scarcely elapsed from the start.'

The celebrating that followed the goal had barely dissipated when Everton got a second, as the *Post* continued:

'Another start from the middle of the field was made ... The ball was worked in front of the visitors' goal, and Watson was seen to let fly and bang went the ball past Unsworth, amidst tremendous cheering. Two goals in less than five minutes looked bad for the Wanderers.'

This breathtaking start rocked Bolton, and for a time they struggled to contain the rampant home forwards. But, frustratingly, Everton were unable to further their lead. As the half progressed, Bolton began to see more of the ball and on a few occasions could have pegged Everton back. As it was, no further goals arrived, and as the sides went in at half-time the scoreline remained 2–0.

In the second period, Bolton appeared better composed and gave the home side much more of a game. Although Everton were resolute in defence, Bolton kept applying the pressure. With a quarter of an hour to go, the breakthrough came when Davenport (from an offside position) smashed the ball past Smalley to get the visitors back into the tie.

Emboldened, Bolton laid siege to the Everton box. But, despite their efforts, that would be as good as it got for the Wanderers. Everton parked the bus for the remainder of the game and resolutely shut out any attempts to find an equaliser. In a hard-fought encounter, and hours of football, Everton had finally emerged victorious.

It had been the first time, in the brief history of the contest, that four games had been required to settle the issue of an FA Cup tie. Everton had made headlines.

But the club would go no further in that year's competition. In the next round, they were drawn against the mighty Preston North End, one of the strongest clubs in the country. On this occasion the favourites triumphed, beating Everton 6–0.

Not that the scoreline mattered anyway. Even if the men from Anfield had won, it wouldn't have counted, as the club was soon under investigation for its own irregularities.

Perhaps disgruntled at their loss, still angry at Everton's complaints regarding player eligibility or irritated that their journey home from Anfield had been marred when their horse-drawn carriage had careered out of control, leading several players to jump for safety, Bolton questioned the legality of the Everton side, arguing that there were irregularities with the registration process.

The FA investigated and ruled in favour of Bolton. Everton were suspended from the competition and Bolton reinstated. For their efforts, they were then satisfyingly battered 9–1 by their Lancashire rivals Preston.

Although Everton's FA Cup 'run' that year ended ingloriously, they had still caused headlines and made others sit up and take notice of what was happening at Anfield. Not only had the club held and then beaten one of the strongest sides in the country, they'd also consistently drawn in sizeable crowds. The four games had been watched by tens of thousands of spectators, the largest cumulative crowd to watch two sides compete in the competition to date.

As football began to develop further, and the idea of a national league gathered supporters, being a competent side that could attract thousands through the gate began to matter. Everton were getting it right just when it mattered most.

v Accrington 2–1

8 September 1888
Football League Division One
Anfield. Attendance: 12,000

Everton: Smalley, Dick, Ross, Holt, Jones, Dobson, Fleming, Lewis, Chadwick, Waugh, Farmer

Accrington: Horne, Stevenson, McLellan, Haworth, Pemberton, Wilkinson, Lofthouse, Bonar, Holden, Chippendale, Kirkham

Referee: J. Bentley

FL12

IT started with just 12. A dozen trailblazers striking out to create what would become the greatest football league in the world (at least until the Premier League ruined the top flight with its orgy of consumption, its vapid razzmatazz and its Jamie Carragher).

Saturday, 8 September 1888 represented a watershed moment in English football. After decades of tournaments, exhibition matches and cup competitions, the game would finally become structured, better organised and more recognisable as the sport that we love and loathe in equal measure today.

For those such as Everton, who formed part of that inaugural band of brothers, the creation of the Football League marked the culmination of a journey that had taken them from knockaround kickabouts down the local park to becoming the elite of the fastest-growing sport in the country.

Why Everton had been chosen while others bypassed was in no small part attributable to the club's hunger to embrace professionalism.

Despite efforts by the FA to uphold the amateur ethos, including the fining or suspending of any clubs who were caught offering players financial reward, in 1885 professionalism had been legalised (as the FA, shaken by threats issued by northern clubs that they would establish a rival football authority, accepted a practice that was widely in illegitimate use anyway).

Throughout, the impetus for this change had largely come from teams of the north-west, specifically those based in Lancashire, who saw that success was there for the taking for those willing to pay for the best.

By accepting this reality, Everton surged ahead of local rivals. The club, according to their biographer, Thomas Keats, 'followed the light'. They sensed the way that football was travelling and took the necessary path. It's telling that former peers that stayed true to amateurism, such as Stanley, Burscough and Earlestown, would fade into obscurity, while Everton thrived in the new football.

The club's embracing of professionalism, combined with Anfield's development and Everton's impressive competitive performances against the likes of Bolton Wanderers (in the FA Cup), Derby County and West Bromwich Albion, caught the eye of one William McGregor, a committee member at Aston Villa and the driving force behind the creation of England's first national competitive league.

Concerned at the disparity in attendances between cup matches and friendlies (the former being much more popular), and aware that clubs who employed expensive professionals needed a guaranteed list of attractive fixtures rather than a haphazard collection of games, McGregor sought to ape what had occurred in county cricket by creating a system of regular competitive matches involving the top clubs, centred around a league structure.

In a move that would have echoes 100 years later when the Premier League was created, McGregor sent a letter to four of the biggest clubs in the country (Preston North End, Blackburn Rovers, West Brom and Bolton) inviting them to form a league where 'ten or twelve of the most prominent clubs in England' could 'combine to arrange home-and-away fixtures each season'. He also asked for their suggestions regarding which other clubs to invite.

If this was modern football, McGregor would probably have called his new venture something awful like 'FL12', 'Premier North' or the 'The Super League' (probably brought to you in partnership with Lloyds Cocaine Tooth Drops). But, luckily, he had a bit more class and so the invites went out for what would simply and elegantly become the Football League.

Were Everton a top club back then? The answer is 'probably not'. What success had been achieved had been local in nature. On a more national level, in the FA Cup, the men from Anfield hadn't progressed beyond the first round.

But that didn't really matter. What McGregor and others really wanted was potential, and that meant clubs from big cities that had embraced professionalism. Although the club was a surprise inclusion in the inaugural league and regarded as one of the weaker members, its prescient realisation that football was changing, that the Corinthian spirit was ebbing away, had given Everton an important advantage.

On the opening day of the season, Everton joined the esteemed ranks of football's elite to take part in a new league that also included Accrington, Aston Villa, Blackburn Rovers, Bolton, Burnley, Derby County, Notts County, Preston, Stoke, West Brom and Wolverhampton Wanderers.

Everton's first opponents were Accrington. Just a week earlier, they had been defeated in a friendly against Everton's great local rivals, Bootle. The need to match what Bootle had done only added to the pressure of that opening day. Around 12,000 turned up at Anfield to watch the match on a balmy September afternoon (although, due to the lateness of Accrington's arrival, it was nearer to 4.30pm before the teams actually kicked off).

Both sides employed variants of the 2–3–5 formation, the 'inverted pyramid'. It was attack minded but with the all-important centre-half (then positioned in the centre of midfield) crucial when the play pivoted.

Despite their potential role as league whipping boys, Everton started on the front foot:

'In the first half the Anfield crew had a decided advantage, and for a considerable time, play was almost entirely in their opponent's quarter. But the splendid defence of the Reds, assisted to some extent by the inaccurate shooting of the home forwards, prevented them from scoring,' reported the *Lancashire Evening Post*.

Profligate in front of goal and squandering superiority: could there be a more Everton way to start the club's Football League career?

As the half progressed, Everton's dominance lessened and Accrington grew into the game. When half-time arrived, with the scores level, the match had become a more even affair.

When play resumed after the break, the sides remained well balanced, and it was unclear who, if anyone, would make the first breakthrough. Fortunately for the majority of those who had come to watch, that particular honour would eventually fall to the home side.

Ten minutes into the half, after a brief spell of intense pressure, the ball fell to Farmer, who whipped in a cross that Fleming met to head home the club's first league goal.

It was a strike greeted by a 'tremendous cheering and waving of hands,' the *Accrington Observer* quaintly reported.

A few minutes after the opening goal, Everton were then the recipients of a huge slice of good fortune. After Horne had gone down low to save an effort by Chadwick, play was stopped when it was apparent that the Accrington keeper was in some discomfort. Ultimately, he had to leave the pitch when it became clear that he was in too much pain to continue.

It would be a further 77 years before a substitute was allowed to come on during a match in English football. In the game's early days, if a player got injured, that team just had to lump it. And so, McLellan went in goal and Haworth dropped back.

Everton faced ten men for the remainder of the match and, as is so often the case, capitalised on the numerical advantage when, not long after, Fleming got himself on the scoresheet once again, meeting a cross from Farmer to make it 2–0. At that point, the home side should have been cruising. But this, even then, was Everton, a club that never likes to take the easy path, never likes to give those watching too much comfort.

After the goal, observed the *Evening Post*, Accrington 'kept up an almost constant pressure, swarming round the Everton fortress with a persistence which was certainly deserving of better luck'.

Crosses rained in, chances came and went, and the away side even hit the bar. It was like watching a Roberto Martinez defence in action: porous to the point of saturation. Eventually, the pressure told and Everton's defence was breached, Holden beating Smalley with a free kick.

But, despite continued pressure from the ten men of Accrington, the home side held out and managed to (just about) register the club's first league win.

In less than a decade, Everton had come a long way. From that first kickabout on Stanley Park, this was now the biggest club in the city and, as part of the new professional elite, could proudly point to that win as proof that they merited their inclusion.

Although they were the victors that day, it was a win that initially didn't yield any points. Amazingly, it was not until a few weeks after the start of the season that it was established that teams would receive two points for a win and one for a draw.

In that inaugural campaign, which was won by an unbeaten Preston, Everton finished the season eighth, chalking up nine wins, two draws and 11 defeats. It might have been unspectacular, but 20 points from a debut campaign wasn't bad for a club widely seen as being slightly fortunate to have been there in the first instance.

It was enough to ensure that Everton would not need to apply for re-election, a fate that befell the bottom four of Burnley, Derby, Notts County and Stoke.

Reservations had existed, and doubt had hovered over Everton's inclusion. But the club had defied and answered the naysayers in the best way possible. Everton had taken to league football. And, in the years that followed, they would only make their inclusion all the more valid.

v Derby County 11–2

18 January 1890
FA Cup First Round
Anfield. Attendance: 10,000

Everton: Smalley, Hannah, Doyle, Kirkwood, Holt, Parry, Latta, Brady, Geary, Chadwick, Milward

Derby County: Bromage, Latham, Ferguson, Williamson, A. Goodall, Roulstone, Bakewell, Higgins, J. Goodall, Milarvie, Cooper

Referee: C. Crump

Cricket Scorelines

FOR all the emotional joy provided by a tight game that is won in the dying seconds, the sense of satisfaction that can be taken from a hard-fought scoreless draw, or the belief that a narrow, against-the-odds victory is one of the sweetest experiences to savour, or sometimes a one-sided beating in which the opposition is decimated, can be just what the fans want.

In Everton's long history, the club has put a fair few sides to the sword. There have been 9–1 batterings of Manchester City and Plymouth Argyle in the league, an 8–0 destruction of Wimbledon in the League Cup and a 10–0 stuffing of Finn Harps in the UEFA Cup (over two legs).

In the modern era (when defences are theoretically meant to be better), Everton have been less adept at handing out absolute kickings. That said, since the Premier League was ushered in, a fair few sides have had six put past them, and both Sunderland and Southampton have shipped seven against the Blues.

But when you're looking for the biggest scoreline, the game that saw not just the most goals scored but also the largest margin of victory, then you have to travel back to 1890 and Everton's first-round FA Cup tie.

Prior to that season, Everton's relationship with the competition had not been a particularly stellar one. The club's record stood as:

1871–1885: Did not take part
1886/87: Forfeited tie due to player irregularity
1887/88: Expelled for irregularities
1888/89: Did not take part

In the 1889/90 FA Cup, Everton were drawn in the first round against fellow Football League members Derby County. At the time, Everton were beginning to catch the eye as one of the more impressive clubs in the country.

After the rather average first season of competitive league football, which had been characterised by a haphazard selection policy that had seen 35 players used in just 22 games, Everton began to recruit with greater clarity, specifically to address the club's misfiring front line. In 1889, the stocky outside-right Alex Latta arrived from Dumbarton Athletic, the diminutive centre-forward Fred Geary came from Grimsby Town, and the free-scoring inside-forward Alex Brady was bought from Sunderland.

In Everton's second league campaign, these three, alongside winger Alf Milward and inside-left Edgar Chadwick (both of whom had been with the club in that first season), took the division by storm.

Everton were in the hunt for the title from the off, and at times produced some blistering attacking football, putting eight past Stoke City, seven past Aston Villa and five past Notts County. Geary in particular had proven to be a canny acquisition and would go on to end the season with 27 goals from just 20 games (in all competitions).

Prior to the tie, Everton sat second in the league, just behind Preston North End, the strongest team in the country. The club's manoeuvrings looked to have worked.

But the opposition that day were no slouches. Fifth in the league and in good form, there were few tougher sides in England for the men from Anfield to face. The draw had certainly not been kind to Everton.

The old and tired cliché 'it was a game of two halves' often gets trotted out when the play differs in character to any degree between each period. It's used as depressingly often as similar phrases such as when a professional centre-forward is described as 'knowing where the goal is', that, in adherence with the long-established rules of the sport, 'goals win games' or that a speedy winger is blessed with 'genuine pace' (as opposed to pace that is somehow artificially created).

Sometimes, though, clichés are applicable, and in this particular case, the head-to-head between Everton and Derby County really was 'a game of two halves'.

On a dull, overcast Saturday afternoon, the pitch slippery after an earlier downpour, the teams kicked off. Derby were instantly on top and within minutes had taken the lead through John Goodall. The away side pressed Everton during the opening exchanges and, on a couple of occasions, could have furthered their lead.

Although Everton were disjointed, after 15 minutes, they strung together a rare coherent attack and Geary levelled the scores. Undeterred by the home side scoring against the run of play, Derby roared back and, according to the *Liverpool Courier*, they 'could not be moved from their advantageous position'. Their pressure proved telling and, after half an hour, John Goodall restored their lead when he got on the end of Bakewell's cross.

Stirred into action, Everton ended the half the stronger of the two sides. They hit the bar twice as their dominance began to mount. Momentum seemed to be with them and, as the break beckoned, Derby were sucker-punched, courtesy of two quick goals from Milward (the left-winger could have had five in the first half but for a lad more luck and some better finishing).

At the break there was nothing to suggest what was to come. Derby had been impressive throughout the first period and were unfortunate to be going in trailing 3–2. But, whether those quick goals before half-time affected their confidence or perhaps they had expended too much energy harrying Everton, in the second period the visitors were blown away.

The turning point arrived 15 minutes into the half. A high shot by Brady should have been easily handled by Bromage in goal. But the Derby keeper opted to punch rather than catch, mistimed his effort and directed the ball into his own net via the bar. Two goals to the good, Everton began to play with exquisite fluency and County's edifice crumbled.

Kirkwood made it 5–2 soon after, before Geary got his second of the match with 15 minutes left. By this point in the game, Everton were virtually camped in the Derby half, as what fight the visitors had displayed disappeared.

With ten minutes remaining, the floodgates opened. Brady made it 7–2, Milward 8–2. Doyle then rampaged through the Derby lines (the crowd audibly laughing at the improbable sight) to make it 9–2.

But still Everton were not finished! In the closing minutes of the match, the prolific Geary had time to get his hat-trick and then his fourth of the game, this latter goal achieved while he was lying on the ground, so hopeless had the Derby defence become.

The final scoreline of 11–2 might not have been a fair one to Derby, but it nevertheless expressed how dangerous the Everton front line could be if given the time and space by a defence (even a talented one from the Football League).

After that hefty win, the club drew fellow Football League members Stoke in the next round and then did what modern Evertonians would expect Everton to do. Despite having dispatched the Potters 8–0 a few months earlier, and Stoke being both bottom of the league and seemingly unable to win a game, Everton went down 4–2 at the Victoria Ground. It was a game where profligacy by the away side combined with a sublime performance by the Stoke keeper conspired to ensure that the FA Cup was done for another year and Everton's disappointing relationship with the competition would continue.

Despite the exit, Everton had still enjoyed an impressive result against a decent Derby side. But how to judge that victory?

Big scorelines were not uncommon in the 1880s and 1890s, specifically in the FA Cup. Along with the mismatch of professional sides meeting amateur ones, tactically these were simpler times. Teams lined up with five (and sometimes six) in the forward line and only two (full-backs) in defence. The game as it was back then still had its roots in the sport that had emerged from the public schools of England, with its emphasis on attacking and dribbling, not defending (which had been seen as ungentlemanly).

On that same afternoon, Preston put six past Newton Heath (the precursor to Manchester United) and Bolton Wanderers beat the Northern Irish club Distillery 10–2. Later in the competition, Bolton battered Sheffield United 13–0, Blackburn Rovers dismantled Bootle 7–0 and Wolves put eight past Stoke.

Contextualised, perhaps putting seven past Sunderland and Southampton in the Premier League era is more impressive? Or better still, beating Southampton 8–0 in the early 1970s, a time when defending was particularly tight?

It's difficult to say which particular result is the most notable. Football has changed so much over the years that any meaningful comparison is largely redundant. There are too many variables to take into account, and so all you're really left with is absolutes. Eleven goals and a nine-goal winning margin, in any era, isn't something to be sniffed at.

What's more, in a competitive match, Everton had never reached those heights previously and would never reach those heights again. The vanquishing of Derby County on that grim Saturday afternoon, in goals alone, remains an apex that stands aloft in the long history of Everton FC.

v Burnley 2–3

14 March 1891
Football League Division One
Turf Moor. Attendance: 10,000

Everton: Jardine, McLean, Doyle, Lochhead, Holt, Parry, Latta, Brady, Geary, Chadwick, Milward

Burnley: Kaye, Walker, Lang, McFettridge, Spiers, Stewart, Haresnape, Bowes, Nicol, Marr, Hill

Referee: C. Hughes

The First Kings of Anfield

AFTER exiting at the hands of Stoke City in the FA Cup, Everton at least had the title to concentrate upon.

As the 1889/90 season had come to a close, the league had become a three-horse race between Everton, Blackburn Rovers and Preston North End. Preston were the favourites. They were the so-called 'Invincibles', the side that had won the 'Double' during the previous season and gone through that particular campaign without losing. They were *the* team to beat.

Although Everton had been pushing Preston hard, the defeat against Stoke in the FA Cup seemed to precipitate a slight wobble. The side dropped vital points during the run-in, with a loss against Accrington proving particularly costly.

Despite this (with Blackburn proving unable to maintain the pace), Everton still pushed North End to the wire and came within a whisker of claiming the club's first title, finishing second, just two points behind Preston. As disappointing as this was, comfort could be taken at Anfield that a warning shot had been fired across the bow of the 'Invincibles' by the Blues.

Although, in this instance, the 'Blues' is too premature a term. The colouring so synonymous with Everton (royal blue shirt/white shorts) was still some way off. Since its foundation, the club had experimented with a variety of different kits and colours, including blue and white stripes, pink and white halves, and black with a scarlet sash. As the 1890/91 season opened, Everton were resplendent in salmon pink shirts and navy shorts.

Everton (the Salmon Pinks?) started the following campaign in blistering form, taking 13 points from a possible 14 over the course of the first seven games. It was a run that included 5–0 demolitions of Wolves and Bolton Wanderers and a 7–0 annihilation of Derby County. Everton took the top spot, a position that was rarely relinquished.

After stumbling slightly in the autumn, and briefly giving the chasing pack hope that the league leaders had lost their way, Everton rediscovered that early form over the winter. It was a run that saw goals spread right across the front line, with the likes of Geary, Brady, Milward and Chadwick all contributing.

But would Everton have enough this time to make it over the line? The fans would have an agonising wait to find out.

The winter that year was an exceptionally cold one. Towards the end of November, a Scandinavian high established itself over England for months. Temperatures plummeted and snowfall became common. In parts of the south-east (the hardest-hit area of the country), temperatures reached as low as −18C.

Although all 12 Football League clubs were based in the less-impacted north and Midlands, many fixtures were still postponed. So dramatic was the effect on the fixture calendar that Everton played their penultimate match in early January and then had to wait two months to complete their season with an away game at Burnley.

In the interim, the mighty Preston, who in January had been off the pace slightly but with games in hand, had put a decent run together and scaled up the table to stand in second place, just two points behind Everton.

Despite the narrow gap, local confidence was high, as the *Liverpool Courier* reported:

'The utmost confidence prevails that Everton will win, and as the Rovers [Blackburn] are completely out of the hunt whilst North End can hardly expect to lower the colours of Sunderland on the banks of the Wear, the prospects of the Liverpool champions are of the highest order. Should they lose even at Burnley and North End win … goal average remains in favour of the Anfield-road team, and although slight, it will nevertheless be enough to secure the honours.'

Everton needed a point to be certain, Preston needed to win and improve their inferior goal average (these were the days before goal difference was used). Everton were the favourites. But even then, this was Everton, a team that could conspire to turn the routine into something much more challenging for the fans.

During the two-month gap between that penultimate match and the final fixture at Turf Moor, the club had remained active. There had been a three-game tour of London and some friendlies against the likes of Rotherham Town, Accrington and Darwen. The team was in good shape and for that final match boasted a strong first XI.

When the day itself eventually arrived, around 2,000 fans made the pilgrimage north. Burnley, secure from the need for re-election in eighth place, should have represented the perfect opponents, being devoid of anything to play for (save professional pride).

But, from kick-off, it was clear that the home side were not participating simply to make up the numbers. Both sides started in a lively manner, with Geary coming close for Everton and Marr for Burnley.

After a fairly frenetic opening 15 minutes, Everton slowly began to assert some dominance. Geary had some decent chances, and Chadwick first forced a smart save from Kaye and then clipped the bar with a strong effort. But, although momentum appeared to be with Everton, as the half-time arrived, the sides nevertheless went in level.

On resumption, Everton carried on from where they had left off. But, despite them looking the more likely to score, it would be the home side who would break the deadlock. Not long into the half, Haresnape got on the end of a rebound to drill the ball past the Everton keeper and put his team in the lead.

Although frustrating for those travelling fans, it wasn't a lead that lasted long, as the *Liverpool Mercury* reported:

'Tremendous was the shout, which acknowledged the drawing of first blood, but well the cheers has subsided, Brady and Latta were away, and Geary getting hold, darted off and equalised in the Everton centre-forward's unique style, such a fine effort evoking a heavy cheer.'

Not long after, it was 2–1 to Everton. Geary attempted a shot which came back to Milward, who had a second go. The ball bounced around the box and eventually found its way past Kaye and into the net, courtesy of the unfortunate Burnley defender McFettridge. Everton were on course for the title and, sensing blood, went for the jugular:

'Everton seemed to have fairly broken up the Burnley formation now, and attacked so continuously that it looked only a question of how many goals they would win by,' reported the *Mercury*.

With the game in control, one hand on the trophy and momentum with them, rather than extend their lead, Everton then conspired to balls things up, as the *Mercury* recounted:

'Burnley, seven minutes from the finish rallied surprisingly. Hill led the way, Haresnape took up the theme, and after Jardine had fisted out he conceded a corner, and from the tussle that ensued, Bowes scored. There was but five minutes left, and on resuming Stewart closed in and beat Jardine with a high shot – amidst a scene of wild excitement.'

Despite a late rally by Everton (including one goalbound effort that got stuck in the mud), the scoreline stayed 3–2.

It looked as though they might have thrown it all away at the very last. In old money, that 3–2 loss now meant that Everton had a goal average of 2.17. Just a 1–0 win for Preston would give them an average of 2.25. Those final ten mad minutes were beginning to look very costly. And yet, as the dejected fans made their way home, news filtered through that Preston had blown it too, losing 3–0 to Sunderland. Everton had got lucky.

On being crowned champions, the men from Anfield became the first club to be awarded the League Championship trophy, which for over a century was presented to the best side in the land (and which is now doled out to the winners of the Championship).

The victors during the previous two seasons, Preston, had to make do with a flag; and, as that was the last time they ever took the top spot, they've not subsequently been able to enjoy the feel of that particular piece of silverware.

The idea of an Everton side resplendent in pink bringing a trophy back to Anfield is strange enough. But to then add to that, the club also struck their own medals for the team. On these, there would be no Prince Rupert's Tower, no 'Nil Satis Nisi Optimum', no symbols recognisable as 'Everton' at all. Instead there was the liver bird. It might have been blue, but it still added an extra element of strangeness to the club's first title win.

But, irrespective of the weird aspects, there was still much to celebrate. In just three seasons Everton had gone from unfancied outsiders, widely thought to not necessarily deserve their place in the league, to champions and vanquishers of the greatest side of the era: Preston North End. The Blues (or the Salmon Pinks) were on the march.

v Bolton Wanderers 4–2

2 September 1892
Friendly
Goodison Park. Attendance: 10,000

Everton: Jardine, Howarth, Dewar, Boyle, Holt, Robertson, Latta, Maxwell, Geary, Chadwick, Milward

Bolton Wanderers: Sutcliffe, Somerville, Jones, Paton, Gardiner, McFettridge, Munro, Willock, Cassidy, Wilson, Dickinson

Referee: S. Ormerod

The Grand Old Lady Is Born

EVERTONIANS are hard-wired to love Goodison and loathe Anfield. But, were it not for the slippery behaviour of one man, the former would not exist and the latter would still be the club's home. And that slippery individual was John Houlding.

Since the game moved from amateurism to professionalism in the late-Victorian era and men with deep pockets became more dominant, those at the top have always been viewed with suspicion by the fans.

Shifty, untrustworthy, duplicitous: these are just some of the more polite terms that have been applied to the money men involved in football over the years.

Although not always fair, there have been enough examples of those running clubs putting their own interests first to ensure that these terms have some basis in truth. And if you want an early example, Everton's one-time president is your man.

He might not have owned the club, but Houlding, a prominent local brewer, loomed large over Everton's early years. Not only was he president, he also established his pub, the Sandon Hotel, as the club's de facto HQ and engineered Everton's relocation to Anfield in 1884.

Although he was initially viewed positively by those he worked with at the club, disharmony eventually began to brew. It was precipitated by Houlding's decision in 1885 to buy the Anfield plot, thereby becoming the club's landlord. Although asked to do this by several committee members (there had been development plans afoot and the possibility of Everton's eviction), his later actions suggested that his motivation might not have been entirely altruistic.

The impact of his growing power at Everton was first felt through a rent increase, which saw the amount that Everton were paying rising from £100 a year in the mid-1880s to £250 by the close of the decade. He also insisted on having a nominee on the club's executive and controlling the sale of refreshments at home matches. There was a sense of a man keen to acquire dominance.

31

Initially, Houlding had the club where he wanted them. The costs of professionalism and the advent of league football meant another move was too much for the club to countenance. Everton were stuck at Anfield and, by extension, stuck with the man from the Sandon. But his benign environment did not last long.

By the early 1890s, Everton were more settled financially. And, just as importantly, they also had a strong and well-organised anti-Houlding faction, led by George Mahon, a prominent Liverpool accountant who arrived on the management committee of the club in 1889.

In 1891, Houlding proposed that Everton should incorporate and buy his land (plus an adjoining plot for development). Although his reasoning was sound (he wanted the club to develop athletics facilities on the adjoining land to create year-round revenue), his price was definitely not.

The committee, and specifically the anti-Houlding faction, felt that the £9,237 price tag (at a time when land prices were falling) was exorbitant. Set within the context of his rent rises, it gave the impression of a man on the make. The proposal was rejected, and, at the same time, efforts were made to try to get Houlding to reduce the rent at Anfield.

Negotiations continued for months, but were fruitless. Realising that the issue was insurmountable, and that an alternative ground needed to be found for the moment when talks inevitably broke down completely, Mahon got to work.

At a special general meeting in January 1892, he revealed what he had found. The alternative was Mere Green field (off Goodison Road), a patch of land on the other side of Stanley Park to Anfield on which Mahon had the option to secure a lease. Houlding's hold over Everton FC was disappearing fast.

In response to his tenants 'doing one', Houlding tried to form a new company called Everton Football Club and Athletic Grounds. Mahon appealed to the FA, stating his belief that the committee, not Houlding, had the right to the name. The FA upheld Mahon's appeal, telling Houlding he could continue to run a football club at Anfield but not under the 'Everton' name.

A few weeks later, at another meeting, Houlding was voted out of the presidency by a landslide.

The proposal to take the lease on the land on Goodison Road was then proposed and subsequently accepted by an overwhelming majority. After this, the club completed its list of Football League fixtures and, at the end of the season, severed its relationship with Anfield and departed for pastures new.

Once there, Everton converted the land and built three stands, two covered, one uncovered, in total accommodating 11,000 people. Goodison Park, as the stadium was named, was the first major football ground built in England.

On visiting the stadium in October 1892, the publication *Out of Doors* wrote: 'Behold Goodison Park! No single picture could take in the entire scene the ground presents, it is so magnificently large, for it rivals the greater American baseball pitches. On three sides of the field of play there are tall covered stands, and on the fourth side the ground has been so well banked up with thousands of loads of cinders that a complete view of the game can be had from any portion. It appears to be one of the finest and most complete grounds in the kingdom.'

The stadium was officially opened on 24 August 1892. And, locally, it was a big deal. There was a lunch at the Adelphi Hotel and then a procession of open carriages to Goodison, where the ground had been opened for all to see. The people came in their thousands. 'From six pm the public entrances kept revolving, registering the throngs,' reported *Cricket and Football Field*.

The inaugural match, the first time a ball was kicked in earnest on that hallowed turf, took place a week later against Bolton Wanderers, with around 10,000 people in attendance.

It might have been a friendly, but, as the *Liverpool Mercury* sensually reported, 'the play at once became of an earnest character, the ball being impelled quickly from end to end. Excitement was thus aroused from the outset.'

Despite the sense of occasion, Everton conspired to make the worst start possible when Bolton raced into a two-goal lead, the first coming via Cassidy and the second Dickinson.

Capitulation seemed on the cards. But the home side rallied, and hope was quickly restored when Geary pulled a goal back, in the process earning himself the honour of becoming the first Everton player to score at Goodison Park.

This was followed not long after with an equaliser, courtesy of Latta. Everton were level but in no mood to let matters rest, as the *Mercury* wrote.

'Everton soon caused Wanderers to beat a retreat, and literally stormed the goal; the siege culminating in Chadwick making his initial goal of the season for his club.'

The interval arrived with Everton leading 3–2, a comeback that had seemed improbable earlier in the half. When play resumed after the break, Everton picked up from where they had left off. Right away the Bolton goal was under attack, and when the home side's hard-working outside-left, Milward, had his shot saved, Boyle was there to slot in the rebound. It was 4–2, with the promise of more to come.

From that point on, Everton had the best of the play. 'They worked admirably together,' reported the *Mercury*, 'the backs having little to do, and the half backs giving their forwards plenty of opportunities to shine, which they did. The ball was passed with readiness and tact, and at times all five forwards touched the sphere in its progress towards goal.'

But, in response, the Bolton defence was resolute; and, try as Everton might, another goal would not come. The game ended 4–2, the kind of result and performance those who had braved the grim weather had come to see.

The friendly had acted as a dress rehearsal to the first competitive fixture at Goodison – which took place against Nottingham Forest only 24 hours later. Over 14,000 supporters this time battled against the wind and rain to watch Everton kick off the new league season with a 2–2 draw, goals coming from Geary and Milward.

Those who were eager to see the club win at their new home would have to wait a bit longer. A few weeks later, Everton crushed Newton Heath 6–0, rewarding the fans' patience with an emphatic win.

Over the years since, Goodison Park has changed and grown, gradually dominating the area. But, regardless of its size, from the very beginning it has held a special place in the hearts of Evertonians. And this has been the case irrespective of how it is regarded by others outside the club.

The ground has enjoyed the status of being one of the grandest in the country, the choice to host FA Cup finals, England internationals and World Cup semi-finals.

But it has also, in the modern era, endured a diminishing in its pre-eminence, stood helplessly as other stadiums have passed it by; watched powerlessly as it has become a slightly antiquated relic set amongst the shiny modern masterpieces that populate the top flight.

Through it all, though, it has remained loved. Few Blues can forget the first time they emerged from the bowels of Goodison, out into the light to take in the glory of the green grass and the thousands of fans that surrounded it; the noise, the heat, the feel of the place; a Grand Old Lady perfect for a Grand Old Team.

v Liverpool 3–0

13 October 1894
Football League Division One
Goodison Park. Attendance: 44,000

Everton: Cain, Adams, Parry, Boyle, Holt, Stewart, Latta, McInnes, Southworth, Hartley, Bell

Liverpool: McCann, Hannah, McLean, McCartney, McQue, McBride, Kerr, Ross, McVean, Bradshaw, McQueen

Referee: J. Lewis

A Rivalry Begins

THE Merseyside derby is a near-perennial fixture in the football calendar, one of the longest-running football rivalries in England. And, like all great traditions, it had to start somewhere.

On 13 October 1894, the first league meeting of the city's footballing giants took place at Goodison Park.

Although it was the first occasion when these two had met in the league, it wasn't their first head-to-head. The date for that was April 1893, and the occasion was the final of Liverpool Senior Cup. The encounter, between Liverpool and what was essentially Everton's reserve team, was settled by a single goal, scored for Liverpool by former Everton player Tom Wylie.

There had also been a Liverpool v Everton head-to-head back in 1885, but this was a charity match to raise funds for Stanley Hospital. And the Liverpool team involved was a collection of local footballers drawn from the ranks of Liverpool Ramblers, Bootle and Cambrian, not the red monstrosity that would go on to torment the Blue half of Merseyside in the distant future.

Although, before the game, there might not have been much history between the two sides to fan the flames of rivalry as we understand it today, there was enough bad blood between the respective boardrooms to ensure that a degree of enmity was in the air.

Liverpool FC had arisen directly from the 'split'. Having seen the money that could be made from the sport, and with an empty ground to fill, John Houlding had responded to his downfall by creating his own football club to fill the void left by the departed Everton. In the spring of 1892, with a loan of £500 from the brewer (which was never paid back), Liverpool FC were conjured into existence.

Although recognised as a football club by the FA committee, Liverpool were initially refused participation in the Football League. But, with their sophisticated stadium (by the standards of the time), Houlding's finance and the organisational skills of John McKenna (the club's first secretary), their case for inclusion could not be dismissed for long.

At the end of the 1892/93 season, Accrington resigned from the Football League and Bootle, who were unable to adapt to the costs of professionalism, lost their place in the second tier. Liverpool applied for both vacant positions and were given the one vacated by Bootle in Division Two.

The club grasped the opportunity provided. At the end of the 1893/94 season, they finished top and then gained promotion to the First Division in the play-offs. It was a victory that set them on a path to an inevitable meeting against their city rivals.

Because of the novelty of this meeting, the nature of the split and the proximity of the two clubs, there was widespread interest in the fixture within the city.

'I never saw such a crowd. As early as one o'clock all streets, for miles around, leading to Goodison Park began to be thronged with men, women, and boys, all tramping to one place. As far away as the Pier Head every tramcar was loaded with excited intending spectators of the game, and these, together with a heterogeneous assemblage of omnibuses, wagonettes, drays, pony carts, hansom cabs, four wheelers, and every imaginable description of wheeled vehicle, formed a huge possession stretching (to take one route alone) from the bottom of Scotland Road right up to the ground,' wrote John Humphreys in the *North Wales Chronicle*.

For those attending, it was expected that they would see an Everton victory. The hosts were overwhelming favourites to win the game. Since joining the inaugural Football League, Everton had done well, finishing runners-up in 1890 and league champions in 1891, and notching up a few top-five finishes in other campaigns.

Importantly, they also entered the derby in scintillating form, having won all seven fixtures played so far that season, scoring freely while remaining resolute at the back. They topped the table and were an early tip for the title.

Liverpool, by contrast, had found the transition to top-flight football a difficult one to adjust to. At that point in the season, they had failed to register a single win and sat fourth from bottom with a miserly four points. They might have beaten Everton in that Senior Cup fixture 18 months earlier, but that counted for nothing in the harsher, cut-and-thrust world of league football.

Aside from home advantage and divergent form, there was also the issue of incentives to bear in mind. So important was victory to the Everton directors, and so palpable the desire to put the club's upstart neighbour firmly in its place, the players were being rewarded with a brand-new silk hat each in the event of an Everton win. As a visiting team, when you realise your opponents are playing not just for 'bragging rights' but also a fancy new piece of millinery, you know you're in for a tough game.

Contrary to the blue and red colours that have long been synonymous with each side, visually the teams lined up that day in a way that would confuse modern onlookers. Everton wore red, while Liverpool opted for pale blue and white halves, something more akin to a Blackburn Rovers strip that has been put through the wash too many times. Red would not become their adopted colour until 1896.

Despite their long-held claims to possess a grand legacy in 'pass and move' football, Liverpool's approach back then could best be described as 'Sunday league'. This was 'kick and rush' at its most elemental. And there was particular emphasis on the 'kick', as Liverpool's confrontational style met Everton's more 'aristocratic' approach with relentless force.

Initially, it was an approach that worked. Tackle by tackle, foul by foul, long ball by long ball, Liverpool edged to dominance, as Everton floundered under their physical onslaught. The visitors had their chances and could easily have gone ahead. But, as their league form had illustrated, being clinical in front of goal was not Liverpool's strong point.

Despite the early dominance of the men in washed-out pale blue and white, it would be Everton who took the lead, when McInnes rose with perfection to head the hosts into a one-goal lead after ten minutes.

For the remainder of the half, Liverpool searched for an equaliser, carving out a number of further chances through their tenacious approach. But it was to no avail. Although at times dominant, they went in at half-time one down.

As the second half commenced, Everton's technical superiority began to make itself felt. Chances for the home side became more regular as Liverpool's momentum visibly ebbed. On 60 minutes, Latta made it 2–0. It was a goal that appeared to put the match beyond the visitors. Liverpool no longer seemed able to trouble the hosts.

As Everton played with ease, a third goal for the home side seemed inevitable. It arrived late on, as a north-west sky unleashed a torrent of rain upon proceedings. Bell, the final member of a Scottish triumvirate that had seized the day for Everton, popped up in the box to make 3–0.

Not long after, the final whistle blew. The Reds had won, to the delight of the directors and fans alike. The local upstart had been firmly put in its place. Silk hats all round!

Despite the comprehensive scoreline, John Humphreys believed that, 'taking the play all through I must express … it was not Everton's defence that saved them from a defeat but the miraculously bad shooting of the Liverpool forwards. This was no doubt due to the tremendous excitement they were labouring under, and no doubt the excitement had a lot of effect on the Everton men. Had Liverpool scored once, their chances of winning the match … would have been five to one.'

But, although he believed that Liverpool had been unfortunate not to have come away with a victory, when pondering the assertion made by Liverpool's Jimmy Ross that the Anfield fixture would go their way, Humphreys strongly disagreed:

'Everton, despite what I have just written, is a better team than Liverpool, and I can hardly believe that at any following match the Anfielders will or can ever again develop such a tremendous amount of steam as they did last Saturday, and unless they do, they stand no chance against their mighty rivals.'

Everton would go on to finish that season as runners-up behind Sunderland. By contrast, Liverpool's poor form would continue, and they ended the campaign bottom of the league (going on to be relegated after a play-off defeat). Although the men from Anfield won promotion straight away the next season, it would be a further three years before they finally beat Everton, a 3–1 win in 1897 at Anfield.

Since that first derby, at the time of writing, 228 meetings between the clubs have taken place in all competitions. Sadly for Evertonians, a pretty dismal performance since the 1970s has seen Liverpool edge ahead when it comes to overall bragging rights. But, for all their crowing, they'll never have that first win, the satisfaction of knowing that when the sides initially met in a contest that mattered, for all Liverpool's kicking and screaming, Everton's class prevailed.

v Newcastle United 1–0

21 April 1906
FA Cup Final
The Crystal Palace. Attendance 75,609

Everton: Scott, Balmer, Crelley, Abbott, Taylor, Makepeace, Sharp, Bolton, Young, Settle, Hardman

Newcastle United: Lawrence, McCombie, Carr, Gardner, Aitken, McWilliam, Rutherford, Howie, Veitch, Orr, Gosnell

Referee: F. Kirkham

The Cup Comes Home

IN the early years of the new century, Everton were erratic. This was a club that could come within a whisker of winning the title (as happened in 1901/02 and 1904/05) but equally be just as likely to find itself mired in mid-table mediocrity (as was the case in 1899/1900 and 1902/03).

Consistency seemed to elude the Blues (and, by this point in time, they were definitively the 'Blues'). And even when greatness was within touching distance, Everton didn't seem to have what it took to grasp it.

In the 1904/05 season, they had come close to securing an historic 'Double' but ultimately faltered, exiting in the semi-finals of the FA Cup to Aston Villa and then being narrowly pipped to the title by Newcastle United (despite topping the table for three months during the run-in).

After those near misses that season, with the talented Alex 'Sandy' Young leading the line and a squad filled with quality, including the lightning-quick winger Jack Sharp, the fast-paced inside-forward Jimmy Settle and the tough-tackling full-back Billy Balmer, Everton were expected to place well in the following campaign.

But, in the league, the Blues once again illustrated how they could confound expectations. In a larger division (now made up of 20 teams), Everton endured another one of those periodic mediocre seasons, finishing in 11th position.

Hopes then turned to the FA Cup and a desire to improve on last season's semi-final exit. Here, Everton were afforded a little bit of luck. The Blues were drawn at home against second-tier outfits in the first three rounds; dismissing West Brom (2–1), Chesterfield (3–0) and Bradford City (1–0).

The quarter-final proved a sterner test, pitting Everton against high-flying The Wednesday. Despite being the favourites, though, the Yorkshiremen were defeated, going down 4–3 courtesy of goals from Sharp, Taylor, Booth and Bolton. It was a win that set Everton on the road to a semi-final head-to-head against city rivals Liverpool.

In those days, Everton didn't carry the baggage that is evident today when it came to derbies. Mentally, Liverpool remained beatable in any game, even one where the outcome seemed more important. In the previous year, the two had met in the first round of the cup and Everton had emerged victorious.

In late March, an uncowed Everton repeated that outcome. Once again, Liverpool exited the competition, this time going down 2–0.

Everton were on their way to London to play in their third final, hoping that 'third time lucky' would prove to be an adage that held weight in this instance.

Their opponents were Newcastle, reigning First Division champions and the previous season's defeated FA Cup finalists.

Although the football world seemed to have Newcastle pegged as the favourites, 'Secretary', writing in the *Liverpool Courier*, refused to be swept along, pointing out that 'luck' particularly in an English Cup final, enters largely into the question, and if Everton are favoured in this respect than the Novocastrians may easily be beaten for the second season in succession.'

This was a time when 'Geordie' was a less familiar term, and instead the denizens of Newcastle enjoyed a collective name that makes them sound more like a kingdom from *Game of Thrones*.

The city, or at last the Blue half, was gripped by cup fever, with thousands making the trip down to London. The trains set off early, and, by 8am, Euston was packed with Evertonians. From there, in the spring sunshine, Scousers and 'Novocastrians' alike made their way south to Sydenham, home of the Crystal Palace (these were the days before Wembley).

Everton, who had been sequestered at their training camp near Epping Forest, arrived from the east, amongst their numbers a confident Will Cuff, the club secretary/manager, who told the *Courier*:

'I was fairly confident that we would beat Liverpool in the semi-final, and I feel just as confident that we shall defeat Newcastle United. Mind you, I do not wish in any way to underrate the ability of our opponents, but I rather fancy our half-backs will not allow the United to settle down to their proper game.'

Both sides could name strong first elevens, as each had rested players over the preceding weeks, putting out teams largely consisting of reserves. So overt had these efforts been that the management committee of the Football League had met a week earlier and fined both clubs £50.

By around 3.30pm, with the ground packed and the skies fully transformed from sunny and blue to gloomy and oppressive, Newcastle kicked off.

The early exchanges seemed to back up the optimism of Cuff, as Everton dominated proceedings. Settle, Young and Taylor all had decent opportunities to put the Blues ahead, and Newcastle were fortunate that their keeper was in good form that day.

What attempts the 'Toon' made to venture forward were largely abortive, frustrated by the Everton defence, which was proving more than capable of thwarting Newcastle's attacking play.

The Cup Comes Home: v Newcastle United (1–0)

'The Novocastrians had certainly not done anything up to this time to justify their favouritism,' reported the *Liverpool Football Echo*, 'Everton having contributed the bulk of the attack.'

But, despite their dominance, Everton had not made it pay; and as the game moved along, Newcastle found their rhythm, putting the Everton back line under greater pressure – pressure that very nearly yielded results when their outside-right manufactured the chance of the half:

'Rutherford managed to slip away by himself and carry the ball along with great dexterity almost into the Everton goal, when the Everton custodian affected a truly glorious safe [sic], to the delight of Everton's supporters who must have thought that it was all over,' reported the *Echo*.

Not long after, the half-time whistle blew and the teams went in level, but with the sense that Everton might have missed their best chance of putting this game beyond the reach of the Tynesiders.

Under an ever-darkening sky, the game resumed around 4.30pm, with Everton playing against the wind.

Where the play had swung from Everton's attacking dominance to Newcastle's in the first half, the second period was characterised by a more defensive approach by both sides, as though neither wanted to be the one to make the first (and possibly telling) mistake.

Perhaps it was this period of play that led the likes of the *Manchester Guardian* and *The Times* to label the final as one of the poorest seen for some time.

Chances became rarer, and the game descended into a defensive stalemate. Of those that did occur, the best fell to Everton, when a cross from Sharp presented Hardman with a glorious opportunity. Frustratingly, he was too slow to react. The Blues then thought they'd got lucky when the ball ended up at the feet of Young, who was able to put it into the net. But the Everton centre-forward was ruled offside.

As the end of the match approached, Newcastle suddenly woke up – attacking with an urgency that had been absent all afternoon. Under the onslaught, it looked as though the Everton defence would eventually succumb. And perhaps it would have done, had the Blues not managed a rare break on the 77th minute, and 'just when success seemed furthest away it suddenly appeared in sight, and this time materialised, with no offside to mar its lustre,' reported the *Echo*.

After an exchange between Taylor and Settle in midfield, the ball came to Sharp, 'who resisted the attentions of McWilliam, and dashing along centred like a flash clean into the goal mouth, Young smartly followed after the leather and finished up by doing the trick in fine style. Needless to say the pant-up [sic] feeling of the vast multitude broke forth in such a volume of sound that it was a wonder the threatening rain-clouds overhead did not discharge their deluge,' the report continued.

41

A renewed onslaught by Newcastle after the goal had to be weathered by the Everton defence. Although it always looked like the Blues might buckle, they held out to the end. Everton had won their first FA Cup.

'On the day's play,' Will Cuff told the local press, 'Everton were the better team. It was a strenuous contest. Of course I am delighted that the Cup comes to Liverpool. This is the fifth year of my secretaryship, and I was never more proud of the team than I am to-day.'

After a league fixture a few days later in Sheffield, the Blues made their way home in a special train, adorned with all manner of flags and banners. On arrival back in Liverpool, as the Everton biographer Thomas Keats later wrote, 'a thunderstorm of cheering greeted Jack Taylor, cup in hand, and his victorious comrades as they stepped from a saloon carriage.'

From there, it was on to Goodison, along streets thronged with jubilant Evertonians. And then, as Keats continued, 'a great reception. More ceremony, more speeches. Refreshments, a lull, fatigue, dispersal; followed by welcome rest after a prolonged hour of glorious life.'

It was deserved. Against most predictions and against the form book, Everton had triumphed, realising the potential of a side that had so often fallen short and proving that sometimes adages can come true, that third time really was a charm.

v Chelsea 2–2

8

26 April 1915
Football League Division One
Goodison Park. Attendance: 10,000

Everton: Fern, Thompson, Galt, Grenyer, Harrison, Weller, Chedgzoy, Parker, Kirsopp, Clennell, Fleetwood

Chelsea: Molyneux, Bettridge, Harrow, Logan, Abrams, Walker, Brittan, Ford, McNeil, Croal, Halse

Referee: R. Harris

Kings of Goodison

AS Edwin Starr rightly pointed out, war is good for nothing (in fact, absolutely nothing, say it again y'all!). Had he been a Blue, he might have also added that it's specifically not great for Everton sides that have just won the league.

After Liverpool, armed conflict must rate as Everton's greatest nemesis. On two occasions, it has torn title-winning sides apart. It might be bottom of the list for unwanted consequences caused by war, but for Evertonians it's been an extra sufferance to add to those manifold others.

Back in the summer of 1914, as the new season dawned, it had been years since the club had won its one and only title. There had been near misses, times when the trophy had been tantalisingly close, but all had come to nothing. In the previous decade, Everton had been runners-up on several occasions, each time faltering when it mattered most.

Amidst all of this, if one adjective could define the club, it would be 'inconsistent'. Good seasons seemed to be followed by mediocre ones, as the club bounced around the table. Consistency and the capacity to build upon promise appeared to elude the men from Goodison.

And often it was self-inflicted.

When Everton had finished second in the 1911/12 campaign, a shortfall almost entirely attributable to a lack of potency up front, the club did not bother to recruit to address that particular deficiency. They sat on their hands, and, as a result, Everton suffered – with the team struggling in the following two campaigns.

Chastened by the slump, a degree of rebuilding did belatedly take place. It was hoped that the arrival of Bobby Parker, a stocky forward from Glasgow Rangers, and Joe Clennell, an inside-left forward from Blackburn Rovers, combined with the growing maturity of young winger Sam Chedgzoy (who had been at Goodison for a few years already), would address Everton's need for greater goals and more attacking fluency and thereby help the club enjoy a better season in 1914/15.

But whether that campaign would reach completion was another issue. The wider political environment had taken a turn for the worse during the build-up to the season's start. After a crisis in the Balkans had triggered Europe's delicately balanced alliance system, Britain had found itself drawn into a European conflict, ostensibly to protect the neutrality of Belgium. In the late summer, as Everton lined up to play their opening fixture against Spurs, units of the British Expeditionary Force were already in France as the country prepared itself for its first continental war in nearly a century.

Calls were made for the FA and the Football League to suspend all fixtures as a mark of respect. But they were dismissed. A variety of factors, including a desire to retain an air of normalcy, the sport's enduring popularity amongst the working classes and an unfounded belief that the conflict would be over by Christmas, ensured that league and cup football continued to be played.

Whether this was good news for Everton, only time would tell. Early on in the season, form was inconsistent, especially at Goodison. Over the course of the whole campaign, only relegated Spurs would win fewer games at home than the Blues.

But there were positives to offset this. The lack of goals that had marred the previous two seasons had been addressed. Parker sparkled and by Christmas had already found the net over 20 times. The side were also particularly effective away from home, winning 11 on the road before the season's end.

As 1915 opened, Everton sat fourth in the table (following some strong form during the late autumn) and optimism filled the air.

'Last season Everton disappointed greatly. This season they are moving ahead steadily, and will shortly be challenging the leaders for top place,' thought the *Liverpool Echo*. 'The club has not won the championship since 1890/91, when 29 points were efficient [sic] to gain the honour, and it is a blow that a club of Everton's resources has so long been unable to take the Consistency Stakes. However, this season looks likely to change the black-looking affair.'

During the remainder of the campaign, against a backdrop of an increasingly gloomy political picture, Everton continued to stay in the title race. And in the cup too. For a time, the prospect of another shot at the 'Double' was on the cards as Everton, fuelled by Parker's goals, remained in the hunt for both domestic honours.

Frustratingly, they would again fall short in the FA Cup, losing 2–0 in the semis to Chelsea. 'In the past Everton gained a reputation for failing at an obstacle which they were expected to clear with comparative ease,' wrote 'Critic' in the *Liverpool Evening Express*. 'On Saturday the Blues were favourites, and their friends believed that they were quite good enough to beat the Pensioners, but the glorious uncertainty of the game was once more demonstrated, and Everton were knocked out. It is no use mincing matters. Everton were well beaten, and Chelsea deserved to win.'

If Everton were to claim silverware that season, they would have to overcome that propensity to falter when it mattered most. Fourth at this point, the Blues chose the perfect moment to find form. Four away wins on the bounce in April sent them to the summit, and, as the campaign came to a close, the runners and riders had narrowed to two: Oldham Athletic and Everton (both level on points with one game left to go).

Oldham faced Liverpool on 24 April. Everton faced Chelsea two days later.

The Blues would need their neighbours to go for the win. Back in those days, the mutual antipathy that characterises relations between the clubs today was largely non-existent. There would be no sense of willing your team to roll over (as was the case nearly 100 years later, when Everton fans were more than happy for the Blues to lose to Manchester City in the latter's fight with Liverpool for the title). Quite the opposite, in fact, as Tony Onslow, author of *Everton F.C.: The Men from the Hill Country – The Development of Everton Football Club During the Reign of Queen Victoria*, explains:

'Rivalry between the fans was limited between the clubs early on. In fact, when you compare what there was to what had existed between Everton and Bootle in the 1880s, it was very tame. There would have been a feeling amongst Liverpool fans that it was a good thing for the city if Everton brought the title home. It was a very different world to the one that we know today.'

Talk before the Liverpool game was all of goal average, the assumption being that Oldham would win, but would need to do enough to improve their inferior goal average relative to Everton's.

Ultimately, such talk was rendered moot. Despite their apparent confidence (and facing a side much further down the table), Oldham lost. Two goals by Fred Pagnam were enough to seal the win and effectively hand Everton the title. Level on points and with a superior goal average, it would now take a catastrophic defeat against Chelsea for Everton to falter.

But the desire existed to win the title on more than goal average. The minimum of a draw would mean Everton had won on points, a much more satisfying outcome for those who had slogged through the long season. And, a victory over Chelsea would also exact some revenge for the FA Cup exit that had taken place a few weeks earlier.

The game itself, perhaps because of the sense that the title race was effectively over, began slowly, with neither side playing to their best.

Ten minutes in, with the first chance of the game, Chelsea threatened to spoil the party when Croal and Brittan worked the ball through the middle and the latter struck a powerful drive that beat the keeper.

In response, Everton rallied briefly, with Clennell and Kirsopp each coming close. Chelsea weathered the mini-storm and then mounted a greater one of their own, when wave upon wave of attacks threatened to extend their lead further. Everton were penned back, unable to put together a coherent attack.

When the half-time whistle blew, the Toffees could count themselves lucky to go in at the break just the one goal down.

After a regroup at half-time, Everton began to play more like champions. Although chances were few, the Blues were seeing much more of the ball, and, with 20 minutes to go, their efforts were made to tell.

'Fleetwood, tired of waiting for his forwards to test Molyneux, and threading his way through, beat the Chelsea goalkeeper with a fast cross-shot,' reported the *Liverpool Daily Post and Mercury*.

After that, Everton attempted to kill the pace of the game and hold on for a point. But, with ten minutes left, a clumsy tackle on Ford by Galt led to a penalty, which Logan converted, putting Chelsea 2–1 up. Everton now had nine minutes to rescue their hopes of winning the title on points. Fortunately for the Blues, they had Bobby Parker:

'Only a minute passed, and then Everton equalised from a corner. Parker hooking the ball into the net in an amazing manner. The pace imparted on the ball was simply astounding, because the ball was high up when Parker got his boot to it. One of the best goals of the season,' reported the *Post and Mercury*.

The game ended 2–2, giving Everton 46 points, one more than Oldham.

The 'Critic' in the *Evening Express* glowed with pride; 'After many years of striving, the famous name of Everton is to be inscribed once more on the Football League trophy. That the success of the club is well merited is acknowledged on all hands ... undoubtedly Everton in my opinion, have proved themselves the best combination of the year, and generally speaking they are very popular winners.'

Sadly for those winners, their defence of that title would have to wait. The First World War, which was far from over by Christmas, showed no sign of abating. In response, all league and cup football was cancelled at the end of the season. It would be August 1919 before Everton took to the field again as champions. The club's momentum irrevocably stalled.

v Burnley 3–1

17 October 1925
Football League Division One
Turf Moor. Attendance: 10,343

Everton: Menham, Livingstone, McDonald, Brown, Peacock, Hart, Troup, Dean, Bain, Irvine, Chadwick

Burnley: Dawson, Blinkhorn, McCluggage, Hill, Armitage, Parkin, Kelly, Cross, Roberts, Beel, Page

Referee: I. Baker

Dixieland Opens Its Doors

WE will never know how good that title-winning side could have been. The war changed everything, and by the early 1920s what magic had existed was largely gone. The four years of conflict had taken its toll, as the players aged and the impetus of the side dissipated. Rather than the club looking up, momentum seemed to be dragging them downwards in the early years of the peace.

Everton were not alone in this. Before the war, a few other sides, most notably Blackburn Rovers and Oldham Athletic, had been enjoying a good spell, consistently residing in the higher reaches of the table. But they too, like Everton, lost that magic over the course of the war, and would spend the years in its immediate aftermath finding life difficult to adjust to. Everton board was initially stirred into action. New players arrived, such as the elegant wing-half Neil McBain, the unfortunately named centre-forward Jack Cock and the inventive Scottish winger Alec Troup. But although there was some initial improvement, by the mid-1920s, with the club flirting with 'the drop', it was clear that Everton were in need of something more.

The club's secretary-manager, Tom McIntosh, set out to find that 'something more'. Luckily for him, it was located just down the road.

William Ralph 'Dixie' Dean, a young forward from Birkenhead, had been turning heads with his startling form at Tranmere Rovers during his short time with the Wirral club. In his first full season at Prenton Park, Dean netted on 27 occasions in just 27 appearances. Along with the glad eye from Everton, he was soon attracting interest from a wealth of other top-flight clubs, including Arsenal, Newcastle United and Liverpool.

But where would he go? The answer arrived on Monday 16 March 1925: the day that Dean of Prenton Park became Dean of Goodison.

'One afternoon,' the man himself said in an interview with the sports writer John Roberts, 'I cleared off to the pictures and when I got home my mother told me Mr McIntosh from Everton had been and was waiting for me at the Woodside Hotel. I ran the two and a half miles there. I couldn't get there quick enough. Mr McIntosh asked me did I want to play for Everton, and that was that.'

Dean didn't even ask how much he was getting paid. He simply said yes, so excited was he to be crossing the Mersey to join the club he'd longed to play for.

Dean was signed for £3,000, no small amount to splash out on a teenager by the standards of the time. But his potential was widely understood, and for Everton, a side languishing near the relegation zone and averaging about a goal per game, his promise of potency was worth the outlay.

But the *Liverpool Daily Post and Mercury*, aware of the pressure the fee might place on the teenager, pleaded for patience, saying, 'It is probably the heaviest transfer fee that has ever been paid for a mere boy. Everton once had another boy on their books who started well but eventually fell through the frailty of human nature and the sickly adulation of the crowd … It is to be hoped the crowd will not make a "god" of Dean. He is very human and has many boy-like touches.'

Although Dean didn't find the net on his debut, he rectified that in his first game at Goodison a week later, when he scored in a 2–0 victory over Aston Villa. It was a goal that earned itself a standing ovation from the Blues in the crowd.

Despite showing flashes of brilliance in his handful of appearances towards the end of the 1924/25 season, and featuring in a squad that had found goals hard to come by (just 40 in the whole campaign), Dean started his first full season at Goodison in the reserves. It would be four games in before he made the starting eleven, and even then he struggled to make an initial impact, scoring just once in his first six appearances.

In mid-October, with Dean now a regular in the side, the Blues visited Turf Moor to face Burnley. Everton (at that point fourth from bottom) were coming into the game on the back of a four-match losing streak (a run that included a 5–1 battering at the hands of Liverpool).

More than ever, the club needed their teenage prodigy to start showing the talent that had won him so many plaudits and admirers at Tranmere. In a frenetic game, Dean did just that, as Everton finally embraced the 'new' way of playing.

This 'new' way had arisen in response to a change in the offside law. At the conclusion of the previous campaign, the International Football Association Board amended the rule to state that to be onside there now only needed to be two opponents between the attacker and the goal line (rather than three, as had been the case previously).

The change in law had a couple of effects. First, it altered the way that many English teams played football. In response to the change, defending players were forced to play squarer to each other and deeper. As a result, attacking players began to use long balls played between the two defenders, and made more use of their wingers who (with only two full-backs being employed) had ample space to cause havoc. Neat passing began to wane as directness and wing play became more effective.

And second, the shift in tactics and greater openness at the back meant that goalmouth action flourished. The number of goals scored in the Football League increased from 4,700 in 1924/25 to 6,373 in 1925/26, as forwards exploited the space they were given.

Different teams responded in different ways to this fundamental shift. Everton were initially slow to see its benefits, failing to exploit a system of play that had the perfect outlet in Dean. By the time of the game at Turf Moor, it was clear that wiser heads had prevailed.

'The Everton men cut out fancy football,' reported the *Daily Courier*. 'Displeasing as this may be to lovers of finesse and pattern-weaving,' it continued, 'these do not get goals under the new order. It was a case of swift one-two from wing to centre … quick passing, swinging the ball about, and no unnecessary dribbling en route to goal.'

But, as effective as this 'new' way of playing turned out to be in that game (and in later seasons), it was the more tactically conservative side who initially took the lead, when Roberts headed Beel's goalbound effort into the net. The home side deserved it, having had the best of the play since the start.

In response, the goal seemed to stir Everton into life, and gradually the away side started to grow into the game, spearheaded by their teenage centre-forward. Thriving on the new, more direct approach, Dean completely altered the complexion of the match, as the *Courier* reported:

'Dean, the 19-year-old centre-forward, carried his honours modestly. His three goals came together. Troup helped him with centres swept in with mathematical precision; Dean banging through without hesitation. Dean was in the picture throughout, enterprising and untiring.'

It was the first time that Evertonians had been given a glimpse of what their new centre-forward was truly capable of, the kind of match-changing impact that could turn a probable 1–0 loss into a 3–1 victory.

The Burnley game became one of those 'I was there' moments. Although all it really amounted to was two points and a single fixture, buried in what would turn out to be an unremarkable season, it was the starting point of a career that would not only shape Everton FC for the following decade but also stand as one of the most remarkable in English football.

Because that hat-trick would prove to be no aberration, no flash in the pan. The touchpaper had been lit. Dean scored three in the following game, a 4–2 win over Leeds at Goodison, the second of four hat-tricks he would nab that season. And he kept on scoring. Soon the cry of 'Give it to Dixie' would ring out around Goodison whenever Everton had the ball, so devastating did he become.

The campaign would end with Dean finding the net 33 times in 40 total appearances. It was the kind of potency that the side had searched for since the war had ended, and a forward the likes of which the Goodison terraces had not seen since 'Sandy' Young had last played for the club back in 1911.

He was a player who would go on to score 37 hat-tricks in his career, more than any English player has managed. He totted up 200 goals in his first 198 games for Everton, the youngest player at that time to have ever reached such a tally in professional football.

But, irrespective of Everton's ownership of one of the most potent attackers in the country, the club was still very much a work in progress. In Dean's first full season, the team netted 72 times, a huge improvement on the previous campaign. But, frustratingly for the fans, this was undone by continued leakiness at the back. It meant that Everton could do no better than finish mid-table.

Everton had performed better than in recent campaigns and in Dean had a genuine talent that a side could be built around. But the rebuilding had to take place. Without it, the best could not be extracted from 'Dixie'. And, despite his manifold talents, he would be unable to carry a side that continually let in such a high number of goals. Further change at Goodison was unquestionably required. Fortunately it soon arrived.

v Arsenal 3–3

5 May 1928
Football League Division One
Goodison Park. Attendance: 48,715

Everton: Davies, Cresswell, O'Donnell, Kelly, Hart, Virr, Critchley, Martin, Dean, Weldon, Troup

Arsenal: Paterson, Parker, John, Baker, Butler, Blyth, Hulme, Buchan, Shaw, Brain, Peel

Referee: W. Harper

Dixie's 60

ALTHOUGH Dean had been scoring for fun since establishing himself as Everton's first-choice centre-forward, the team had not prospered. The Blues ended the 1926/27 campaign in 20th position, one place off 'the drop'.

Despite Dean's contribution that season (albeit more limited than desired, after he spent a chunk of the early months of the campaign recovering from a serious motorbike accident), the team's total goal tally deteriorated from the previous year, and at the back they were porous, shipping a greater number of goals than both clubs that were relegated.

In response, the board began bringing in recruits to address Everton's problems. At the back, to plug up a defence that was worryingly leaky, Warneford 'Warney' Cresswell was signed from Sunderland, a player who subsequently became known as the 'Prince of Full-Backs'.

Then, from Stockport County, Everton brought in the talented outside-right Ted Critchley – providing Dean with a source of delivery to match that he had been receiving from the diminutive Troup on the left.

As an investment to end the club's permeable defence and get even more out of Dean, it was one that yielded spectacular dividends.

After a patchy start, form picked up dramatically, and by the end of November Everton were top.

Although they were unquestionably tighter at the back, a key reason for the club's ascent up the table was the form of Dean, which was mesmerising.

With the deliveries provided by Everton's wide men, Dean was on fire. By the end of that same November, the colossus of Goodison had played 15 games and found the net 27 times, including hat-tricks against Portsmouth, Leicester City and Manchester United.

Tentatively, Dean had his sights on the English goalscoring record, which had recently been set by George Camsell of Middlesbrough, who had scored 59 goals during the 1926/27 campaign (albeit in the second tier). With just over a third of the season gone, he was nearly half-way there.

Over the months that followed, despite a winless streak that lasted from mid-January until the end of March, Everton remained in the hunt for the title. It was a sustained assault, attributable in no small part to Dean's continued potency.

By late March, after bagging a brace in a 2–2 draw against Derby County, he reached 45, claiming the record for most goals in a First Division season (previously held by Ted Harper of Blackburn Rovers).

As the season closed, both the club and Dean (although he slightly less so) were still well positioned to claim their respective titles. In the league, with three games to go, it was a head-to-head battle between Everton and Huddersfield Town for the title. In the goalscoring stakes, Dean needed nine more goals to beat Camsell's record. For Everton's unstoppable centre-forward, it was a tough proposition but not one beyond his skills.

Dean bagged two in a 3–2 win over Aston Villa and then followed this with four in a 5–3 victory over Burnley. At the same time, Everton pushed further ahead of Huddersfield, and, after the Yorkshiremen lost their penultimate match of the season (a game in hand away at Villa), the title was Goodison bound.

The presenting of the trophy would have been exciting enough for Evertonians. After all, it was the first time in over a decade that the club had won any silverware. But there was also the issue of Dean's record to consider. Three more goals were needed to best Camsell, and there was just the one game left to do it.

But would the great man play?

In the penultimate match of the season, Dean had sprained a leg muscle and limped off. With Saturday approaching and the leg continuing to give him some jip, Everton's trainer/physio Harry Cooke sprang into action.

'From the Wednesday night until the Friday, he was with me at home, my home in Alderley Avenue, Birkenhead,' Dean told John Roberts. 'Old Harry kept putting clay plasters on [the muscle] until the Friday night, even leaving one on overnight as well. Old Harry cured it and on the Saturday, of course I was fit.'

On the day itself, although the official attendance was said to be 48,715, it's thought that around 60,000 (nervous) Blues crammed into Goodison to witness history being made.

Did the man himself share those nerves? Like he did at every home game, Dean caught the number 44 tram from Water Street, got off and walked along Goodison Road, chatting all the time to fellow fans. He was relaxed, motivated and, as he revealed to John Keith in *Dixie Dean: The Inside Story of a Football Icon*, confident in his abilities:

'I need three goals against Arsenal, who were the greatest club in the land. But that didn't worry me whatsoever, I always used to think, "I'm better than you."'

Despite Arsenal taking a quick lead through Shaw, the hopes and dreams of the fans were given a huge boost not long after, when Dean opened his account with a typically powerful header.

Minutes after Arsenal had kicked off again, the man himself was brought down in the box by Butler, who had been drawn into a reckless tackle. Penalty to Everton!

There was only person to take it. Goodison held its breath.

'I intended to place the penalty in the corner,' he later recalled. Instead 'it went in-between the keeper's legs. It wasn't one of my better kicks.'

Not that it mattered. Camsell's record had been equalled. And, with most of the game remaining, Dean needed only one more to nudge out in front.

As the crowd waited for him to strike again, Arsenal levelled. With the title secured and that scoring record exercising minds, it was one of those rare occasions at Goodison when the opposition's efforts to secure victory hardly mattered.

What was of more concern to the increasingly agitated crowd as the minutes ticked along was the growing impregnability of the Gunners' defence, which seemed determined to spoil the day. No matter what Everton threw at it, the back line remained resolute.

And then, with around four minutes left, Everton won a corner. Troup trotted out to take it. As the ball came in, 'Dean was in the midst of a bunch of players – friend and foe, and when it was a case of whose head was going to reach the ball first, it was a foregone conclusion it would be Dean's. He nodded the ball into the right hand corner of the net,' reported the *Football Express*.

Goodison exploded. It was a noise so loud, so the story went, that it sent the pigeons around the Pier Head scattering off into the sky.

'You talk about explosions, and loud applause; we have heard many explosions, and much applause in our long pilgrimage, but, believe us, we have never heard such a prolonged roar of thundering, congratulatory applause before as to that which ascended to heaven when Dixie broke the record,' Thomas Keats later wrote.

Along with that unprecedented roar, in the immediate aftermath of the goal Dean got to experience another 'first', as he later recalled to John Keith:

'Somebody ran on the pitch and stuck his whiskers in my face and tried to kiss me. Well! I'd never seen a supporter run onto the field until that day.'

This excitable Blue was then grabbed by the collar and pushed into the hands of a nearby policeman by the referee.

By contrast to the level of excitement in the crowd, the reaction of Dean and his fellow players was more measured. The man himself merely bowed to Goodison in response to his goal and then received a succession of handshakes from his team-mates (and the Arsenal keeper).

'There was no pulling me about and all that in those days, there was a bit of a knock on the shoulder or a touch of the hand or something but there was never any of this here love-making going on,' he later told John Roberts.

The remaining minutes of the match passed by in a deafening whirl of noise as the crowd sang and cheered without pause. When the end came, the pitch was flooded with Blues eager to celebrate not just the club's first title win that decade but also the remarkable achievement of their beloved centre-forward.

Not that they would find Dean. Just prior to the game's conclusion, the hero of the hour had already made a quiet exit, as he later confided to John Roberts: 'I turned round to the referee and I said: "Look, I'm going off, if you don't mind, tell them I'm going off for a 'Jimmy' or something." And he said: "Listen, if I were you I'd be in there now." I went off, and that was that, because I would have got murdered.'

Although Arsenal had managed to sneak a late equaliser through Shaw, it did nothing to diminish the celebrations amongst the crowd. They had witnessed something truly remarkable.

Since that glorious day, although there have been great centre-forwards at Goodison and elsewhere within the game, none have come close to what Dean achieved. Football might have been different back then and the likelihood of scoring such a haul more realistic, but that shouldn't undermine what he did.

Despite the game's more open nature, it was immeasurably rougher. Football during the inter-war years was tough, and centre-forwards took the kind of punishment that would make modern players run to the referee in tears.

Scoring 60 goals in that era took skill, determination and an unerring eye for goal. Dean had the lot and did something memorable with them. And, more importantly, he did it all in a Blue shirt, playing for the club he loved.

v West Ham United 6–1

16 April 1932
Football League Division One
Goodison Park. Attendance: 26,997

Everton: Sagar, Williams, Cresswell, Clark, Gee, Thomson, Critchley, Dunn, Dean, Johnson, Stein

West Ham United: Hufton, Goodacre, Chalkley, Norris, Barrett, Cadwell, Wood, Yews, Watson, Phillips, Morton

Referee: J. Whittle

Champions Again

OFTEN the game that actually wins the title is not the best one during a title-winning campaign. And that was certainly true when Everton became champions in 1932.

After a swashbuckling season, one in which Everton at times destroyed opposing sides, the club rather limped home over the line, defeating Bolton Wanderers 1–0 in a scrappy game which the *Liverpool Post and Mercury* described as 'the kind of match one generally associates with relegation problems rather than winning league championships'.

And, by that point in the club's history, Everton had certainly learned a thing or two about 'relegation problems', not least during the period sandwiched in between the title wins of 1928 and 1932.

For a time in the late 1920s and early 1930s, there existed two different and wildly contrasting versions of Everton. There was the side led by the talismanic Dean, which was capable of laying waste to all comers. And then there was the side that played without Dean, which consistently struggled, so over-dependent was it on him.

The cost of this over-dependence had been felt a few years earlier, when an injury-afflicted couple of seasons for their dominant centre-forward had seen Everton struggle and eventually drop into the second tier – the first time that had ever happened to the club. Everton had powered back immediately, but, once again, done so with Dean fit and leading by example.

While in the lower division, changes had been made to the squad with the aim of addressing its weaknesses.

The addition of the powerfully built centre-half Charlie Gee (bought from Stockport County), the acquisition of talented inside-left Tommy Johnson (from Manchester City) and the improved form of the tricky inside-right Jimmy Dunn (who had finally cemented a place in the first team) had gone some way to addressing Everton's shortcomings, albeit in a lower division. The test now would be to see if this more complete approach could be translated to the top flight.

Everton began the campaign well and by the end of September sat in sixth place. Although impressive, it wasn't a flawless start. There were defeats against Manchester City and Derby County and continued references in the local press to the lack of connection between the full-backs and the half-backs (defence and midfield to modern readers).

But any concerns were blown away by a period of form characterised by a spate of goalscoring that stands as one of the most impressive in Everton's entire history. In roughly a six-week period, Sheffield Wednesday were dispatched 9–3, Newcastle United 8–1, Chelsea 7–2 and Leicester City 9–2.

'It is remarkable', wrote John Peel (no relation) in the *Post and Mercury*, 'how Everton have reduced good sides to mere commonplace combination on their own ground in recent weeks.'

It was a run that took the club to the top of the table, a position barely surrendered for the remainder of the campaign. Although the rampant goalscoring eased, the victories continued to pile up, and several sides were still sent packing by fairly hefty margins, such as Middlesbrough (5–1), Blackburn Rovers (5–0) and Sheffield United (5–1).

Of the 'Dixieland' era, this was Everton's most complete side. They were more resilient at the back, conceding just 64 goals all season. They scored freely, finding the net on 116 occasions (a higher figure than in the breathtaking 1927/28 campaign). And they were less reliant on Dean too. In the previous title-winning season, Troup had come closest to Dean in the scoring stakes with ten goals (50 fewer than Dixie). In the 1931/32 campaign, Johnson chipped in with 22 and White with 18. These two complemented Dean's more modest (yet still hugely impressive) 45. In this side, Everton's other forwards were shouldering much more of the burden.

As the run-in approached, Everton welcomed West Ham United to Goodison Park. The Blues were within touching distance of an improbable title. Improbable, because it would mean that Everton would become only the second team to have won the league straight after being promoted (the other being Liverpool in 1906).

On the back of a nine-game unbeaten run, a surge in form that had done much to put them in a position of strength in the title race, the Blues were also in good spirits, as 'the Pilot' of the *Evening Express* had discovered when he had accompanied them on a short break a few weeks earlier:

'"We are the lads from Goodison Park – ooh! Rah! Rah! Rah! Rah!" With this battle cry Everton are marching forward to the attainment of the dearest ambition – the winning of the Football League championship. It was only last week-end, while I was touring with the Blues that I learned of this collegiate war cry. It awakened the tranquil townsfolk of Reigate as we motored through to Brighton for the invigorating brine-baths. It is no exaggeration to say that I was deeply impressed with the splendid feeling of comradeship, which pervades the entire team ... A happier or better band of players it would be impossible to find They are practical jokers everyone; and few people escape the gentle, harmless leg pulling, but still those same men are determined to bring that championship to Liverpool.'

Against West Ham, Everton ran out unchanged, while the visitors made drastic alterations, with three outside-rights included in the attack. This, combined with the Hammers' lowly position in the league, suggested an easy win for Everton. But their opponents were fighting for survival, making them a tricky adversary to play against. West Ham were hovering above the relegation zone and keen to reverse a run of dismal form. The Hammers were also one of only a handful of teams that had beaten the Blues that season.

From the off, it was evident that here were two teams with something to play for, with both sides carving out early chances. As it was, much to the delight of the Goodison crowd, Everton were the first to draw blood:

'Stein ran for a bouncing pass, and by a gentle header raced passed Goodacre and cut to the goal line. He made a low centre, which Barrett allowed to pass between his legs, and Dean being on the spot banged the ball into the net under Hufton's falling body,' wrote 'the Pilot' in the *Evening Express.*

On the front foot, Everton continued to press and, just a few minutes later, extended their lead when Stein bagged a second for the Blues. He had Dean to thank for the chance, who had gathered a bouncing pass, drawn the defence to him and then placed a square ball across to the running Stein. The Scot gave Hufton no chance with his left-footed shot.

If any of those gathered believed that Everton were in for an easy ride, West Ham were soon to prove otherwise (in the first half, at least). They came back at Everton, putting pressure on a back line that appeared tentative and surprisingly vulnerable. And, around 20 minutes in, they got their break when Wood's cross was turned into his own net by Cresswell.

Although Everton were the more threatening of the two sides, hitting the woodwork and making Hufton the busier of the keepers, West Ham remained dangerous, and when the half-time whistle blew, with the scoreline 2–1, it was unclear who would come out on top.

West Ham had worked tirelessly in the first half, making life hard for the Everton front men, while breaking decisively to put the opposition defence under pressure. Perhaps they had expended too much energy, or perhaps, ultimately, the gulf between these two clubs that the table illustrated made itself felt. Whatever the reason, the second half could not have been more different from the first.

'West Ham were hardly seen, and it almost developed into a case of Hufton against Everton ... Everton were right on top, and really it only seemed a question of how many they would get,' wrote 'the Pilot'.

Two quick goals 15 minutes into the half, one from Johnson and the other from Dean, did little to help the cause of the Hammers. At 4–1 and facing a rampant Everton, there seemed no way back into the game for them.

'And once Hufton's superlative display had been curbed ... the London side collapsed' reported 'Bee' in the *Post and Mercury*.

Dean scored again on 75 minutes, and Johnson nicked his second of the day in the dying minutes (illustrating how his presence in the side had done much to provide Everton with another valuable goal outlet).

At the end, Everton's 6–1 victory put them in a commanding position in the league. The title was theirs to lose. And, despite some ropey form thereafter, they put it beyond dispute in that dismal match against Bolton towards the end of April. The game's solitary goal came from Dean, when he headed Critchley's cross just inside the far post. It would be the only time Everton would find the net in the club's last four games (as though that deluge against West Ham represented the last hurrah of that season's free-wheeling side).

For the fans, the title victory capped the end of one of the most dramatic rollercoaster rides ever endured by any English football club. From the summit of Division One, down to Division Two and then back to the summit of the top flight in just a few seasons. Being an Evertonian had become an exercise in masochism.

v Manchester City 3–0

29 April 1933
FA Cup Final
Wembley Stadium. Attendance: 92,950

Everton: Sagar, Cook, Cresswell, Britton, White, Thomson, Geldard, Dunn, Dean, Johnson, Stein

Manchester City: Langford, Cann, Dale, Busby, Cowan, Bray, Toseland, Marshall, Herd, McMullan, Brook

Referee: E. Wood

Stein, Dean, Dunn!

I N the 1932/33 season, Everton's title defence never really got going. A stuttering start and some disappointing autumn form meant that by Christmas, the Blues were well off the pace; any sense of becoming champions again was unlikely.

And so hopes turned instead to the FA Cup. By 1933, it had been a generation since Everton had won the trophy. The inter-war years had not been a particularly productive time for the Blues in the competition. In the 1920s, the best they managed was one solitary quarter-final appearance, and they were more commonly found exiting in the early rounds.

Despite the club's patchy league form that season, the Blues still boasted a decent side and in all probability were one of a handful of clubs thought best placed to have a run at Wembley.

For some reason, where the league was a struggle, the cup seemed to offer respite. Everton recaptured their form from the previous campaign and swept aside teams with comparative ease. Leicester City and Bury were dismissed in the early rounds before Luton Town were battered 6–0 in the quarter-finals.

The only potential hurdle on the road to Wembley turned out to be West Ham United, whom the Blues met in the semi-finals at Molineux. The Londoners were at that point struggling in the nether regions of the second tier.

After Everton had taken an early lead, West Ham had responded strongly. For the want of some better finishing, the Hammers should have been able to pull out in front. As it was, they had to wait until just after half-time merely to draw level.

After that, they continued to dominate but ultimately came to pay for their profligacy. Everton took an undeserved lead seven minutes from time, when Critchley's effort hit the goalkeeper and then deflected in off the chest of West Ham defender Jim Barrett. With that, the Hammers were out.

At Wembley, Everton would meet Manchester City in an 'all-Lancashire final'. It was a head-to-head regarded by the *Evening Express* as one of the most closely pitted to have ever taken place.

'For 33 years – with intervals – tomorrow's Cup finalists have fought their battles and now, with a record of 50 games played against each other in league football, the difference is only three goals and four league points. This is the most remarkable case of equality in the whole of Football League history.'

Tens of thousands of Blues headed down to Wembley come the day itself. From midnight onwards, specially laid-on trains brought the travelling fans southward, packed to capacity. They steamed out of Lime Street, and by 9am thousands had reached the capital – all buoyed, no doubt, by the stirring words of their captain:

'I am full of hope that we shall be able to bring the cup to Merseyside. This is no idle statement and if I know my colleagues, they will have no stone unturned in their endeavour,' Dean told the local press. Adding, 'If we should fail, our supporters can rest assured that it will not be for want of trying. Tomorrow we go on the field to bring honour to Everton.'

Despite the club's disappointing league form, the Blues were the favourites that day. They were recent champions, led by the talismanic Dean, and most believed that a full-strength Everton side had the edge, especially when it was confirmed that City would be without their star centre-forward, Fred Tilson, who was out injured.

With both teams traditionally running out in variants of blue, the FA ruled that each should submit an alternative to play in. City opted for red and Everton, white shirts, black shorts and black socks with royal blue trimmings. For the first time in English football, the players were also numbered, Everton wearing 1–11 and City 12–22 (making Dean the first player to wear the number nine shirt).

Reminiscing years later in the *Liverpool Echo*, goalkeeper Ted Sagar provided an illuminating description of how some of the players prepared for the match.

'It is just about half an hour before the start that dressing-room excitement reaches its peak. Smoking in the dressing room is barred before a match and more particularly before a cup final, but even that strict disciplinarian, "Warney" Cresswell, felt it necessary to have a quiet pipe in the corner of the dressing room and nobody said him "nay" (as a matter of fact I had a cigarette with him).'

With pipes extinguished and ciggies put out, the teams eventually took to the field, and, in front of nearly 93,000 fans, City kicked off.

'Manchester City started as though they were going to swamp us, and I think that during that critical period we had to thank more than anybody Willie Cook, who had to face the City "flyer" and match-winner, Eric Brook,' remembered Sagar years later.

But Everton soon settled, and for much of the game City's approach was largely reduced to one of containment – their back line working like dervishes to limit the likes of Dean, Stein and Johnson. The marking of Dean in particular as an unenviable job, as Matt Busby, a member of City's half-back line, later put it:

'To play against Dixie Dean was at once a delight and a nightmare. He was a perfect specimen of an athlete, beautifully proportioned, with immense strength, adept on the ground but with extraordinary skill in the air.'

City worked hard to restrict Everton and, as half-time approached, must have thought they would at least go in level. There might have even been a belief that luck was on their side when Dean uncharacteristically missed a golden opportunity from a few yards out with the goal at his mercy.

'Oh, Mr Dean,' lamented the clipped tones of the commentator, 'what an open goal to dream about for the rest of your life.'

But this was to prove merely the warning shot. A few minutes later, City's defences were finally breached when 'Britton controlled the ball in masterly style, definitely made it his own, and then banged across one of those sweeping centres which always prove so menacing,' reported 'the Pilot' in the *Evening Express*.

Langford was caught in two minds, with Dean and Stein bearing down on him.

'Dean's worrying tactics enabled the ball to pass through a bunch of players to Stein, who after tapping it down with his left foot screwed it into the net with his right,' he continued.

After the break, the game continued as it had done in the first half, with Everton seeming far the more likely to find the net.

They probed continually and, on the 62-minute mark, finally found success when Britton beat Bray before banging the ball into the centre.

'Langford did not seem to know whether to catch the ball or put it over the top,' wrote 'the Pilot'.

Dean made the most of the keeper's procrastination, leaping to head both the ball and Langford into the net. It was a goal that bore similarities with Andy Gray's against Watford in the 1984 FA Cup Final: a powerful Everton centre-forward physically dominating an opposition goalkeeper.

Two–nil up and with just over half an hour to go, Everton seemed content from that point to sit back and protect their lead. And, for a time, City attempted to grasp the opportunity presented, pushing forward and threatening Everton with more regularity.

But, despite their toil, it would be the Toffees who would next find the net. With eight minutes of normal time remaining, a corner taken by Everton's young outside-right, Albert Geldard, was lofted in with precision to Dunn on the edge of the six-yard box. There, the Everton inside-right headed the ball, watching as it sailed into the bottom corner of the net, giving the keeper no chance.

Despite a few belated efforts by City, the game was over. When the final whistle went, few could deny that the stronger side had won.

'Dean then led his men in Indian file to the Royal Box and was presented with the Cup by the Duke of York amidst enthusiastic cheering. The Manchester players meanwhile stood on the field and joined in the applause. Dean waved the Cup to the spectators when he was given possession, and he came down from the box his face wreathed in smiles,' wrote 'the Pilot'.

Everton had achieved something remarkable: Second Division champions, First Division champions and then FA Cup winners in three consecutive years. It was a triumvirate that the city turned out to celebrate, as Ted Sagar recalled to the *Echo*:

'On our home-coming on the Tuesday night we were given a tremendous reception by huge crowds who lined the route from Lime Street Station to the Town Hall where we were received by the Lord Mayor and Lady Mayoress.'

The players travelled to the Town Hall in the original four-in-hand carriage which had carried the victorious 1906 team (and was driven by the same driver, Mr Jack Pagenham).

'We had to appear on the Town Hall balcony with the Cup,' continued Sagar 'and more than one, including Billy Dean himself were in tears at the warmth of the reception. Thousands more lined the route to the ground and it was estimated that 60,000 more were waiting inside the ground for us. Certainty [sic] nothing like it – not even the two Armistice nights – has been seen in the City before or since.'

v Sunderland 6–4

30 January 1935
FA Cup Fourth Round Replay
Goodison Park. Attendance: 59,213

Everton: Sagar, Cook, Jones, Britton, Gee, Thomson, Geldard, Cunliffe, Dean, Stevenson, Coulter

Sunderland: Thorpe, Murray, Hall, Thomson, Johnston, Hastings, Davis, Carter, Gurney, Gallacher, Connor

Referee: E. Pinkston

Cup Thriller

SOME games are 'great' because they represent tangible achievement, like a title win, European success or the capture of a domestic cup. Others are 'great' because with hindsight they come to mean something, like the moment a season turned around, the debut of a terrace legend or matches that embody the essence of a great side.

And then there are those games that are great simply because they're good to watch.

In the 1934/35 season, Everton played four matches against Sunderland, and three of those games saw seven goals or more. Few followers of football (aside from anyone under the age of ten and the people who run Sky Sports) equate goals with greatness. After all, a tight goalless draw can be more thrilling than an easy 5–0 victory. But one of these high-scoring games, against Sunderland, was a belter – an unpredictable and thrilling ride, one in which those watching had no idea what was going to happen next.

After dispatching Grimsby Town in the third round of the FA Cup, Everton were drawn away against Sunderland in the fourth. This was no easy tie. The Wearsiders were widely regarded as one of the best teams in the country (they would go on to finish second that season).

But, irrespective of their unfancied status, on a pitch that had been battered by snow, sleet and frost, Everton took the game to Sunderland and, were it not for an outstanding display by their keeper, could easily have emerged victorious. As it was, the game ended 1–1, which meant a replay a few days later back in Liverpool.

Although Sunderland were amongst the title favourites, possessed the best away form in the country and had recently beaten Everton 7–0 at Roker Park, Dean told the local press that he thought the Blues had a good chance.

'We have a hard fight in front of us – a cup final could not be more exacting – but we have the ability and the spirit to bring success.'

The fixture might have been arranged for a Wednesday afternoon, but nevertheless tens of thousands flocked to Goodison.

'Tramcars from town, packed to capacity were still arriving until almost three o'clock, half an hour after the kick off,' reported the *Evening Express*.

These late arrivals joined the swelling ranks of those who found their entrance barred, so popular had the game become. 'Thousands of people were unable to gain admission to the Everton ground and for a long time hundreds stood outside the closed entrances on the chance of room being found for them,' the report continued.

The first match had come in for some criticism from the press, largely because of the propensity of both teams (but particularly Sunderland) to play the man rather than the ball.

With this in mind, the referee, Ernest Pinkston (a man known pejoratively as the 'Sergeant Major'), gathered all 22 players in the centre circle prior to kick-off and warned them that a similar approach would get them sent off immediately.

Whether the warning from the 'Sergeant Major' was a deciding factor (or maybe these two teams just found their rhythm), what followed was a game packed with quality football, thrilling moments and an outcome that few could have predicted at the start.

From the beginning, both sides attacked with intent. Although Everton had started brightly, Sunderland had the better of the early chances and the Blues were fortunate that Sagar was on form in goal. But, despite Sunderland's greater threat, it was Everton who would take the lead:

'It was a joyous move,' wrote 'the Pilot' in the *Evening Express*. 'Coulter out on the wing, turned the ball in to Stevenson, who wheeled completely round, giving Murray and Thomson the dummy, he then came through with a shot. The ball was parried; Dean tried to drive it home; then Coulter hooked the ball out of Thorpe's reach, a foot inside the far post.'

Undeterred, Sunderland responded strongly, coming close on a number of occasions. They were particularly unlucky not to level after Connor's wonderful shot beat Sagar only to come back off the bar. Gurney breasted in the rebound, but the luck was with Sagar, who managed to grasp the ball on the line.

Once again, despite Sunderland having the better of the play, it would be Everton who claimed the next goal, when they broke from a Sunderland corner. 'The ball was taken down by Stevenson and swept to his right. Geldard centred and, with the defence watching Dean, Coulter had nothing to do but to beat Thorpe at short range' reported the *Sunderland Daily Echo and Shipping Gazette*. With 15 minutes left in the half, Sunderland continued with the same energy, this time matched by Everton (who appeared to have grown in confidence).

Both teams had further chances, with the best one falling to Sunderland when Thomson was forced to clear off the line after Sagar had nearly parried Carter's shot behind him into his own net.

Although leading, Everton had ridden their luck at the back, and a goal for the away side always seemed to be on the cards. It arrived just before half-time:

'From a throw in on the left, Connor went through and lobbed over the ball, which Gurney back-headed to Davis. The outside-right was unmarked, and he crashed the ball into the top of the net, giving Sagar no chance,' reported the *Evening Express*.

The second half carried on in the same manner, with both teams passing neatly and playing at a high tempo. As was the case with the first period, Sunderland had the better of the chances and Everton were once again grateful to their keeper for the maintenance of their lead, notably a magnificent save from Carter that would have beaten lesser men.

Although Sagar was good, he was helped enormously by Sunderland's profligacy in front of goal, specifically that of their centre-forward, Gallacher, who at one point put a gilt-edged chance wide that was easier to score than miss.

As the game edged into the final 15 minutes, it looked as though Sunderland might rue not taking their chances, after Everton nudged further in front.

'The ball had been whipped out to Connor,' wrote 'the Pilot', 'but Cook made a wonderful tackle, carried the ball along by a series of headers and then lobbed it into the centre. Dean tried a header, but was bumped by an opponent. The ball dropped and Stevenson coming in full pelt flashed the ball into the back of the net with a terrific shot.'

The game should have been out of Sunderland's reach. But the Wearsiders refused to give up. They continued to pile forward and eventually were rewarded for their efforts when Connor made it 3–2 around the 80-minute mark.

In a game filled with so many chances, few would have backed the score to remain the same.

With just 30 seconds left, Sunderland's tenacity was rewarded when Connor lobbed the ball into the middle. Sagar rushed out to meet it, but misjudged its flight slightly. A few yards ahead of him stood Gurney with his back to the goal. Sensing the opportunity presented by the keeper's rare error of judgement, the Sunderland forward attempted an audacious overhead kick, connected perfectly and levelled the scores, pushing the game into extra time.

It's a testament to Everton's resilience that despite squandering a two-goal lead, they came out in the first period fighting. Within two minutes, this sense of determination paid off as Britton lobbed the ball into the middle of the box. There, Dean was on hand to head it across to Coulter, who drove the ball past the Sunderland keeper from close range.

In keeping with the theme of the match, inevitably, the visitors came back, as Connor levelled to make it 4–4. With the game neatly poised, Sunderland then threatened to do something they hadn't done all afternoon: take the lead. Gallacher, hoping to atone for his earlier wastefulness, found himself unmarked in the box and managed to put the ball in the back of the net. But, to Sunderland's dismay, he had moved too early and the goal was ruled offside.

Some of the freneticism of the game seemed to dissipate after this point, as perhaps the players finally began to tire. But although the prospect of another replay appeared to be on the horizon, Geldard chose this moment to make his mark on the tie, crashing the ball into the net from a corner.

Everton defended resolutely for the remainder of the match as Sunderland vainly attempted to level. Their efforts, understandable as they were, left them exposed at the back; and, with time nearly up, Everton got the opportunity to let Sunderland taste what a disheartening last-minute strike felt like, as Geldard shot from distance to nab his second of the game. The goal made it 6–4, and this time Sunderland had no further answers.

When the end arrived a minute later, those at Goodison could breathe a sigh of relief and celebrate not just the fact that their side had gone through to the next round but also that the fans had witnessed something remarkable.

As John Peel (still no relation) wrote in the *Liverpool Post and Mercury*: 'There have in the past been many exciting cup-ties played on Merseyside, but never has there been a more thrilling struggle than that in which Everton defeated Sunderland yesterday in the fourth-round replay by six goals to four. Whatever cup-ties are talked about in years to come this one will hold a prominent place in competition history.'

v Leeds United 7–1

3 March 1937
Football League Division One
Goodison Park. 17,064

Everton: Sagar, Jackson, Cook, Britton, Gee, Mercer, Geldard, Lawton, Dean, Stevenson, Gillick

Leeds United: McInroy, Sproston, Gadsby, Edwards, Holley, Mills, Powell, Ainsley, Hodgson, Furness, Buckley

Referee: B. Amos

Master and Apprentice

'**G**OOD luck to you. But you'll never be as good as Dixie.'
It might have been a throwaway comment, but the bus conductor who guided 17-year-old Tommy Lawton on his first trip to Goodison Park, and who saw him off with that parting pearl of wisdom, summed up what many Evertonians felt (or feared). The teenage prodigy, bought for £6,500 from Burnley (a huge sum for someone so young), had big shoes to fill.

Lawton might have been young and raw, but he came with an impressive record. His 560 goals in three years of schoolboy football had brought him to the notice of several Lancashire clubs. Burnley were the ones who captured his signature, and, after featuring as an amateur, he made his professional debut for the Clarets against Spurs aged 17, banging in a hat-trick in the process. A few months on, 25 appearances and 16 goals to his name, he was at Everton, a big-money fee hanging over his head, and training with his idol Dixie Dean.

Tall, slim and with slicked-back, brilliantined hair, Lawton had the makings of the perfect centre-forward. Quick and decent in the air, he also possessed a hard, accurate shot, which had been honed at Turf Moor. It was one that adhered to the principle of 'low and hard' – struck with unwavering accuracy.

At the time that Lawton arrived at Goodison (January 1937), Everton were in the process of transition. Although some of the old guard remained from the team that had claimed the 1933 FA Cup, such as Britton, Cook and Sagar, there were younger players coming through, part of the process that saw the club try to shake off the mediocrity that had beset it in the mid-to-late 1930s.

The most dominant figure remaining from the old guard was unquestionably Dean. For over a decade he had loomed large over Goodison, a name that became intertwined with Everton's own. Despite him being only 29 when Lawton was bought, Dean's majestic powers were on the wane. Injuries had begun to take their toll, and, with them, Dean had lost some of his pace and movement. Yet he retained an unerring eye for goal and continued (if at a lesser volume) to find the net. In the season that Lawton arrived, Dean scored 24 goals in 36 league games, not a bad return for a supposedly 'fading' star.

During Lawton's early time at Goodison, Dean was still very much the focal point of Everton's forward line, and so the young lad from Farnworth initially spent time in the reserves.

His earliest chance to shine in the first team came in an away game against Wolves (Dean was being rested for an upcoming FA Cup tie). On a boggy pitch, Everton were battered 7–2. Although the debutant did manage to get on the scoresheet (via a penalty), it was hardly the most impressive of starts.

Dropped for the subsequent cup game against Spurs, his cause for future inclusion was given a boost after another lacklustre performance by the first team, one in which Everton had narrowly gained a 1–1 draw (through a last-minute equaliser) and ended the match fighting with the opposition. The directors demanded change, and, in the replay, 'master' and 'apprentice' took to the pitch for the first time, with Lawton playing outside-left.

In a match that at one point Everton had led 3–1 (only to end up losing 4–3), Lawton impressed from the off. He got his second senior goal when he put the Blues one ahead with a shot that 'Bee' in the *Liverpool Echo* described as 'so hot and fast, so rushing that the goalkeeper Hall saw nothing of it'.

The story goes that, on seeing the back of the net rippling, Dean turned to Joe Mercer and said 'Well, that's it. That's the swansong, that's the end of it.' The 'master' had seen the writing on the wall. The time of the 'apprentice' was clearly at hand.

Not that the 'master' had been anything other than generous towards his future replacement. On their first meeting at Goodison, Dean had taken the youngster to one side, put his arm around him and said, 'I know you're here to take my place. Anything I can do to help you I will. I promise, anything at all.'

Despite the club boasting arguably the two best centre-forwards to grace English football in the 1930s, Evertonians would only get to see them play together on nine occasions in total. And only one of those would result in victory. But at least it was a healthy one.

Leeds United visited in the spring of 1937, the Blues mid-table, the Yorkshiremen skirting with relegation. At that point, impressively, Everton were undefeated at Goodison. Were it not for a much patchier away record, the Blues could have been challenging for the title.

Although it was a fine and dry day, heavy rain during the week had taken its toll on the pitch, as 'Bee' perfectly illustrated:

'When Dean and Willie Edwards came to toss up they found the conditions too severe to allow the task to move off. Trying to find a better bit of turf, they were baulked in their desires and eventually Dean tossed the coin up on the back of his hand.'

The conditions made the opening minutes of the game scrappy. Everton's first three attempts at through balls all got stuck in mud, so appalling was the pitch anywhere except the wings. Eventually, though, as 'the Pilot' explained in the *Evening Express*, one team adapted:

'They [Everton] could do what Leeds were unable to do, judge the pace of the ball in the mud. After a rather scrambling opening they gradually got on top, and remained there.'

Everton began to build momentum, with Dean and Geldard coming close early on. Leeds's fragility was evident throughout. Their defence, described by 'Bee' as being in a 'state of coma', could not cope with Everton's front line. Holley, who was tasked with marking Dean, had an especially torrid afternoon.

Goals were in the air, and eventually the first arrived courtesy of the 'master', when Dean, 25 yards out, belted the ball into the top right-hand corner of the net.

But, despite Everton's dominance, at 1–0 Leeds had chances to get back into the game. Powell and Hodgson both tested Sagar, and Mercer had to clear one Leeds corner off the line. That second Everton goal was sorely needed, and, ten minutes before the interval, the 'apprentice' provided:

'There had been a corner and Lawton, usually a very fast shooter, seemed to hesitate in order to find a vacant spot. So soon as he had espied the left-hand corner of the goal he let out the shot that has made him famous and scored a neat goal,' reported 'Bee'.

Although largely outplayed, at 2–0 Leeds were not out of the game as the teams went in for the break. A better performance in the second period could have redeemed matters. Instead, what they offered was utter capitulation.

In the second half, what edifice Leeds had displayed simply crumbled away. In part hampered once reduced to ten men through the loss of the injured Sproston, the Yorkshire side also lost what little organisation and discipline they had enjoyed.

Geldard made it three on 67 minutes. Stevenson made it 4–0, and then Gillick 5–0 not long after. Hodgson, in what could barely count as consolation, then brought it to 5–1, after which Everton continued to press their advantage, with Dean and then Stevenson making the final score 7–1. It was a consummate performance, one so dominant that Sagar only touched the ball twice during the entire half (albeit once to pick the ball out of the net).

Dean and Lawton had linked up well together throughout, the pair clearly a difficult prospect for any defence to handle. But, as dazzling as the partnership had been, for 'master' and 'apprentice', that was as good as it got together on the pitch. The 'Dixieland' era was coming to a close. Dean had fallen out with Theo Kelly, the recently appointed, ruthlessly ambitious, club secretary. As their relationship soured, and Lawton's ability became more evident, the new secretary felt emboldened to do what would have once seemed unthinkable.

Three matches into the 1937/38 season, Dean was dropped. He barely featured again and spent much of the remainder of his time with Everton in the reserves (falling one short of 400 first-team appearances).

His last game in a blue shirt came in the Liverpool Senior Cup semi-final against South Liverpool at Holly Park. Thousands turned up to see Dean play (proving his continued 'box office' appeal). Although not at his best, the 'master' still found the net, scoring the final goal in Everton's 4–1 victory.

A few days later, fans and the football world alike were stunned when it was announced that Everton's legendary centre-forward had been sold to Notts County. Neatly, from Kelly's perspective, the fee was £3,000, exactly the same amount as Everton had paid Tranmere Rovers for the young Dean all those years ago.

Dixieland had closed its doors. With the 'master' gone, it was now the time for the 'apprentice' to shine.

v Sunderland 6–2

10 April 1939
Football League Division One
Goodison Park. Attendance: 46,016

Everton: Sagar, Cook, Greenhalgh, Mercer, Thomson, Watson, Gillick, Bentham, Lawton, Stevenson, Caskie

Sunderland: Heywood, Feenan, Hall, Housam, Lockie, Hastings, Duns, Carter, Robinson, Smeaton, Burbanks

Referee: J. Mellor

War Time Blues

THE 1937/38 season had been a frustrating one for Everton. Although the team had scored freely, with Lawton proving to be a capable replacement for Dean (finishing as the First Division's top scorer), Everton had ended the campaign just three points off 'the drop'.

Everton were a young side and unquestionably one in transition, which perhaps contributed to their underwhelming season. But a change was on its way. In the summer of 1938, the team participated in a tournament at Ibrox, which necessitated a month away together in Scotland. As Lawton later wrote in *When the Cheering Stopped*, it was a transformative period:

'We began to know each other as people, not just players. People with different personalities, faults, varying moods, likes and dislikes … a wonderful blend developed between the players, which resulted in a far closer team spirit.' Allied to this closer sense of unity, there were other changes to the side. The mercurial yet gifted winger Torry Gillick became a regular. The energetic and determined inside-right Stan Bentham graduated into the first team. And Tommy Watson, who had actually been with the club since 1933, would gradually make the role of 'twelfth man' his own, providing vital utility cover for the side.

Everton started the 1938/39 season well, winning the opening six games (including an away victory at champions Arsenal). The club was flying high:

'I know it is early to talk and much may happen before the end of the season draws nigh, but I am much more hopeful than I was this time last year,' wrote 'Stork' in the *Liverpool Echo*, capturing the mood of the time.

Everton were one of a small number talked of as possible title contenders. But the expectation of any club grasping that mantle was shrouded in doubt. The prospect of war with Germany again loomed in Europe, as Nazi expansionism threatened the uneasy peace that had existed since 1918.

Prime minister Neville Chamberlain might have secured a peace deal from Hitler at Munich towards the end of September, but there remained anxiety in many circles that war, at some stage soon, still seemed inevitable.

As it was, the season continued under this shadow and Everton remained in the hunt. The side, although less dominant than had been the case in those opening weeks, had improved dramatically compared with the previous campaign. And Lawton led by example. Everton's in-form front man would finish the campaign as the division's top scorer again.

After a slight wobble around Christmas, Everton got back to winning ways, and, following a 3–0 victory at Anfield in February, they topped the table – a position that the club never looked like giving up.

While others faltered, Everton were imperious. As the finishing line approached, the Blues had lost only one league match in 1939 (to their title rivals Wolves) and drawn two.

'Everton's success is a triumph of pure football ability,' wrote 'Ranger' in the *Echo*. 'Whenever they have appeared they have won praise by their craft and artistry. After their visit to Highbury early in the season the Arsenal programme the following week went into eulogies about them. The same thing has happened elsewhere several times.'

In early April, Everton faced Sunderland at Goodison. It was a game where the Blues knew that victory would make the title a near certainty. Wolves, their nearest rivals, had dropped off the pace and were increasingly reliant on Everton stumbling to have any hope of catching up.

Sunderland's league powers had diminished since their title-winning heyday. By that point in the season they were languishing in the nether regions of the table, an opponent ripe for the picking.

But, regardless of their travails, Sunderland initially suggested that the day might not be Everton's. A flurry of attacks, led by the energetic Duns, briefly had the home side worried.

However, against the run of play, Everton struck after 12 minutes when Caskie's inch-perfect corner (which had resulted from Hall's cack-handed clearance) was met by the head of Bentham, who butted the ball past a helpless Heywood in goal.

At 1–0 up, the momentum switched and Everton began to pile on the pressure. The chances started to build in number, the standout one being a blistering volley by Lawton from just inside the box which sailed narrowly over the bar.

In response, Sunderland vainly attempted to get back into the game, with everything that was good about their play originating from the inventive Duns. Sagar saved well from one of his efforts, and, had Smeaton and Robinson been more alert, they each could have turned in a dangerous cross from him too.

Despite their efforts, though, it would be Everton who scored next, not long after the half-hour mark.

'The ball was lobbed into the goalmouth. Heywood and Lawton went up for it together, the Everton man nodding the ball back to Bentham, who crashed it into the net at lightning speed,' wrote 'Stork' in the *Echo*.

Everton were good for the lead and deserved to go in at half-time ahead. Yet Sunderland had not been without threat, and, as if to underline that point, on the stroke of half-time, Housam scored for the Wearsiders, heading in Duns's corner.

Over the course of the 1930s, Everton had put big scores past Sunderland with surprising frequency, to the point where the Wearsiders might have feared an avalanche of goals every time they went a few behind the Blues. On the strength of the first-half display, such an outcome would have seemed unlikely. But, in the second period, everything changed. Sunderland wilted, and, in response, Everton went up a gear.

'At 50 minutes Stevenson scored a picture goal,' reported 'Stork'. 'Gillick was the starting point, and his centre was helped on by Lawton, which left Stevenson with a marvellous chance, which he took finely to score it.'

Ten minutes later, the floodgates opened. Caskie scored Everton's fourth with a header. Two minutes after that, a defensive error by Sunderland let in Lawton, who drove the ball home to make it five.

By this point the visitors looked broken, all shape and organisation gone. But, although the chances of further Everton goals seemed more and more likely, in the end there would be just the single addition. Bentham, who had gone off for a time to have a head wound seen to, came back on to nab Everton's sixth after some great work by Lawton, who all but single-handedly created the chance. It crowned an unlikely hat-trick for the wing-half.

In the dying seconds of the game, Duns got Sunderland's second, a just consolation for the tireless work he had put in.

Through that victory, Everton had made their position in the league exceptionally strong; the likelihood of the title coming back to Goodison was now a near certainty.

It might have taken a few more days, and included a goalless draw against Preston North End and a 2–1 defeat against Charlton Athletic, but Everton were eventually crowned champions in late April.

The Blues would technically remain the title holders for the next eight years. As had been the case when Everton had won the league in 1914, conflict changed everything. Although the 1939/40 season was permitted to begin in late August, just a few weeks into the campaign the political climate darkened considerably. In early September, after the Nazis had invaded Poland, the UK and France declared war on Germany. With the country at war, the FA and the Football League cancelled what was left of the season.

When the league resumed in 1946, Everton's all-conquering side would be without Lawton and Mercer, both of whom had left to join other clubs. Without them, and with the years of conflict robbing the team of any momentum that could have been built, Everton were a shadow of the side they had been. Once again the fans and the players were left with a sense of 'what might have been'.

'They were a bloody good side,' Lawton later wrote, 'and the next year we should have won the league again, the FA Cup and the bloody Boat Race if they'd put us in it.'

As the 1940s bled into the 1950s, Everton struggled. Final positions took on a downward momentum. Not for the first time in the club's history, war had negatively impacted on Everton's fortunes. No other club in Europe has such a close correlation between title success and the outbreak of armed conflict.

It makes you wonder how people felt a generation later in 1962, when Everton were once again looking capable of mounting an assault on the title. Around that time, reeling from the horror of the Cuban Missile Crisis, with the world's superpowers still contemplating the possibility of initiating World War III, perhaps more than one neutral might have been hoping Everton would stumble, so potent a portent of all-out conflict had the club's title successes become.

v Manchester United 2–1

14 February 1953
FA Cup Fifth Round
Goodison Park. Attendance: 77,920

Everton: O'Neill, Clinton, Lindsay, Jones, Parker, Farrell, Lello, Eglington, Hickson, Buckle, Cummins

Manchester United: Wood, Byrne, Aston, Carey, Lewis, Chilton, Cockburn, Pegg, Berry, Rowley, Pearson

Referee: H. Beacock

The Cannonball Kid

IN the early 1950s, Goodison was ruled by a board which seemed determined to hold on to the austerity aesthetic that had so characterised Britain in the late 1940s: the culture of 'running a tight ship', of 'every penny counts', of 'make do and mend'. In short, they were tight-arses.

As such, like had not been replaced by like, and instead the club's prevailing ethos was to put faith in youth (augmented by cheap acquisitions from the lower leagues and Ireland).

The result, inevitably, was disaster. Deteriorating form led eventually, humiliatingly, to relegation. The club ended the 1950/51 season bottom of the First Division, consigning the Blues to their second spell in the second tier.

Down there, life proved tougher than expected, and, for a time, Everton laboured. At one point, early in the second campaign, the Blues were bottom – thoughts of an unprecedented drop to the Third Division North haunting those who followed the club.

Although silver linings were hard to find, a few did exist. The approach of the board might have been largely disastrous, but that isn't to say that the faith in youth didn't sometimes bear fruit. Young players such as T. E. Jones, John Willie Parker and Dave Hickson started to make their mark on the first team.

Of these, Hickson was unquestionably the highlight for the fans. Ask any Evertonian who followed the club in the 1950s to name their idol and they will invariably point to the 'Cannonball Kid'.

'He was an old-fashioned centre-forward. With his a towering blonde quiff, his physical style and a decent eye for goal, Hickson gave us Evertonians something to get excited about in the dark days of the early 1950s. And they were dark. It was a very tough time to be a Blue,' remembers lifelong Evertonian John Flaherty.

Hickson was tenacious to the point of self-harm, putting his head in places where others might be wary of putting a foot. In was a level of commitment appreciated by the Goodison faithful, who responded to a player that appeared to give his heart and soul for the club every Saturday afternoon.

'I think Evertonians, as much as they appreciate skills and dexterity, have always taken to their hearts players that give their all for the club. And Hickson was the embodiment of that sort of player,' continues John.

It was an approach probably best summed up by Hickson's own iconic quote, when he said:

'I would have died for Everton. I would have broken every other bone in my body for any other club I played for but I would have died for this club.'

Hickson sealed his reputation for tenacity in a game that also represented another of those bright spots during the bleak 1950s: Everton's fifth-round FA Cup tie against First Division champions Manchester United.

After some difficult times during the inter-war years, including a few spells in the second tier, Manchester United had emerged as a football force in the immediate post-war era. Under the management of former Liverpool right-half Matt Busby, United had consistently pushed for the title since top-flight football had resumed in 1946. In 1952, after several near misses, they had eventually clinched it.

On paper, the tie looked relatively straightforward (in so much as an FA Cup game can ever be), the reigning champions playing a side languishing in the second tier.

But, despite their threat, United were enduring a tricky season of their own, struggling to recapture their title-winning form. And, as 'Stork' reported in the *Liverpool Echo*, Everton were not to be underestimated:

'Manchester United will have to sit up and take notice of this Everton team which has not lost a game since January 3. For it has become a competent footballing side with a high degree of confidence in itself.'

In the cup, Everton had dispatched Ipswich Town (3–2) and Nottingham Forest (4–1) in the opening rounds, while United had struggled against Millwall (1–0) and then taken two stabs to dispose of amateur side Walthamstow Avenue (5–2). If form could count for anything, Everton were certainly worth a flutter.

Then again, any punter who had done so would certainly have been cursing that decision if the opening exchanges had been anything to go by.

'United, while not playing as good football as they used to do 12 months ago, still looked the more dangerous side. When they attacked, it was usually with all forwards up, whereas Everton's attack frequently saw the inside men well back and the half backs after their defensive efforts unable to lend a hand,' wrote 'Ranger' in the *Liverpool Football Echo*.

Eventually United's attacking momentum gave them the advantage, when Rowley put them ahead around the 25-minute mark, seizing on a rebound after the Everton keeper could only parry Berry's effort away.

The goal, far from disheartening the hosts, seemed to spur Everton into action. Buckle came close on two occasions, and both Chilton and Carey had to make last-ditch interventions to prevent Everton scoring. But the

Blues would not be denied for long, and, ten minutes before half-time, they levelled.

'The start of the movement was a very clever pass by Cummins to Hickson, who was in the outside-right position. Hickson quickly transferred the ball to Eglington who came in to round Aston and then score with a grand right foot shot from ten yards' distance,' reported 'Ranger'.

Five minutes from the break, with the game hammering back and forth, Everton appeared to have been dealt a devastating blow when Hickson dived to connect with a cross, receiving a boot to the head for his troubles. With blood streaming from a cut above his left eye, he was ordered off the field.

Half-time came and went, but without Hickson initially remerging. But, unbeknownst to the crowd, the 'Cannonball Kid' was being patched up by Harry Cooke. To the relief of those (home fans) crammed into Goodison, a few seconds after the Everton side had run out on to the field, that recognisable blonde quiff emerged from the tunnel, replete with a hastily stitched-up wound above his right eye.

Shortly after he returned, as Hickson described in *The Cannonball Kid*, a second collision, this time with the post, almost spelled the end of his game that day:

> There was blood and all that everywhere. At this point the referee, Mr Beacock of Scunthorpe, suggested to Peter Farrell [the Everton captain] that I should leave the field.
>
> 'He'll have to go off,' said the referee. 'He can't go on with an eye like that. He's not normal.'
>
> There was no way I was going off the pitch, no way at all.
>
> 'I am normal,' I told him. 'Tell him I'm normal, Peter, tell him!'
>
> 'Of course you are Dave,' said Peter.
>
> 'There you are, Ref,' I said. 'I'm staying!'

Blood oozing from his wound, Hickson continued, a decision that paid off not long after, as the man himself later described:

'On 63 minutes came the game's decisive moment. I took Tommy Eglington's pass on my chest, beat one man, sidestepped another and hammered a right-footed shot beyond the reach of Ray Wood and into the net. Goodison erupted in celebration. It was a wonderful moment.'

The remainder of the game was confidently and competently seen out by the home side. 'Nobody', wrote 'Ranger', 'seeing Everton for the first time for a couple of months would recognize them as the side they were around about the turn of the year. They fought grimly and resolutely for every ball. They were going to it more quickly than the opposition, and they were swinging it about nicely and their defence covered up even more convincingly than United's.'

Everton could have extended their lead on several occasions, with Hickson and Parker each having good opportunities. But that extra goal, although sought for, was ultimately not needed. The Blues ended up 2–1 victors, with a huge debt of gratitude owed to their tenacious centre-forward.

'Hickson was the man of the attack. His grit and determination carried him through despite his handicap and he still chased the ball as though his very life depended on it,' reported 'Ranger', later adding, 'When the final whistle went O'Neill dashed half the length of the field to throw his arms around Hickson, the hero of a wonderful win.'

Evertonians have always loved their centre-forwards. And, for many, that was the day that Hickson was truly taken into the bosom of the faithful. For as much as the fans respect a forward for his guile, his craft, his skill, they want something more. They want to believe that he feels what the supporters feel, that he loves the club, that he would spill blood for the shirt. Hickson embodied everything that Evertonians want from those who lead the line.

His performance, and those of his team-mates, had earned the Blues a famous win. But there was only so much sunshine to go round that season. Despite the victory, Everton would not make it all the way to Wembley. Although the cup run continued, the Blues faltered in the semis, losing 4–3 to Bolton Wanderers (despite a valiant fightback from 4–0 down).

'It wasn't to be. Which was a shame,' admits John Flaherty. 'But lucky for us, things were about to get a whole lot better. We were about to see the team get back to where they rightfully belonged.'

v Oldham Athletic 4–0

17

29 April 1954
Football League Division Two
Boundary Park. Attendance: 30, 072

Oldham Athletic: Burnett, Smith, McGlen, Lowrie, Naylor, Whyte, Walker, Harris, Hardwick, McIlvenny, Brierley

Everton O'Neill, Moore, Donovan, Farrell, Jones, Lello, Wainwright, Fielding, Hickson, Parker, Eglington

Referee: A. Baker

Back in the Big Time

DESPITE the high of beating the champions in the FA Cup, Everton had ended the 1952/53 season in the doldrums, languishing near the bottom of the league (finishing 16th, the club's lowest-ever position in English football). Superficially, the chances of promotion looked remote.

Look a little deeper, though, and the green shoots of recovery *were* evident. The team was more settled, and the genesis of a decent side was beginning to take shape, with the likes of Hickson, Parker and Jones growing in confidence.

There was also, as Dave Hickson explained in *The Cannonball Kid*, an emergent sense of team camaraderie, underlined by a grim determination to reverse the club's fortunes.

'After our FA Cup run and the disappointment of finishing so far down the Second Division, there was a real resolve among us to get Everton back where they belonged in the top flight. We sat down at the start of the 1953/54 season and resolved to do it. I think the spirit was all over the club.'

Strong from August onwards, the Blues remained one of a handful of clubs seriously vying for promotion. And, in contrast to the dirge that had characterised recent campaigns, Everton were also playing attractive, swashbuckling football. Along the way, teams were often dispatched by scorelines more redolent of the Dean era (6–1, 6–2, 8–4).

A key element in this cavalier approach was the partnership that developed between Hickson and Parker.

'He was an excellent inside-forward,' Hickson later wrote of Parker. 'We had a good working relationship and with that you always know what the other fellow is doing … John Willie was really my partner in crime. We each knew what we were going to do.'

The pair netted over 55 league goals between them during the campaign, a key element in the push for promotion. With that kind of potency, the Blues should have been comfortable champions. But, Everton being Everton, the club nearly conspired to throw it all away. A dip in form during the run-in saw the race go to the wire. As the final game approached, Everton sat outside the promotion positions.

Above them were Leicester City (56 points) and Blackburn Rovers (55). Importantly, both had played their final games, giving Everton (who had 54 points) the opportunity to leapfrog Blackburn and in the process get back into the top flight. If the Blues managed the improbable feat of winning 6–0, that would also be enough to see them crowned champions.

'There aren't a lot of Blues left who can remember what it was like to be in the Second Division,' says John Bohanna, who first began following the club in the 1940s. 'It was tough. Ever since, whenever we have been down near the bottom of the top flight, I've had cold sweats and sleepless nights because I know what the reality of relegation is like. We had to get out of that league. It was as simple as that. The last game of the season was as important as any that has taken place in Everton's long history.'

In their way stood Oldham Athletic (already relegated to the Third Division North) and an away fixture at Boundary Park. Should Everton achieve promotion, it would restore the club as the kings of the city once more. Although this was still the age of 'friendly rivalry', when Blues and Reds would regularly go to each other's games, there was just enough competitive spirit between the two clubs for Evertonians to take satisfaction from the fact that Liverpool would be heading down just as Everton returned to the top.

That the club was in any position at all to countenance the idea of promotion was thanks to Hickson's contribution in the season's penultimate game, as the *Liverpool Echo* reported:

'Hickson has scored many extremely valuable goals for Everton but none of greater significance than his splendid header at the 38th minute against Birmingham. Had it not been for that goal, we should not now be caring two straws about the game at Oldham, as Everton's promotion chances would have been extinguished.'

The game was a late kick-off, so the exodus from Liverpool began early. People took the afternoon off, and by early evening Oldham town centre was awash with Evertonians.

'Oldham had never seen anything like it,' remembers Tony Onslow. 'We were there mob-handed. They tried to stop people bunking in to the ground by putting tar on the walls. But it made no difference. The young kids just put newspaper over it and climbed over. The tar still got all over them, though. There was a report in the local paper the next day that referred to the Blues as the "tar babies" of Everton.'

Inside, the Everton enclosure was soon full to bursting point, and people were beginning to spill out on to the track that surrounded the pitch. There are conflicting reports regarding how many fans actually turned up to watch the match, but most figures put it around 40,000 (the numbers possibly swelled by followers of Blackburn, who also had an investment in the outcome).

'It was certainly packed. And in the end there were many who didn't get in. It was the kind of thing that you just would never see nowadays,' Tony continues.

In a boost to the Blues' promotion chances, Cliff Britton was able to name his strongest starting eleven after Wainwright, Fielding and Eglington, all of whom had suffered knocks in the previous match, had recovered and come through training unscathed.

Although a win of 6–0 remained a tall order, even against a side devoid of motivation, early signs of an easy and significant victory were promising, as 'Ranger' reported in the *Liverpool Daily Post*:

'It was Parker who set Everton on the road to victory when he gave them the lead in the seventh minute after Moore had centred the ball from long-distance and Hickson had headed it forward. Parker took advantage of a partial slip by the Oldham defence to nip in quickly and head it home.'

Everton barely gave Oldham the opportunity to breathe after that. The Blues were rampant and, as if to underscore this, got their second not long after. The goal came via an error by the Oldham keeper, Burnett, who misjudged a speculative long ball from Jones. He failed to reach it and, under pressure from Hickson, flapped desperately at thin air, watching helplessly as the ball dropped behind him into the net.

But Everton weren't done. Soon after, Parker nipped in to side-foot the ball into the net after Burnett had dropped Fielding's shot. Everton were 3–0 up and Oldham hadn't even attempted an effort on goal. With only 26 minutes gone, 6–0 suddenly didn't seem wholly unrealistic.

Before the sides went in for the break, Everton found the time to add one more to their tally when Hickson ran half the length of the field, beat three men and drove the ball out of Burnett's reach.

'It was a goal that sealed promotion in the minds of anyone watching. Everton had been breathtaking and Oldham non-existent. I think at that point most Blues in the ground thought we could go on and finish top,' says Tony Onslow.

The game was all but over. All Everton needed to do now was come out in the second half and maintain the same tempo, and the league title would likely be theirs. But Everton couldn't quite manage that.

'After the entrancing football which Everton had served up in the first half the second portion was something of an anti-climax. The visitors appeared to slacken off considerably in their efforts and allowed Oldham to take the upper hand for quite lengthy spells,' wrote 'Ranger'.

Despite Everton's dissipating momentum and Oldham's resurgence, the Blues still had chances, with Eglington coming close and Burnett pulling off a couple of fine saves from Hickson. But the zip and swagger had gone from their game, and, as the match continued, the likelihood of a 6–0 victory began to recede.

Not that the assembled Evertonians were too bothered. The 4–0 win still meant promotion, enabling the club to jump above Blackburn into second place.

'There were scenes of tremendous enthusiasm as soon as the final whistle went,' reported 'Ranger'.

The Blues who had invaded Boundary Park let themselves go deliriously. 'Thousands of them swarmed on to the pitch and hoisted Farrell the Everton captain shoulder-high carrying him in triumph to the entrance to the dressing room,' he continued.

For Dave Hickson, whose goals and work ethic had done so much to get Everton back into the top flight, that moment is one that remained with him for his whole life, as he recalled in *The Cannonball Kid*:

'It was the highlight of my career,' he wrote. 'Even now when people stop me and say, "Hi, Davey", I think it's because they look back at the time when we got them back up to where they are now. I think people remember that time, even if they weren't around to see or experience it. Evertonians are very good with their history and there's a sense of recognition that I was part of a side that got them back to where they belong. They've been very close to going down again a few times, but they've got through it. I'm proud that Everton have sat in the top flight for six decades following our efforts.'

v Fulham 4–1

11 May 1963
Football League Division One
Goodison Park. Attendance: 60,578

Everton: Dunlop, Parker, Meagan, Labone, Gabriel, Kay, Scott, Stevens, Young, Vernon, Temple

Fulham: Macedo, Cohen, Langley, Mullery, Keetch, Robson, Key, Brown, Cook, Haynes, O'Connell

Referee: R. Windle

The Mersey Millionaires

EVERTON'S return to the First Division in 1954 hadn't initially been a resounding success. During the remainder of the 1950s, the club had struggled and spent most of its time skirting around the lower regions of the table.

But as the 1960s dawned, change was in the air at Goodison Park. 'John Moores, founder of the Littlewoods empire, had started investing in the club, a process that would culminate with him becoming chairman in 1961,' says Greg Murphy, who wrote an expansive analysis of Everton's boardroom from the 1960s to the 2000s in the Everton fanzine *When Skies Are Grey* a few years ago.

'Moores had a simple aim,' continues Greg, 'to restore Everton to the elite of the game. And he was going to do this by underwriting investment in players, developing the stadium, improving the club's commercial performance and getting the right people in charge on the playing side.'

When Moores had first taken control at Everton, the man in the managerial hot-seat was Johnny Carey.

'Although not a popular figure with the players, Carey played an expansive style of football that was open and enjoyable to be part of,' says Derek Temple, who made his debut for Everton in 1957. 'It made for a good side, although not a great one. I think we were entertainers but not necessarily winners. It was the sort of side that could be great to watch but which doesn't win titles.'

Moores wanted more than to be simply entertained. He wanted silverware. After a catastrophic run of form during the 1960/61 season, a dismal slump that had seen Everton's incipient title hopes disappear, Carey was sacked.

In his place came the Sheffield Wednesday manager, and former Everton player, Harry Catterick.

'Harry had done great things at Wednesday,' says left-half Tony Kay, who played for Catterick at both Everton and the Yorkshire club. 'You have to remember that they had finished runners-up in the league in 1960/61 behind the magnificent Spurs "Double"-winning side, which was no small achievement. He was highly regarded and you could understand why Everton prised him away.'

Like Carey, Catterick was never a particularly popular manager with his players, as Rob Sawyer, author of *Harry Catterick: The Untold Story of a Football Great*, explains:

'He was a product of his times, a man who had grown up in the more austere environment of the 1920s and 1930s; very old school. He believed that the manager didn't mingle with the players. He was the absolute boss and they were employed to do his bidding. Admiration and respect for him was mixed with a sizable dose of fear – few players felt much fondness towards him at the time.'

On arrival, Catterick recruited sparingly but judiciously, seeking to create a side that was more resilient.

'Harry tried to put together a side that was "complete", that possessed less weak links,' thinks Kay. 'In particular, he recognised that the Blues had a soft underbelly and perhaps lacked that touch of nastiness that all great sides have. He created a side that could measure up to most in the physical stakes.'

Although Everton finished only in fourth during Catterick's first season in charge (one place higher than Carey the season before), there was a sense of upward momentum about the team.

'They were simply a better team,' argues David France, author, football historian and founder of the Everton Collection. 'There was a sense of solidity about them, a feeling this was a team (and a manager) that understood how to win games and manage a season. You had the feeling at Everton that the only way was up, that the club was really going places.'

And so it proved. As the 1962/63 campaign began, Everton started well and remained in the higher reaches of the table throughout the season, giving the fans the belief that here was an Everton side that finally, realistically, had a shot at the title.

'The only worry', explains John Flaherty, 'was that perhaps we lacked experience. Although unquestionably steelier, this was a side unused to big occasions and the pressures involved in going for big prizes.'

And then there was the weather to take into account. Bearing similarities to Everton's successful 1890/91 title-winning campaign, the 1962/63 season was blighted by an uncommonly cold winter.

In parts of England, it was one of the coldest winters since records began. Rivers, lakes, and even in places the sea, froze over. Snow lay on the ground for months, and for several weeks the football calendar was blighted.

Although it affected everyone, the fixture pile-up created by the harsh winter made the league more unpredictable. There were so many games rescheduled for April and May that if a club unfortunately chose that period to have a poor run of form, it could significantly affect what might otherwise have been a good season.

Fortunately for Everton, the pressures of hunting for the title and the added stress of the fixture pile-up were competently navigated. As the season came to a close, the Blues found themselves in a three-horse race with Leicester City and Spurs for the club's first title in a generation.

'We played Spurs at home in the April in a game that was vitally important,' remembers David France. 'Despite boasting the likes of Jimmy Greaves, Dave Mackay and Terry Dyson, the recent "Double" winners were outplayed by us. Although just the one goal separated the sides [Alex Young's], the scoreline flattered Spurs. We had dominated them. It was the performance of champions.'

The impact of beating and outplaying Spurs was tangible. As the season came to a close, Everton were imperious: strong, confident and at times unplayable.

'We knew we were good,' says Tony Kay, 'and as the season's end neared, all we had to do was trust in our ability, maintain concentration and take each game as it came. It also helped that we looked the better side of those chasing the title.'

Spurs and Leicester were faltering, the long season taking its toll. The Foxes, in particular, appeared to buckle when it mattered most, taking three points from their final six games.

As Everton's final fixture came around, the Blues were top of the table. A win at home against Fulham would cement matters mathematically and bring the title home.

'What a time to be at Goodison that day,' recalls France. 'I felt blessed somehow to be part of the tens of thousands who were there watching that game. There was something magical in the air that afternoon. The atmosphere was almost overpowering and is not something I have ever forgotten. The roar that greeted those players as they came out was breathtaking.'

In front of more than 60,000 fans, the game began. 'Fulham were no pushovers and boasted some decent players, such as Robson, Haynes and Cohen, remembers Derek Temple. 'They might not have enjoyed the best of seasons but we could take nothing for granted. We had to be at our best.'

The players and the crowd were given a huge boost after just five minutes, when Everton went ahead through Roy Vernon.

'Parker put the ball through to him on the edge of the penalty area and he collected it off Mullery, dribbled through, drew Macedo out of the goal and put the ball over the line,' reported Michael Charters in the *Liverpool Echo*.

Everton were dominant and within minutes had got a second, once again through Vernon. 'It was the start everyone had wanted. We were just a few minutes in and cantering towards the title. Goodison was shaking,' remembers David France.

Although Fulham threatened to spoil the party when they pulled one back though Key after 20 minutes, their goal was an aberration. The London side were never really in the game, and, not long before the break, Scott effectively killed them off when he restored Everton's two-goal advantage.

'At half-time it felt like the celebrating had already begun,' recalls lifelong Blue John Monro. 'We had been so good, you just felt like the day was ours.'

In the second half, although not as clinical as in the first, Everton continued to dominate, with Vernon and Young combining consistently to make life uncomfortable for the Fulham defenders.

'With five minutes to go Vernon scored his third,' wrote Charters. 'A long clearance from Dunlop was headed through by Young. Vernon chased it.'

Although Mullery was with him, Vernon won the chase and then drew 'Macedo out of the goal and sent the ball over the line from a narrow angle'.

When the referee signalled the end of the 90, Goodison revelled in victory. 'As a supporter, I had not experienced anything like that before,' explains John Monro. 'It felt great to be back on top again. It was no wonder people were on the pitch dancing.'

For the players, the feeling of being champions was equally satisfying. 'I recall being up in the old Main Stand after the game with the team, the champagne flowing and cigars being passed round and remember just feeling great,' says Tony Kay.

Everton had come a long way in a short time. The days of struggling in the second tier with a team made up of youngsters and lower league 'finds', a board hamstrung by self-imposed austerity and the weight of expectation hanging heavy over Goodison now seemed like a distant memory.

'Everton were the "Mersey Millionaires", a side on the up, backed by the deep pockets of John Moores,' says Greg Murphy. 'For the first time in a very long time, the future looked very bright.'

v Leeds United 0–1

7 November 1964
Football League Division One
Goodison Park. Attendance: 43,605

Everton: Rankin, Labone, Brown, Gabriel, Rees, Morrissey, Temple, Pickering, Vernon, Young, Stevens

Leeds: Sprake, Reaney, Bell, Bremner, Charlton, Hunter, Giles, Storrie, Belfitt, Collins, Johanneson

Referee: K. Stokes

The Battle of Goodison

TO many modern fans, reared on a game where crowds are often dispassionate tourists, players overly protected and referees the agents of the authorities' aims to make football as bloodless as possible, the past must look like a foreign country.

The days of swaying crowds seething with a palpable sense of malign fury, defenders who would soften forwards up with a vicious tackle to 'let them know they're there' and officials who seemed to be more generous in their definition of what constituted 'contact' in the term 'contact sport' are long gone (at least in the higher reaches of the game).

For all the club's School of Science aspirations, back when football was a more raucous affair Everton could give as good as they got. It was an attitude that in the mid-1960s produced a match that is one of the most memorable to have ever taken place at Goodison.

At that time, Leeds United were on the rise. Under the management of Don Revie, the Yorkshiremen had just climbed out of the Second Division and were on the way to becoming one of the dominant football forces of the decade. Although undoubtedly blessed with talented players, such as Bobby Collins, Johnny Giles and Billy Bremner, they were also a side that was developing a reputation for aggression.

The FA had labelled Leeds 'the dirtiest side in the country', and, in their official journal, pointed to evidence that cited them as having the worst record for players cautioned, censured, fined or suspended in the Football League.

The former Leeds centre-half Jack Charlton provided a revealing insight into the Elland Road mentality in his eponymously titled 1996 autobiography. In a telling account, he related a story in which the young Leeds midfielder Jimmy Lumsden, while receiving physio treatment, had told Charlton and Revie how in a recent reserve match he had gone in over the top of the ball during a challenge, injuring his opponent in the process. According to Charlton, Revie had 'murmured approvingly'.

Despite United's refutation that they were a dirty side, there remained a perception that the FA had got it right, and whenever Leeds played there was a sense that opposition teams took to the pitch expecting and preparing for a fight.

This had certainly been the case when Everton had met Leeds in the FA Cup at Elland Road earlier in the year: a bad-tempered and fractious 1–1 draw that had reflected poorly on both teams. Leeds had set the ball rolling with some vicious fouls and then Everton had responded in kind, both sides ratcheting up the aggression as the match progressed.

When the clubs met in the league later in the year, it seemed that memories of that FA Cup clash were fresh in the minds of those both watching and on the pitch.

'There was certainly a tense atmosphere that day,' remembers David France. 'You felt that it wouldn't take much to get the crowd riled up.'

The game had barely begun before the tackles started flying in. Pickering was clattered by Bremner. Seconds later, Charlton suffered a similar fate at the hands of Gabriel. Battle lines had been drawn.

But the 'Battle of Goodison', as the game subsequently became known, really burst into flames on the four-minute mark when Giles, notorious amongst opponents for going over the top of the ball, left his stud marks on the chest of Brown, tearing his shirt in the process.

'I was stood in the Boys' Pen and watched as Sandy Brown took his revenge, catching Giles with a good left hook that floored him,' remembers Stan Osborne, one-time Everton apprentice and the author of *Making the Grade*, a memoir about his time with the club and his life as an Evertonian.

Brown received his marching orders, and the Goodison crowd roared in protest. It was a decision that coloured all that followed.

'Leeds were rough, but after a while it almost didn't matter. Every tackle they made, clean or not, was met with fury by us,' recalls Stan.

The temperature rose as blood boiled. Any Leeds player who ventured too close to the crowd ran the risk of being pelted by coins. Life was particularly tough for the Leeds keeper, Gary Sprake, who was probably pelted with enough spare change to buy himself a few drinks if he'd had the inclination to pick it up.

When it came to the rough-and-tumble on the pitch, Everton might have being missing their very own 'hard man' in Tony Kay, but the Blues still had enough about them to meet Leeds kick-for-kick:

'We had players such as Jimmy Gabriel, Johnny Morrissey and Dennis Stevens to give the likes of Norman Hunter, Jack Charlton and Billy Bremner a run for their money,' remembers Kay.

Catterick was the kind of manager who wasn't afraid to mix it up. The addition of more bite to the squad was one of the things that set him apart from Carey.

'I remember watching the tackles raining in, and with half an hour gone it was almost a surprise that Brown was the only player sent for an early bath!' recalls Stan Osborne.

Amongst all the kicking, some football was actually played, and after 15 minutes Leeds capitalised on their numerical advantage to take the lead.

From a free kick far out on the right wing, Collins swung the ball high into the heart of the Everton area. Rushing in at speed, Leeds full-back Willie Bell met the ball perfectly, his header flashing into the net. It was a great finish from a player always willing to supplement the attack.

But, as good a footballer as Bell could be, he also possessed a nasty streak, and, ten minutes before the break, revealed it at its worst when a chest-high tackle on Temple provided the moment that ensured the game would pass into infamy.

The Everton outside-left was knocked unconscious. The crowd seethed in response. Missiles were hurled down on to the pitch, Leeds players were spat at, intermittent fights broke out. Such was the level of hostility, the referee marched both teams off the pitch so that the players and fans could cool down. It was the first time that had ever happened in an English league game.

'I was stretchered off and was lying in the dressing room,' recalls Temple, 'when all the players came in after he'd [the referee] told them to go off. I heard him talking to the two managers, saying "I'm calling the game off. There is going to be a riot out there." Both managers said there *will* be a riot out there if you don't get those players out on that pitch!'

The referee lectured the players during the halt in proceedings, entering each dressing room and telling the teams that if their behaviour didn't improve they would be reported to the FA.

Outside, for a time, nobody knew whether the game had been suspended or abandoned. Despite the break, according to Horace Yates in the *Liverpool Echo*, the crowd remained agitated to say the least:

'Fights were breaking out in the crowd while they waited for the game to resume and this incident was the most sensational I have seen in my years of watching football.'

After five minutes, it was announced on the loudspeakers that play would soon restart, although the fans were warned that the match would be abandoned if more missiles were thrown.

Ten minutes after they had trooped off, the players returned. Temple and Bell (the latter had hurt himself in his disgusting challenge) came back too.

But, despite the referee's warnings, little changed on the pitch. Some of the tackling, specifically by Hunter and Vernon, remained exceptionally aggressive, and the game seemed to be powered by an undercurrent of venom and animosity.

Hunter was booked, and Bremner, Collins and Vernon warned for dangerous play. Astonishingly, no further players were sent off. Perhaps the referee didn't want to risk antagonising the crowd any further, so close to the precipice of further violence did those on the terraces appear.

Despite being a man down and unable to play their natural game, Everton refused to submit throughout and were constantly on the hunt for an equaliser. But, although they chucked everything they had at Leeds, Revie's men hung on grimly to the end.

Throughout the entire game, the kicks and fouls barely relented, ending with 19 transgressions inflicted by Everton and 12 by Leeds.

'And in response, the hostility that seethed through the crowd continued too. It was so bad that, after the game, there were mounted police outside to disperse us. It was the first time I had ever seen that at Goodison,' remembers Stan Osborne.

Unsurprisingly, the press reacted negatively to what had happened. This 'unhappy day for English football' was labelled by the Sunday papers as 'vicious' and 'spine-chilling'. Blame for what had occurred was apportioned equally, with the players, the fans and the referee castigated for the role they played.

Inevitably, the FA responded. Evertonians can probably guess what happened next. When the FA disciplinary committee met in December, it suspended Sandy Brown for two weeks and fined Everton £250 for the behaviour of their fans. Revie's men emerged unscathed.

Or did they? 'The events of that day cemented the reputation of Revie's United in the minds of many for years to come – that they would stop at nothing to win a game,' thinks David France.

However, irrespective of their darker side, Revie's men could play and over the following decade were never out of the top four (an achievement unachievable via brute force alone).

Certainly, John Moores wasn't put off by the 'Battle of Goodison'. Years later, prior to Catterick's removal from the manager's job, the newspapers were filled with rumours that Revie had been offered a record-breaking annual salary plus a massive signing-on bonus in an attempt to lure him to Goodison.

The deal never came off. Revie opted to turn down Everton's offer and stay at Leeds, citing 'personal reasons' for his decision. For a time, though, the move had been on. There was a moment, however brief, when the School of Science was close to metamorphosing into the School of Hard Knocks.

v Sheffield Wednesday 3–2

14 May 1966
FA Cup Final
Wembley Stadium. Attendance: 100,000

Everton: West, Wright, Wilson, Gabriel, Labone, Harris, Scott, Trebilcock, Young, Harvey, Temple

Sheffield Wednesday: Springett, Smith, Megson, Eustace, Ellis, Young, Pugh, Fantham, McCalliog, Ford, Quinn

Referee: J. Taylor

Trebilcock's Double

FORGET England, forget a gleaming Jules Rimet, forget Nobby Stiles's nauseating little jig – in the eyes of Evertonians, 1966 means just one thing; the club's greatest moment in the FA Cup. For the fans, that year is about Trebilcock not Hurst, Temple not Peters, Catterick not Ramsey.

In the mid-1960s, Everton were in transition, moving from the side that had won the league in 1963 towards that powered by the 'Holy Trinity' of Harvey, Kendall and Ball that would lift the title in 1970.

Prior to the final, 1966 had been a difficult year, the low point in that transition. With the team adrift in the league and knocked out of the Fairs Cup in the second round (courtesy of Újpest Dozsa), the FA Cup represented Catterick's last chance at redeeming the season.

For Evertonians it was also the opportunity to restore some local pride. Under the helmsmanship of Bill Shankly, Liverpool, long the city's junior club, were threatening to upstage Everton locally. Two titles and an FA Cup victory since they had been promoted from Division Two a few years earlier represented a warning shot sent across Stanley Park towards Goodison. Liverpool were on the rise. Everton had to respond.

The Blues' road to Wembley that year had been an impressive one. Before a ball was even kicked in the final, the club had become the first since Bury in 1903 to reach the closing stage without conceding a single goal.

And that was no mean feat, as, through the various rounds, Everton had met some impressive and determined opponents, most notably a Manchester United side in the semis that boasted the likes of Denis Law, Bobby Charlton and Nobby Stiles.

Everton had won that game 1–0, Harvey's late strike booking the club a place at Wembley.

Prior to the great trek down to the capital, the minds of Evertonians were exercised by two things: the line-up and getting a ticket. The latter was tricky. With just a 15,000 allocation, most Blues had to barter, blag or beg a ticket from whatever source possible.

'I hitch-hiked down to London, with no ticket,' recalls David France. 'When I got there, touts were selling them for ten times their face value. For me, that was the equivalent of a week's wages. But it was a cup final, so you had to go.

'Although, when I saw people climbing over the walls to get in, it did make me think I might have been better off trying that instead.'

When it came to the final eleven that would take on Sheffield Wednesday, although it was widely thought that Tommy Wright and Fred Pickering (both of whom had only recently returned from injury) would start, Evertonians could never be sure that Catterick, a manager not immune to pulling the occasional surprise out of the hat, wouldn't do something unexpected.

On the Friday lunchtime before the game, Wright, Pickering, Sandy Brown and Mike Trebilcock (Everton's rookie centre-forward) were called into a meeting with Catterick, as Trebilcock recently recalled to the Everton Former Players' Foundation (EFPF):

'He [Catterick] said, "Look, at a time like this, decisions have to be made and I'm the one who has to make them ... Sandy, I'm leaving you out and putting Tommy back in" (which we all knew anyhow). And then he said "Fred, I'm leaving you out and putting Mike in." Well, if the saying is "You could fall off the back of your chair", then that's what I felt like.'

It was a bold move. Pickering, an England international and Everton's top scorer, was being replaced by a young rookie who had made just a handful of appearances for the Blues.

Although a shock, to those who had been paying attention, the decision had already been signposted. A week earlier, Catterick had told journalists, 'I feel he (Pickering) is not playing with the confidence he was showing in his play before he was injured.'

Catterick was the kind of manager who would prefer to pick a player who was fit rather than one that might be more 'talented' but was not performing to the best of his ability.

With the line-up confirmed and tickets obtained, thousands of Blues packed into Wembley on that blazing-hot Saturday afternoon, hoping to see the team claim the cup for the first time in 33 years.

'The atmosphere inside was breathtaking,' recalls Stan Osborne. 'To a 13-year-old lad like myself there was something magical about it. The twin towers, the sight of all those Blues, the sounds of our songs drowning out the Wednesday fans. It's almost indescribable.'

Sadly for those who had travelled down, the chances of a happy outcome seemed slim early on when, just four minutes in, Everton found themselves 1–0 down after McCalliog's effort cannoned in off a defender's heel.

Rocked by the opening goal and bamboozled by Wednesday's 4–3–3 formation, Everton were second best throughout the first half, despite Young having a goal controversially ruled out for offside after 15 minutes.

When half-time arrived, Catterick's men were fortunate to go in only 1–0 down. Talking years later to Charles Lambert, the *Liverpool Echo* journalist, Catterick revealed how he attempted to motivate his players.

'I am looking round the dressing room,' he said, 'and I can't see many people who are going to be coming back here. This must be your last chance of a cup winner's medal at Wembley. What are you going to do about it? Go out there and roll your sleeves up.'

Irrespective of Catterick's best efforts, all hope appeared lost around 15 minutes into the second half, when Ford latched on to a rebounded effort to put Wednesday two ahead.

'I remember fellers leaving at that point, just getting off,' says Stan. 'You could see why, two down and outclassed. But lucky for them, they couldn't get out, couldn't get through the crowd. If they had managed to, then they would have missed out on one of the FA Cup's greatest fightbacks.'

Catterick's gamble was about to pay off in dramatic style. Within the space of five minutes, the game was turned on its head. First, Temple set up Trebilcock and the youngster made no mistake from 12 yards to make it 2–1.

Then, a few minutes later, Scott launched a free kick into the Wednesday area, which was poorly cleared. The ball fell to Trebilcock, who crashed it home from just inside the box to draw the scores level.

At that point, Wembley was treated to one of the most infamous pitch invasions in cup final history, when Eddie Cavanagh ran on to celebrate.

'As soon as that ball hit the net, I was on me bike,' he recalled in *Three Sides of the Mersey.* 'I'd seen Trebilcock and I went for him first. Well, he didn't know me but I grabbed him, pulled him on the ground. He shit himself because he didn't know me. We all played in blue and white, didn't we? Sheffield were in blue and white, and we're in blue and white, so he didn't know who I was. When I got him down, I was coming across then to Westy. I was going to say, "Gordon, for God's sake don't let no more in, we'll get that now." But I'd seen this busy [sic] came after me and he caught up with me and got me by the coat. But I just took it off!'

The sight of the 'busy' floundering and falling while grasping at a now Cavanagh-less coat warms the heart to this day. The invader was eventually caught by another policeman, pinned down by more and escorted out of the ground (although he later got back in).

Cavanagh's exuberance while in full flight seemed to capture what every Evertonian must have been feeling. The cup was back on and momentum with the Blues. At 2–2, it was clear that the nature of the game had changed.

Sheffield Wednesday began to panic. Chasing a winner to claim a cup that they believed was theirs just a few minutes earlier, they committed too many players forward and began to leave things open at the back. There were spaces that Everton could exploit.

'I was playing outside-left,' recalls Derek Temple, 'but not seeing much of the ball. It wasn't a rigid system, so I wandered towards the old inside-right position where there was a bit of space. When Colin Harvey hit a long ball, Gerry Young, their "sweeper", appeared to have it covered, but the ball slipped under his left foot and into my path. I already had two yards on him and he was never going to catch me! I had three options: chip the keeper, try to round him or simply belt it. In the end, the keeper made my mind up by standing his ground and not coming out too far. It sat up for me so I hit it cleanly; he dived the right way but the pace beat him.'

There were 15 minutes remaining. The Everton half of Wembley was alive, songs filling the air. The other half, mirroring their team on the pitch, was visibly shell-shocked. After the third goal, Wednesday were broken, and Everton saw out the remainder of the game with ease.

When the final whistle arrived, Evertonians could revel in their first FA Cup success in decades, the players could celebrate an unbelievable comeback and Catterick could take pleasure in a gamble that paid off.

'That was my greatest moment,' he later confided to Charles Lambert. 'The cup hadn't been to Everton for many years and it was wonderful to bring it back to Merseyside.'

It would be another 18 years before Everton repeated the joy of an FA Cup Final win. And not since would the fans enjoy (or endure?) a final with so much high drama.

'It was a great spectacle. Very exciting and a bit of a thrilling ride for the fans,' admits Derek Temple. 'But, as the old saying goes, "Wembley is the greatest place to win and the worst place to lose." As exciting as it was to watch, it was the winning that mattered.'

v Sunderland 4–1

16 May 1967
Football League Division One
Goodison Park. Attendance: 30,943

Everton: West, Wright, Wilson, Hurst, Labone, Harvey, Ball, Husband (Brown), Young, Gabriel, Morrissey

Sunderland: Montgomery, Irwin, Parke, Todd, Kinnell, Baxter, Gauden, O'Hare, Martin, Herd, Mulhall

Referee: J. Thacker

The Golden Vision

'IF Dave Hickson is Everton's most-loved player and Dixie Dean their most iconic, it's no exaggeration to say that Young is their most adored. He is to Everton what Kenny Dalglish is to Liverpool or Éric Cantona to Manchester United,' wrote James Corbett in *The Blizzard*.

Evertonians have always loved their 'Number 9s'. They like them big, strong and willing to die for the shirt. Think back and you can see a 'type' that Blues fall for: Dean, Lawton, Hickson, Royle, Latchford, Sharp, Gray, Ferguson, Campbell. They are the kind of forwards that leave centre-halves black and blue come Sunday morning.

When it comes to adoration, Alex Young is unquestionably part of that list. But he sits uneasily amongst such company because Young was no battering ram – not big or strong.

And, although clearly infatuated with the club, not necessarily someone who would put his face where others fear to tread.

'He was slight, nimble and delicate,' recalls George McKane of the Everton Supporters Trust, 'someone who had the build of a winger or inside-forward.'

Young didn't fit into the traditional mould of the 'archetypal' Everton number nine. And yet, he was adored nonetheless.

'He was a one-off; a supremely gifted player, the likes that you rarely see,' continues George. 'He had a beautiful touch and could ghost past big lumbering centre-halves with ease (the kind with hairy arms and Desperate Dan chins) and had the knack to be in the right place at the right time. When you watched him in action, it was an honour. Like a lot of Blues of my age, he was just an idol. We treated him like a god. He was known as "The Golden Vision", and, with his blonde hair, sublime talent and grace, it fitted him perfectly.'

Although adopted by Evertonians, the moniker did not originate from within Goodison. Instead it was coined by Danny Blanchflower, captain of both Northern Ireland and Bill Nicholson's great Spurs sides of the early sixties. In Young he believed there was something beyond football:

'The view every Saturday that we have of a more perfect world, a world that has got a pattern and is finite,' said Blanchflower. 'And that's Alex, the Golden Vision.'

Young was born in Loanhead, Midlothian in 1937. His talent with the ball saved him from a life 'down pit', and by the age of 18 he was playing for Hearts. In five years at Tynecastle, Young found the net 71 times in 155 appearances, helping the 'Jambos' to win the title in 1957/58 and again in 1959/60. Inevitably, clubs south of the border had their interest pricked by this emerging talent.

Everton and Preston North End led the pack, with the latter in pole position. Hearts accepted Preston's bid, and Alex Young agreed personal terms. But the move never went through, as the man himself revealed in an interview with the NSNO website back in 2008.

'I went to Preston, and they said that they were gonna give me £3,000. That was a lot of money then, you could buy a house with that – plenty money. I said, "Well, if you do that then I will come to you"; that was the first meeting. The next day, the manager, the Preston manager came again and said, "The directors won't give you £3,000, it's £2,000", so I said, "Everton's giving me £2,000, I'll go to Everton."'

And with that, in November 1960, Everton signed a Goodison legend and Preston missed out on a centre-forward who could have transformed their fortunes.

Although injuries marred his first season with the Blues, flashes of what he could do were noted by those watching. 'Young is a thoroughbred, a great mover with the ball, fast, active, razor sharp in his reactions,' reported the *Liverpool Echo* after one impressive performance.

He soon got over his fitness issues and for the next three seasons was unassailable; his form breathtaking.

'He formed a great partnership with Roy Vernon,' says George McKane, 'who always has to be remembered for the work he did with Young, and the pair of them helped us reach heights that hadn't been seen at Goodison for some time.'

The pair netted 116 league goals between them over three seasons, lifting the club to the higher reaches of the table and helping Everton clinch the title in 1963.

Around this time, while in his pomp, Young was simply sublime. As Mickey Blue Eyes reminisced on ToffeeWeb, to watch him was to be in the presence of something majestic, almost spiritual. He first saw Young on a wintry afternoon against Leeds, the Golden Vision marked by two snarling defenders.

'Alex killed the glistening orange ball to feet in a flurry of snow crystals,' wrote Mickey.

The Leeds defenders closed in, one lunging to clatter the delicate Scot.

'Except the tackle arrived in empty space. Alex was gone!'

For a microsecond, the defenders looked at each other. 'Over the years,' continued Mickey, 'I got used to that look on opponents' faces. It was an almost comical combination of bafflement, fury and hapless despair. Seeing Alex play for the first time was like an epiphany. You wanted to shout, "Hallelujah!"'

Picking one game to illustrate the majesty of Young is a tough challenge. He excelled so often, delighted the crowd with such frequency, was so majestic that you could fill a book with them. But one game does stick out.

At the close of the 1966/67 season, Everton hosted Sunderland at Goodison. The Blues, still in transition, were on course to finish sixth. Sunderland, not long out of the second tier, were in the bottom eight but safe. There was little but pride riding on the game. Few expected much. What they got was a pleasant surprise – an Alex Young masterclass.

'Young beat Sunderland almost on his own that night,' wrote Brian Labone in his autobiography, Defence at the Top.

From the very first kick, as Michael Charters wrote in the *Echo*, the Golden Vision was a nuisance:

'Young came back to lead the line and, given the freedom of the park by the inept Sunderland defenders, he spread destruction through their ranks with his wonderful ball distribution, artistry and sheer cheek.'

He zipped, danced and buzzed around the pitch, linking with his team-mates, creating chances for others and accepting some for himself.

'It was obvious that Young was going to enjoy himself and Sunderland should have appreciated that to give him the space they did was tantamount to football suicide,' continued Charters.

Were it not from an inspired performance from Montgomery in the Sunderland goal and an apparent desire by Everton to walk the ball into the net, the Blues should have been out of sight before the half-hour mark, so dominant and threatening had they been. As it was, *it took Everton 41 minutes to go ahead.*

Unsurprisingly, considering that he had been at the heart of everything good Everton had produced, Young played a part in the opener when he slid a delightful pass to Morrissey to put him one-on-one with the keeper. Although he scuffed his shot slightly, the effort still had enough on it to beat Montgomery. It was a goal that gave Everton a deserved half-time lead.

In the second period, Everton's dominance continued, and, inevitably, more goals arrived. The second came not long after the restart, when Young and Husband combined well to get the ball wide to Ball. His low centre was met spectacularly by Morrissey, who volleyed Everton into a 2–0 lead.

Minutes later, Harvey made it 3–0, converting a cross from Husband (who had been threaded through by Young) to put the game beyond Sunderland.

Although the visitors pulled one back through Martin after 70 minutes, it was a rare foray forward against a tsunami of Everton attacks.

'I would need columns of space to detail all the Everton moves which brought goals or near misses,' wrote Charters. He added, 'the near complete absence of anything from Sunderland gives an idea of how they were outplayed and outclassed.'

As the game ebbed to a close, Montgomery rugby-tackled Wright to the ground, and Morrissey was able to get his third from the spot. But, although he had completed his hat-trick, Alan Ball wanted the match ball to go to Young, so peerless had his performance been – a dazzling display of grace, vision and skill.

Frustratingly for those consistently thrilled by Young, such afternoons were to appear with less frequency from then on. After that season, his strike rate declined and his powers appeared to wane. Although still loved, the hints of decline that had only fleetingly been felt before became more pronounced.

Everton were changing, and the side that had been so synonymous with Young was on its way to being replaced by the one that would come to be characterised by the 'Holy Trinity'.

In May 1968, after eight years in which he had delighted the fans, the curtain came down on one of Goodison's most cherished careers. Young left to become player/manager with Northern Irish club Glentoran. Following a brief stint there, he then moved on to Stockport County, where, after 23 games, a knee injury eventually forced his retirement aged 32.

Although he was no longer part of life at Goodison, his memory lived on amongst those who had watched him play, their adoration undimmed as the years passed. It was a love perfectly encapsulated by Bill Kenwright, who said this after Young's death in 2017:

'Legend is a much and often overused word these days. But no one at Goodison will argue that today we have lost one of the greatest of them all. Without any doubt the finest "true" footballer it has ever been my privilege to worship. And those who were lucky enough to have seen Alex play did worship him. Our own Golden Vision. A title accepted immediately. No question. As night follows day he was Golden … he was visionary.'

v West Bromwich Albion 2–0

1 April 1970
Football League Division One
Goodison Park. Attendance: 58,523

Everton: West, Wright, Kenyon, Brown, Kendall, Ball, Harvey, Royle, Whittle, Hurst, Morrissey

West Bromwich Albion: Osborne, Hughes, Wilson, Fraser, Robertson, Merrick Cantello, Suggett, Astle, Brown, Hope

Referee: L. Callaghan

The Holy Trinity

AS the 1960s came to a close, Catterick's process of transition at Goodison was starting to bear fruit. Slowly a side emerged that not only looked like it had what it took to match what had been achieved in 1963, but also looked as though it could go even further.

'It was a side that bristled with talent,' remembers the former Everton defender Roger Kenyon. 'Along with the players who had been there for a while, like Gordon West in goal and Brian Labone at the back, Catterick brought in some great new players, such as Alan Ball and Howard Kendall, and promoted youngsters from the club, including Colin Harvey, Joe Royle and Alan Whittle. It took a while to take shape, but when it started to, you felt there was something special there.'

During the latter half of the 1967/68 season, the first signs that Catterick was on to something good began to emerge. Everton reached the final of the FA Cup (dominating West Brom but unfortunately losing), and, in the league, finished fifth, just six points behind winners Manchester City.

'Everton had always been a good footballing side under Harry,' remembers former Everton centre-forward and manager Joe Royle, 'but around that time, something started to click. We were playing some wonderful football and that only got better in the season that followed.'

In terms of aesthetic beauty, the 1968/69 season is regarded by many as one of the finest ever seen at Goodison.

'They were a wonderful footballing side,' thinks John Daley, who first began going to Goodison in the 1950s, 'one that played without inhibition and which were a joy to watch. But also, perhaps because they lacked maturity, one that couldn't always grind out a result or make dominance count.'

Despite this, as the 1968/69 run-in approached, Everton were just about in with a shout at the title. But a few injury issues, a fixture pile-up and a touch of inexperience in the squad conspired to halt any assault at the top. Everton drew too many of those remaining matches and ended up third, ten points behind winners Leeds United.

'Even though the end of the season was slightly frustrating,' recalls Joe Royle, 'there were still plenty of positives. We felt like the side was gelling and as the following season started, we were strong contenders early on.'

Between the season's beginning and Christmas, Everton were in impressive form. Title rivals, such as Manchester United, Leeds and Newcastle, were all defeated as dominance on the pitch was translated into victories.

'And Everton found the resilience to grind out wins when free-flowing football proved less easy to conjure up too,' remembers Stan Osborne. 'They were a perfectly balanced side. You had that blend of youth and experience, grafters and genuine stars that any side that wants to win the title needs.'

Within this side, subsequent focus has tended to concentrate on the so-called 'Holy Trinity' of Harvey, Kendall and Ball, the midfield trio that blended together so perfectly and which seemed to be the very embodiment of the School of Science mentality.

There was Ball, a bundle of energy who covered every inch of the park and drove play forward; Harvey, a player blessed with incredible close control; and Kendall, a tenacious tackler who read the game beautifully. For a triumvirate, they had the lot.

Goalkeeper Gordon West once told the *Liverpool Echo*: 'They were the only three-man team to have won the League championship! Seriously, Kendall, Harvey and Ball were the best midfield unit that I have ever known. I used to stand back and marvel at them – I had very little else to do.'

But, as good as they were, and they were magnificent, they were not alone. 'That side was packed with talent, from front to back,' says Roger Kenyon. 'When you think about the likes of West in goal, Labone at the back and Joe up front, to name but a few, you start to realise just what a great team it was.'

It was probably just as well that Everton were not *so* reliant on the 'Holy Trinity' anyway, as over the course of that season they played together on only 20 occasions, with injuries and suspensions taking their toll.

'Along with those who regularly started,' argues Stan Osborne, 'Everton were lucky that they had lots of players who could come in and do a job. Tommy Jackson was the perfect example of that. He's a player who came in and understudied for the likes of Ball and Kendall and who did a great job, keeping the momentum going. Unheralded and underrated but vitally important nonetheless.'

Playing a notional 4–3–3 formation from the off (which could convert to a 4–4 2 in defence if Morrissey dropped back), Everton were sensational that season: fast, organised and strong.

'People have used the phrase, in relation to Everton, of "instant football",' said Catterick in an interview with ITV. 'I think', he continued, 'it is a compliment because we believe in quick play, quick, accurate passing and possession until we can see an opening and then striking as quickly as possible. Instant football means, in effect, that you have got quick control and the ability to part with the ball quickly and accurately.'

But, as good as the side was, it was still young, still a work in progress and still capable of faltering. Despite Everton's magnificent form during the first half of the season, a dip after New Year saw the Blues surrender top place to Leeds. It was a setback that Catterick sought to remedy with a touch of tough love, as Stan Osborne recalls:

'I remember approaching the dressing room after a disappointing 1–1 draw with Forest and hearing raised voices. Inside, the players were getting a rollicking off Catterick and Wilf Dixon [his coach]. I remember the door bursting open and Harry emerging, looking furious. He turned back and with a parting shot said, "If you think that sort of performance is going to win us the league, then you lot have got another thing coming." It might not have been pretty, but it had the desired effect!'

Everton's form improved dramatically in response, recapturing the momentum of the early season. The Blues went on a commanding run, and reclaimed top spot in the process.

'There was a 2–0 victory against Liverpool in March at their place,' recalls Joe Royle, 'with goals from Alan Whittle and me, when I think we all thought that the title could be ours. We were playing so well and winning really important games. As good as our rivals were, I think we knew that we were something special by then.'

Whittle's contribution during the run-in was another testament to the strength of the squad that Catterick had put together. A graduate of the youth system, who only got a prolonged run in the first team because of a long-term injury to Jimmy Husband, Whittle hit a rich vein of form, scoring freely as the title race narrowed.

After a tight 1–0 victory away at Stoke City at the end of March (the goal coming courtesy of Whittle again), Everton were poised to capture the title. A victory over West Brom in the next game at Goodison would confirm things.

As an apprentice, Stan Osborne was lucky enough to witness first-hand how the players prepared for the encounter:

'It was interesting to see the contrasting approaches. You had the likes of Royle, Harvey and Morrissey just having a laugh. Ball, full of enthusiasm, was geeing people up. Then there were those like Sandy Brown and John Hurst, who were quiet and brooding. There were so many differences.'

The midweek game pulled in nearly 60,000, turning the ground into a cauldron of noise. 'It was a hell of an atmosphere to come out to,' recalls Joe Royle. 'One of the best I experienced as a player or a manager.'

Prior to the match, West Brom's manager, Alan Ashman, told the press that 'Everton will have to fight!' if they wanted to claim the title. And he wasn't wrong. The Baggies took to the Blues, kicking lumps off the title hopefuls.

This approach, combined with evident anxiety amongst the Everton players, made for a nervy start.

'It doesn't matter how close that title was,' remembers John Daley, 'you still have those doubts, the horrible feeling that we could throw it all away. Lucky for us, then, that we had a forward who was really on form.'

On 20 minutes, Whittle popped up to provide Evertonians with a much-needed tonic to steady those nerves, pouncing on Colin Harvey's rebounded shot, and smacking the ball past Osborne in goal.

With the nerves settled slightly by the strike, as Charters wrote in the *Echo*, the home side began to find its rhythm.

'Everton's performance against West Bromwich at Goodison last night was full of the brilliance that has established them as the superb footballing side, a side which plays the game with a skill and speed as fine as anything we have seen in many years.'

But, for the celebrations to really begin, Everton really needed another. Fittingly, considering their association with that team, it would come from a member of the 'Holy Trinity'.

On the 65th minute, Harvey picked up the ball just outside the box. 'First he moved towards goal,' wrote Horrace Yates in the *Liverpool Daily Post*. Then he 'changed his mind and veered out, as though to bring Morrissey into play. Seeing Morrissey was covered, he doubled back to the edge of the penalty area and while on the run sent a crashing drive soaring into the net.'

The game was all but over after that. Everton saw out the remaining 25 minutes efficiently, as the crowd produced a ceaseless cavalcade of noise.

'The atmosphere was incredible,' remembers John Daley. 'There were chants of "Ever-ton", "We are the champions" and "We're on our way to Europe" ringing out. You must have been able to hear it from miles away.'

After the final whistle, the players did a lap of honour, soaking up the adulation from the thousands who had crammed themselves into Goodison.

'The sense of elation was palpable, whether you were a fan or involved with the set-up,' remembers Stan Osborne. 'And we felt it was just the beginning. We had a young team and there was every reason to believe that this side could dominate for years to come. Things could only get better. It was a great time to be a Blue.'

v Borussia Mönchengladbach 1–1

(2–2 on aggregate; Everton win 4–3 on penalties)
4 November 1970
European Cup Second Round, Second Leg
Goodison Park. Attendance: 42,744

Everton: Rankin, Wright, Newton (Brown), Kendall, Kenyon, Harvey, Whittle (Husband), Ball, Royle, Hurst, Morrissey

Borussia Mönchengladbach: Kleff, Vogts, Müller, Sieloff, Wittmann, Dietrich, Le Fevre (Wloka), Laumen, Köppel, Netzer, Heynckes

Referee: A. Sbardella

Penalty Kings

I T might not have enjoyed the allure that it possesses today, but success in Europe still mattered in the early 1970s. Although the league title remained the focus for domestic clubs, increasingly, doing well in Europe (and specifically the European Cup) came to be seen as a marker of a great side.

After the disappointment of exiting at the hands of Inter Milan in 1963, Everton got a second bite at the European Cup in 1970.

And, for Catterick's men, the value of participation had actually become incrementally *more* important as the season progressed.

'Far from dominating the league, as had been predicted following our stylish capturing of the title during the previous campaign, we'd struggled,' says Roger Kenyon.

In part, this was attributed to a 'World Cup hangover' suffered by those amongst the squad (the likes of Ball, Labone and Wright) who had accompanied England to Mexico '70. They returned jaded, as is often the case after international tournaments.

But the squad also suffered its fair share of injuries, and several players failed to reach the heights of the previous year too. Most notably, the 'Holy Trinity' were far from the devastating force they had been when Everton had been storming their way to the title.

By accident rather than design, then, cup competitions, foreign and domestic, grew in importance as a way of redeeming the season.

Everton's European adventure had begun easily enough with a routine 9–2 aggregate victory over the Icelandic champions, Keflavik. In parallels with 1963, when Everton had faced Inter (albeit in the preliminary round), the Blues were then drawn against an exceptionally strong European side, in this case Borussia Mönchengladbach.

Bundesliga champions and a side that would, along with Bayern Munich, dominate German football in the 1970s (and feature prominently on the European stage too), they were arguably one of the strongest teams in the competition.

'It was certainly a test for us,' says Joe Royle. 'But that wasn't necessarily a bad thing. We wanted to test ourselves against the best and felt, despite struggling that season, we had what it took to beat anyone.'

After a 1–1 draw at the Bökelbergstadion, in which Kendall grabbed an all-important away goal for the Blues, the West Germans came to Goodison for the return leg in November.

'It was a big game,' says David France. 'Although it might not have had the glamour of the modern-day Champions League, having the German champions visit Goodison, especially under the lights, was something to look forward to. There was a big crowd, the atmosphere was fantastic, and there was a sense that we were in for a special night.'

For the thousands who had turned up, the game could not have started any better. With just 23 seconds on the clock, an aimless long ball was poorly dealt with by the visitors, the clearance finding its way to Morrissey on the left wing. From the edge of the area, Everton's industrious outside-left then drew two defenders towards him and clipped the ball towards goal.

'The goalkeeper, Kleff, who ended up having one of those nights when almost nothing would get past him, made his one mistake and misjudged the ball entirely, and in it bounced,' remembers Royle.

Was it a shot? 'It was,' says Royle. 'You could ask Johnny yourself but if you do, you'd better duck. Of course it was a shot.'

Everton had the perfect start: ahead and still possessing that all-important away goal. But there was no sense of the side resting on its laurels.

'You couldn't,' says David France. 'The visitors were a good team, and we knew that they were going to come at us and that they would have chances.'

Although limited in their forays into the Everton half, the Germans remained dangerous. 'You always had the sense that they had a goal in them,' he continues. 'They looked good on the ball and carried that air of threat. You knew you were in a game when you watched them. A goal always seemed possible.'

With ten minutes to go before half-time, a German free kick, some distance out from the 18-yard box, was curled in by Netzer. There, six yards out, the ball found an unmarked Laumen, who headed towards the Everton goal. At near point-blank range, Rankin managed to pull off an excellent save, but unfortunately the parried ball dropped down and bobbled in front of the empty Everton net. Of those in the box, Laumen was the fastest to react, pouncing and poking the ball over the line.

The aggregate scores level, Everton had little option but to continue to press forward in the hope of recapturing the lead. But if the Blues had got lucky early on in the game with Kleff's mistake, good fortune seemed to desert the home side from that point as the German goalkeeper put in an outstanding performance, thwarting Royle on numerous occasions and pulling off a wonderful double save after successive efforts from Kenyon and Kendall.

'It was frustrating, but sometimes that just happens,' says Royle. 'Don't forget, Andy Rankin in our goal had a decent night too, so overall both teams probably felt a bit frustrated.'

With honours even after 90 minutes, the match went into extra time, where the sodden pitch and tired legs seemed to sap the energy from the game. The play became more ragged and clear-cut chances fewer. Not that there weren't a few 'heart in the mouth' moments, notably Kleff's scrambling save from Husband's goalbound effort and Laumen's looping header which hit the Everton bar.

'It was one of those games that could have gone either way but where a draw was probably a fair result,' admits John Monro.

But there was no possibility of it ending that way. When the end came, it brought with it a novelty: the first-ever European Cup penalty shoot-out.

'Even if you didn't value the European Cup as much as the league or the FA Cup, by that point, the whole ground was desperate for Everton to go through,' remembers David France.

What the fans probably didn't want, though, was Joe Royle taking that first penalty. Never a forward renowned for subtlety, Royle opted to smack the ball as hard as he could.

'Raw power can work. On this occasion it didn't. The keeper saved it, giving me the dubious honour of being the first person to miss a penalty in a European Cup shoot-out,' says Royle.

After this, Sieloff and Ball both converted, before Laumen put his kick wide, leaving the scores level.

'It was incredibly tense to watch,' remembers David France.

Morrissey put Everton ahead before Heynckes drew the Germans level. Then Kendall and Köppel both converted to make it 3–3 with one penalty to go each.

Up stepped Sandy Brown to attempt Everton's fifth. In the goal, crouched, his boots nearly sinking in the mud, Kleff attempted a slight little knee-wobble, a Bruce Grobbelaar tactic long before Grobbelaar made it unpopular. Brown turned his back on these antics, walking away from the ball.

He then turned back to face the Gwladys Street, strode purposefully towards the spot, and belted his effort past Kleff, ridiculing the German's diversion attempts in the best way possible.

That left Müller against Rankin to see if Everton would progress or if the Germans could push this to sudden-death.

'I remember him running up,' says John Monro, 'the crowd around me surging forward to get a better look. He hit it low and to the left. But Rankin read it and palmed the ball away. It was an incredible moment. You'd have thought we won the competition by the reaction of the crowd (including myself).'

Riding high on self-confidence, with thoughts of a possible final flittering through their minds, Everton were next drawn to face Panathinaikos in the quarter-finals.

'I think, at that point, we thought we could go on and win the thing,' admits Roger Kenyon. 'Regardless of our indifferent league form, we were probably the strongest team left. But it wasn't to be.'

The Greeks were battered at Goodison, but somehow managed to earn a 1–1 draw (vitally nicking an away goal). This meant the Blues would need to take the game to Panathinaikos in the away leg to continue on their European adventure.

On a terrible, dusty playing surface, in front of an exceptionally hostile crowd (one that drenched the Everton bench in spit) and ruled over by a referee whose impartiality has long been questioned, the Blues stumbled, the game ending goalless, meaning they were knocked out on the away-goals rule.

A season that had promised so much was effectively ended a few days later when, exhausted after their Greek Odyssey, Everton were knocked out of the FA Cup by Liverpool at the semi-final stage.

'For me, I think that was the moment that the great Catterick side died,' argues Joe Royle.

Within the year, Ball was sold, rumours of dressing room dissent had spread, and Everton went from a side that had been predicted to excel in the league to one that now had one eye on the relegation zone.

'You can never know what would have happened had we got through against Panathinaikos or Liverpool,' says Royle. 'Either could have been the spark that brought things back to life. But in the end, those two results killed the side off. And it's a pity, because the talent was there to do remarkable things, as we proved against Borussia Mönchengladbach. That was no small achievement. One of those great Goodison nights that lives long in the memory.'

v Aston Villa 2–3

13 April 1977
League Cup Final Second Replay
Old Trafford. Attendance: 54,749

Everton: Lawson, Robinson, Darracott, Lyons, McNaught, King, Hamilton, Dobson, Latchford, Pearson (Seargeant), Goodlass

Aston Villa: Burridge, Gidman (Smith), Robson, Philips, Nicholl, Mortimer, Graydon, Deehan, Little, Cropley, Cowans

Referee: G. Kew

The Blues Fall a Little Short

THE 1970s were a challenging time for Evertonians: a time when hope, belief and optimism gave way to the modern Everton tropes of pessimism, frustration and despair.

Catterick left the manager's post in April 1973 after failing to halt the club's slide towards the nether regions of the table. Ill health, growing tactical conservatism and discord on the terraces eventually proved too much for the board to tolerate.

His replacement, Billy Bingham, initially showed promise. Although the football his sides produced was more organised and percentage oriented than Catterick's, Everton came close to winning the title in 1974/75 (blowing it by faltering as the season closed).

But, as the mid-1970s wore on, his approach began yielding diminishing returns.

With Everton sliding down the table once again and the Goodison crowd unimpressed by the dire football they were being forced to swallow, Bingham was shown the door.

In January 1977, the board then turned to the well-regarded Newcastle United manager, Gordon Lee.

'I always liked Gordon, as did others,' says former Everton midfielder Martin Dobson. 'He was honest, had a dry sense of humour and clearly loved the game.'

Lee was charged with the task of bringing back the glory days by the Everton board. And glory was sorely needed. While Everton had underachieved, Liverpool had been dominant in the 1970s, scooping up silverware with disgusting ease.

'It was a tough time, when broad shoulders were needed,' says John Black, who has been a regular at Goodison since the early 1970s. 'As everyone of my era will readily remember, there were more than the fair share of gobshites ready to taunt you every Monday morning, the common denominator being that not one of them actually went to the match (it was ever thus).'

Everton needed success. And when Lee took over, the domestic cups were the only options left available. Fortunately for the Blues, in a campaign dogged by poor form in the league, the cups appeared to offer some respite.

'I went to every game on the 1976/77 League Cup run,' says 'Regular Street Ender', Trevor Edwards, 'and had watched a struggling team in the league vanquish the likes of Cambridge United, Stockport County, Coventry City and Manchester United with ease.'

With the club's new manager in the hot-seat, Everton came through a tough semi-final against Bolton Wanderers to book a place at Wembley, where they would face Aston Villa.

Under the management of Ron Saunders, Villa had already won the League Cup a few seasons earlier and were in the process of becoming a strong force in the top flight (one that would ultimately win the title in the not-too-distant future). In short, they represented a considerable obstacle. But not one that was insurmountable.

'I still remained confident we could beat them,' continues Trevor. 'After all, we had Dobson, we had Latchford, Lyons, Goodlass and King. I remember that my dad had a banner made for me that said, "Toffees can lick 'em all", which made the TV coverage. It summed up our confidence. At no point, pre-match, could I conceive of us losing.'

When the teams took to the Wembley pitch in early March, nobody watching knew that they were about to witness the beginnings of what would become one of the most epic cup encounters of all time.

Although also, initially, one of the dullest. Despite some of the country's most exciting attacking talent being on display, such as PFA Player and Young Player of the Year Andy Gray and the sublimely mercurial Duncan McKenzie, the match was a stale non-event, the first 0–0 draw since the final had moved to Wembley in 1967.

'I remember two things from that final,' recalls Graham Ennis, co-editor of *When Skies Are Grey*. 'First, the game had to be stopped during the second half because one of the marching band who had been on the pitch at half-time had lost a spur from his boots. And second, at one point Everton mistakenly put out two players wearing the number two shirt. That's how boring it was.'

A few days later, on the Wednesday, the teams met again, this time at Hillsborough. The game might have been an improvement in quality, but, as the minutes ticked along, a breakthrough looked unlikely. That is until two Everton players intervened to breathe drama into proceedings.

With ten minutes left, to the dismay of the travelling Blues, Roger Kenyon put the ball into his own net, giving Villa the lead. Focused by the deficit, Everton found the gear they had been searching for since the first ball had been kicked at Wembley and laid siege to the Villa goal. In the dying seconds of normal time, McKenzie played in Pearson, who was then able to pick out

Latchford through a melee of players for the Everton number nine to smack the ball home.

'What a moment that was,' says Dave Kelly, chairman of the Blue Union. 'You can't beat a last-minute goal. I think we hoped that it would be the catalyst to spur us on into extra time; that it might deflate Villa a bit. But the extra half-hour ended without any further goals. With the scoreline still level, that meant another replay and the guarantee that this would now go down in the history books as the longest final in British football history.'

Due to a fixture pile-up, it would be a further month before the teams met again, this time in mid-April at Old Trafford. In the interim, both sides had been in fairly good form, if not exactly flying then difficult to beat. Gordon Lee had brought some stability to Everton, and there was confidence that the cup could still come back to Goodison.

In a match played with more energy and at a higher tempo than the earlier games, from the off both sides appeared willing to have a go, although Everton were the more dominant. In the first period, half-chances came and went, the thousands of Evertonians packed into the Stretford End tense with anticipation.

With the interval nearing, the deadlock finally broke. After a foul given away by Nicholl, the resultant free kick was looped into the box, where Ken McNaught outjumped his markers and managed to direct a header down in front of the opposition's goal.

'It seemed like the entire Everton team were lining up to get the ball over the line,' recalls Brendan Flynn, who had been following the Blues since the 1950s. 'In the end it was Latchford who got the final touch, sweeping the ball past the helpless Burridge in goal. For the first time in this epic encounter, Everton had the lead.'

In the second half, Villa, orderly and composed throughout, came back at Everton strongly. The Blues did well to check their opponents' attempts to force their way back into the match and, with just ten minutes remaining, must have felt like they had one hand on the trophy.

And, when Everton feel like that, you almost always know what's coming next. First, Nicholl, from about 30 yards out, let loose a swerving drive that caught David Lawson unaware and flew in, just inside the post.

'Then,' says Brendan, 'minutes later, we watched on with horror as Brian Little outmuscled Neil Robinson in the box and squeezed a shot under the body of the advancing Lawson. That was a horrible moment. You could feel those around you just deflate.'

But, amazingly, the twists and turns were not over. Not long after, improbably, Everton fought back. With the Villa fans jubilantly singing 'We Shall Not Be Moved', an Everton corner was swung into the box.

After some head tennis, the ball fell to Mick Lyons. 'Amongst a scramble of players,' says Dave Kelly, 'he managed to put it past their keeper and the whole of the Stretford End exploded. It was a wonderful moment. You couldn't help thinking, as the celebrations were going on, that the advantage, mentally, was with us now.'

When the whistle went, it had been 300 minutes of play and still the sides were level. And that meant another period of extra time.

Perhaps that last extra bit of effort had taken it out of Everton, because, as the additional period wound along, it was Villa that looked the stronger. Yet, despite their growing dominance, chances were few. Everton were still in the game, and as the final minutes approached it looked as though nothing would separate these two sides.

And then Villa got a huge slice of luck. Attacking the Everton end, a cross came in from Smith out on the right.

'I think it took a deflection off Ronny Goodlass,' recalls Martin Dobson, 'bobbled into our six-yard box, and there Darracott, Robinson and the keeper all left it for each other. Brian Little, unmarked, reacted faster than anyone else and smacked the ball into the back of the net. The goal came so late that we had no time to respond, and when the referee blew a few minutes later, that was that.'

After five hours of play, it was a desperately cruel way to lose. 'I'd got myself convinced that year that our name was on the cup,' says Dave Kelly. 'So it was a devastating blow that we had fallen short. But I suppose it set me up for a lifetime as an Evertonian.'

Everton had been part of a titanic struggle and participated in arguably the most memorable League Cup Final to have ever taken place. But they had emerged with nothing.

Ten days later, the Blues had a second chance to go back to Wembley, when they faced Liverpool in the FA Cup semi-final at Maine Road.

With ten minutes to go in that game and the score 2–2, Bryan Hamilton deflected a Duncan McKenzie header into the net. To everyone watching, it was a perfectly legitimate goal. Alone, referee Clive Thomas believed an infringement had taken place and ruled the goal out, despite having no clear sight of the incident. The game ended 2–2, and Liverpool went on to win the replay 3–0.

'You could sum the 1970s up in those few games,' says George McKane sadly. 'It was a decade of sheer frustration. We had our moments back then, times when success was within touching distance. But it just never seemed to happen for us.'

v Chelsea 6–0

29 April 1978
Football League Division One
Goodison Park. Attendance: 39,500

Everton: Wood, Robinson, Pejic, Lyons, Wright, Buckley, King, Dobson, Latchford, Telfer, Thomas

Chelsea: Bonetti, Locke, Harris, Swain, Droy, Wicks, Finnieston, Wilkins, Langley, Lewington, Walker

Referee: P. Willis

Bobby Latchford Walks on Water

AMONGST the cavalcade of big number nines taken to the hearts of Evertonians, Bob Latchford has a special place.

'At a time when we looked enviously across Stanley Park at the success that we had once thought was ours to take,' says Brian Viner, author of *Looking for the Toffees: In Search of the Heroes of Everton*, 'a time when people would go into school and work and endure the daily smugness of Liverpudlians, a time when you felt so much in Liverpool's shadow, Bob Latchford was something magical, a class player that Liverpool didn't have. And that mattered.'

Latchford had arrived at Everton from Birmingham City in 1974, in a deal that was both headline grabbing and contentious. The transfer fee of £350,000 was a British record. But the deal itself was not cash alone. It was a player-plus-cash offer, with Everton offering £80,000 plus Archie Styles and, most controversially, Howard Kendall.

The letters pages of the *Liverpool Echo* were inundated with complaints and outrage at the move, illustrating how highly Kendall was still regarded amongst Evertonians. It placed an extra level of expectation on the head of the new arrival, who was already feeling the pressure of that transfer fee, as he recently explained to the *Football Pink*:

'I carried the burden until I got my first goal for the club. I didn't score in my first two games for Everton, but then I opened my account against Leicester City and the great weight was lifted.'

And once he got going, Latchford kept at it. In that first campaign, he managed more than a goal every other game (a rate he roughly kept up throughout this Everton career), helping haul Everton up the table and providing a vital outlet for a team that had struggled to score before his arrival.

'He was great to watch,' remembers Viner. 'He didn't score great goals, like bending free kicks or thirty-yard screamers. But he was big, strong and powerful and read the game superbly. He seemed to always be in the right place at the right time – a natural born goalscorer.'

First under Bingham and then under Lee, Latchford provided the kind of firepower that could lift a side, giving it the realistic prospect of challenging for the title and collecting silverware.

But, although they came close on several occasions, his time with Everton would never be marked by top-level success. And so he had to make do with a different kind of glory and achievement for which Evertonians, and those outside the club, know him best for.

Ahead of the 1977/78 campaign, the *Daily Express* had offered a £10,000 prize (no small amount by the standards of the time) to the first player that scored 30 league goals in the First Division that season. Latchford, despite topping the Everton scoring charts three years in a row and bagging 17 league goals in the previous year, was not considered a favourite by the bookies.

'I think us Blues gave him a better shot. We were playing good football and he seemed as decent a bet as anyone to reach that target first,' remembers Dave Prentice, lifelong Blue and the *Liverpool Echo*'s head of sport.

Although his failure to get on the scoresheet in the first three games of the season might have dented any initial confidence, Latchford did eventually start to pick up goals.

'He would go a few games without scoring and then bang in four against QPR or three against Coventry. So, just when you thought he might not do it, he'd suddenly and dramatically remind you just what he was capable of,' continues Dave.

Along with Everton's more attack-minded football that season, which inevitably gave the club's forwards more opportunities, Latchford also benefitted from the arrival in the summer of Dave Thomas from QPR.

'Thomas was a fantastic winger and he could put a cross into the box on a sixpence,' remembers Viner. 'He was the perfect supplier for a forward like Latchford, someone who was so predatory in front of goal. The two of them seemed to understand each other, know exactly what the other had in mind. It was one of Gordon Lee's better moves.'

Despite Latchford's potency and Everton's sparkling form, the 1977/78 season ended up being a frustrating one for Evertonians. A hoped-for title challenge had stuttered, and, as the run-in approached, the Blues fell off the pace against eventual winners Nottingham Forest. Although European football was ultimately secured, the fans were left with the lingering sense that the side could have done much more.

To make matters worse, Liverpool had once again reached the final of the European Cup, where they had the opportunity to defend their title against the unfancied Club Brugge.

'The sole silver lining for us Blues was Latchford,' argues Brian Viner. 'As the season had closed he'd got closer and closer to the magic number. By the end, a home game against Chelsea, he needed two goals to get himself over the finishing line. For Evertonians back then, him doing that would be our "title", our "European Cup". It was that important.'

On the day itself, Latchford recalls feeling pretty relaxed. 'I was very calm all day,' he recently told Toffee TV. 'I woke up very calm, which is unusual as I always had a little bit of tension … but on that day, nothing. Just a total calm. I knew I was going to get the two goals.'

Although he might have been eerily calm, for those in the ground, it was a different story:

'There was a palpable sense of tension in the air,' recalls Dave Prentice. 'You could feel it. 40,000 nervous fans crowded into Goodison on that Saturday afternoon to see if Everton's number nine could reach that magical target.'

Everton made mincemeat of the Londoners that day, dominating them throughout. 'We strolled to 2–0 lead within 15 minutes,' continues Dave, 'and it could have been more. Chelsea were overwhelmed and Everton were magnificent. But the strange thing was, I don't think anyone really cared about winning or losing. They had come to see Latchford score and so when Dobson and Wright got the opening goals, the crowd wasn't that bothered.'

The scoreline remained the same until the 54th minute, when Neal Robinson, the 21-year-old rookie right-back, scored his first (and what would prove to be only) goal for the club.

'You have to feel for him,' says Brian Viner. 'What should have been a glorious moment for the youngster was marred slightly by the muted reaction. By that point we were all starting to get a bit impatient and were even less interested in other players scoring than we had been at the start of the match!'

Although Everton were rampant, and Chelsea largely passive, as the minutes ticked along it looked to those watching as though Latchford might fall at the final hurdle.

'We were just beginning to think it wasn't to be,' remembers Brian Viner, 'when Mick Buckley put a cross into the box and Latchford was able to get on the end of it to get his 29th. The noise from the crowd was incredible. You'd have thought it was a cup final or something.'

Mick Lyons added a fifth not long after, leaping in front of Latchford to head home from a corner. Everton's stalwart centre-half then further tested the patience of Everton's centre-forward when he got up top again, latched on to a loose ball and thundered a shot against the crossbar.

In an interview with the writer and Evertonian Andreas Selliaas, Latchford revealed that his response to Lyons's effort suggests that the pressure was finally getting to him:

'Mick Lyons is the toughest player ever to play for Everton and I've never had a negative word to say against him, before or now. But the pressure was immense that day to get to 30, and when Mick hit the crossbar instead of passing, I shouted at him "Fuck off, Lyonsy, and stay in our half!"'

Luckily for Latchford, it was advice that his captain opted to ignore. 'I think we were all starting to think it might never happen when fate intervened,' remembers Brian Viner.

Chelsea centre-half Micky Droy challenged Lyons in the box, and the Everton captain went to ground. In all honesty, it was a bit of a soft pen, but it didn't matter. The referee signalled to the spot and Goodison roared its approval.

It's remarkable that nearly all of the goals Latchford had scored to that point had come from open play. Penalties were not usually his responsibility. But this opportunity wouldn't be passed. There was only one man to take that spot kick. He duly stepped up to grasp his date with destiny.

Latchford took up the story in *A Different Road*: 'Martin Dobson took me to one side while Chelsea began to protest. "Just keep your head down and blast it," he whispered. I followed his advice. I thought about exactly where I wanted to put the ball – to Bonetti's right-hand side. There were no nerves. The excitement cancelled out my fear and I was feeling numb. I was simply waiting for the whistle. This was my big chance. The ball left my right foot, I closed my eyes and then heard the Goodison roar. Elation. Relief. Satisfaction. I ran to the supporters and sunk to my knees. As fans ran on to the pitch, my team-mates ran towards me. The fairy tale was complete.'

It was not the greatest penalty that you'll ever see, but it did the job. Everton were 6–0 up and Latchford had got his 30.

'I think up to that point, that was my greatest moment as a Blue,' says Brian Viner. 'I had never experienced an atmosphere like it. The whole place was rocking. You have to appreciate how important that goal was. In a decade when so little had gone right for Everton, that was a moment to truly cherish. Bobby Latchford walked on water. And he was ours!'

v Liverpool 1–0

28 October 1978
Football League Division One
Goodison Park. Attendance: 53,141

Everton: Wood, Todd, Pejic, Kenyon, Wright, Nulty, King, Dobson, Latchford, Walsh, Thomas

Liverpool: Clemence, Neal, Kennedy (A.), Thompson, Kennedy (R.), Hansen, Dalglish, Case (McDermott), Heighway, Johnson, Souness

Referee: P. Partridge

King(s) of Liverpool

YEARS without a win, the sense that Liverpool always have the measure of Everton, the fear that a battering is on the cards. If this all sounds depressingly familiar, it's because it is. Everton's modern malaise in Merseyside derbies is nothing new. In the 1970s, the picture was every bit as bleak.

When Liverpool visited Goodison in the autumn of 1978, it had been 362 weeks since Everton had bested them in a head-to-head.

'People moan, justifiably, about us rarely beating Liverpool nowadays,' argues Dave Kelly, 'but back then you also have to take into account that not only could we not defeat them, we also had to watch as they won everything. So you have to put the lack of derby victories in that context too. When it came to Liverpool, the 1970s were a very dark time for Evertonians, probably the worst ever endured.'

Despite Everton's often erratic form during the 1970s, prior to that derby, matters on the pitch had been looking up. Since Gordon Lee had arrived, Everton's outlook had improved markedly. Although in its relative infancy, the 1978/79 season was looking good for the Blues.

'There was extra spice to that game because both teams were at the top of the table,' says Martin Dobson. 'Liverpool might have been in their pomp but because our form was so good, we fancied our chances. Gordon [Lee] had got us playing well and we had nothing to fear.' But, irrespective of the Blues' improved form, amongst the supporters there was a sense of unease that would be familiar to those who follow the club today.

'Liverpool were so good back then, and their record in derbies so impressive,' recalls Phil Redmond, co-editor of *When Skies Are Grey*, 'that you went to those games fearing that we could get turned over, even if things *were* going well on the pitch. It was a bit like it is nowadays. They had a psychological hold over us.'

On an unseasonably hot October afternoon, 53,000 crammed into Goodison to watch what *Match of the Day*, in a rare example of pre-Sky hyperbole, billed 'THE MATCH OF THE SEASON!'

'I remember there being a huge build-up to that game,' continues Phil. 'It felt like a cup match. I was sitting in the top balcony, down by the Street End. After playing footy in the morning, I got down there early enough to see all kinds of "entertainment" on the pitch, the weirdest of which was the police dog displays. The club was really making the effort beforehand for some reason.'

Liverpool were unchanged from their previous game, boasting the side that had taken the league by its throat. Everton, by contrast, had one key absence, with Mick Lyons out injured; Roger Kenyon was deputising at centre-half.

'You look at those two sides', remembers Brian Viner, 'and in one, Liverpool's, there are no weak links. In Everton's, the likes of Roger Kenyon, Mickey Walsh and Geoff Nulty suggested a side that couldn't match Liverpool player-for-player, so would have to work a lot harder for any chance of a win.'

A raw and raucous atmosphere in Goodison seemed, as it often does on derby day, to be reflected in what unfolded on the pitch. From kick-off, the play was frenetic; tackles flew in, movement a blur, the rhythm of the game played at the highest of tempos.

Watching those two sides, you would never think that Liverpool were the kings of Europe and Everton their overshadowed neighbours. Recent history seemed to mean nothing as the Blues took the game to Liverpool with an attacking display that would shame some modern Everton sides. In a first half that rang with blood and thunder, it was the home team that always seemed to carry the greater threat.

Aside from Graeme Souness's speculative effort at the Everton goal, Liverpool offered very little. The chances, when they arrived, fell instead to the Blues. Latchford came close early on, putting a header wide and later forcing a smart save from Ray Clemence. He then had the best chance of the half when a mix-up between Clemence and the Liverpool defence presented him with a tricky header into an open goal. Agonisingly for those watching behind in the Gwladys Street, the ball trickled inches wide.

'Even though this was Liverpool,' recalls Phil Redmond, 'the kind of side you could imagine getting outplayed and still nicking a jammy win, at half-time it felt good that we had been so much better than them. Despite yourself, you had that weird feeling, something that very rarely occurs for us, that maybe this could be our day.'

Under a floodlit pitch, this time switched on to compete with the sunlight, Everton (attacking the Park End) started the second half strongly. Almost immediately, a sublime cross by Walsh nearly put Nulty in. But, although he flung himself at the ball, the Everton midfielder couldn't quite get his head to the cross.

It felt like the game's momentum was with Everton and that a goal was on its way. But it would take a moment of magic for one to be conjured up. And, on this occasion, the magician in question was Andy King.

King was just 19 when he had moved to Goodison from Luton Town in April 1976 for £35,000. Almost on arrival, he was taken to the hearts of Evertonians.

'There was just something about him that we loved,' remembers Dave Prentice. 'Maybe it was his chirpy, effervescent personality or maybe it was because he "bought" into Everton. It was clear very quickly (and later confirmed by the many kind things he's said about the club) that he became an Evertonian once he had arrived. I think the fans always have a soft spot for those who choose to become a Blue.'

Always capable of a moment of magic, this busy midfielder was about to score his most memorable goal for the club.

'I remember Mike Pejic looping a ball into the box which was headed down,' says Brian Viner. 'I could just about make this out through the glaring sun.'

The ball bounced right outside the box, where it was met by the onrushing King. The midfielder adjusted his body to account for an awkward bounce and then let fly. To the delight of every Blue inside the ground, he caught it sweetly. The ball flew over the fingertips of a beaten Clemence and exploded into the top corner.

'To this day I can see the ball curling away from Clemence,' remembers Mike Constantinou, who was stood in the Lower Gwladys Street. 'As soon as it was hit, you just knew. Cue complete euphoria and insanity. The Old Lady was at her best and was shaking, we were all just being carried around in waves of people, arms around each other, fists clenched. It was complete bedlam.'

A tale later told by King to TalkSport, possibly apocryphal, possibly not, gives a beautiful illustration of the difference between the two clubs at the time.

'The story goes, and it's true,' he recounted to Richard Keys, 'that Souness, as I'd hit it, said "you've missed". I turned to him as it went into the top corner and said, "I did. I was aiming two inches to the left."'

Whether true or not, the story has a nice ring to it, contrasting the effervescent glee of the underdog with that of the dour, unsporting sourness displayed by the perennial winner.

In response to being one down, Liverpool (inevitably) upped their game and, not long after, nearly silenced Goodison when Johnson put the ball in the back of the net. Most Evertonians probably think otherwise, but sometimes the officials can come to the rescue in derbies. The flag went up before Johnson had struck, and the goal was ruled offside. With that, Liverpool's brief resurgence started to run out of steam.

As the game edged towards conclusion, it was Everton who would come closest to scoring, when Thomas had his goalbound shot cleared off the line by Hansen (who opted on this occasion to use his foot rather than his hand).

'When the 90 minutes was up, Goodison went mad,' remembers Brian Viner. 'I think that we gave more voice that day than we had six months earlier when Latchford scored his 30th. Goodison was hysterical. We'd actually been singing 'Bobby Latchford walks on water' during the game. But for the remaining half-hour or so, the ground shook to a chorus of "Andy is our King, oh Andy is our King, oh Aaaandy is our King!"'

After the game, as jubilant Blues danced around their hero, *BBC North West Tonight*'s Richard Duckenfield stuck a microphone under the nose of King. 'Andy King …' he began, before a local bizzie hovered into view and started to barge the pair down the nearby players' tunnel. 'Can you get off the pitch!' barked the bizzie, making his allegiances plain for all to see.

The supporters never got to hear Andy King's immediate thoughts. But that might be just as well, as his goal probably said more than any words could.

'In a time when Evertonians had so little to cheer, that was an unquestioned highlight,' argues George McKane. 'The 1970s, specifically when it came to Liverpool, had been really hard for us. It's probably difficult to explain to modern fans what it felt like to live so comprehensively under their shadow. So, to beat them, finally, was magical.'

Blues of all ages got to experience something that had been denied them for so long: a proper post-match gloat.

'After so many Monday mornings going into school and having to put up with their smug faces,' remembers Phil Redmond, 'it was great to go in and give the Reds in my class loads. The novelty of the experience was made all the sweeter when you saw just how pissed off they were.'

Although, according to Phil, the reaction of some was a bit of an eye-opener for one so young:

'I think that was the first time that I really realised what a bunch of shitehawks they really are. I had a go at one mate and he shot back sourly, "How many European Cups have you won?" Typical Redshite, can't lose graciously, not even the once.'

v Liverpool 2–1

24 January 1981
FA Cup Fourth Round
Goodison Park. Attendance: 53,804

Everton: Hodge, Ratcliffe, Bailey, Wright, Lyons, Ross, McMahon, Eastoe, Varadi, Hartford, O'Keefe

Liverpool: Clemence, Neal, Thompson, Irwin, Cohen, Kennedy, Dalglish (Case), Lee, Fairclough. McDermott, Souness

Referee: C. Thomas

Varadi's Meat Pie

GORDON Lee's tenure as Everton's boss has enjoyed some revisionism in recent years. The top-four finishes, the cup runs, the derby wins – it's all been dusted off and if not exactly put on the mantelpiece, then at least no longer locked away in the cupboard of perpetual shame.

But revisionism can be a dangerous thing. Because sometimes, the passage of time can erase just how bad an era felt. And as the Lee era came to a close, it was as wretched as anything endured under the dog days of Walter Smith or Roberto Martinez.

'Although the Lee era had started brightly and for a time we had thought that he was building something good, by the end it was tough,' remembers George McKane. 'It was a bleak time. Liverpool were flying and we'd just endured a decade of frustration, false dawns and disappointment. Any glimmers of hope, any moments of happiness, were few and far between. And because of that, when they did appear, we grabbed on to them.'

After finishing third and then fourth during his first two full seasons in charge, Everton under Lee had then slumped to 19th in his third. In the campaign that followed, Everton were largely poor and, by January 1981, sat mid-table, out of the League Cup and saddled with a manager rapidly running out of both ideas and friends.

'Gordon Lee was never that popular with the fans,' continues George. 'In his first few seasons, the runs at the title had helped us accept him slightly, but we'd never taken him to our hearts. As the form deteriorated, there was very little goodwill on the terraces to sustain him. He was just an unpopular manager with a team that looked to be going nowhere.'

Just to kick Everton (and Lee) when they were down, the footballing gods, in their infinite wisdom, then decided to draw the Blues against Liverpool in the fourth round of the FA Cup.

As the 1970s bled into the 1980s, Liverpool had remained difficult to beat. 'Andy King's winner had not been the turning point,' remembers John Daley. 'Although we had notched up some draws, wins since had remained elusive, and, before the game, the bookies had Liverpool as the overwhelming favourites.'

For many Blues, memories of the last time the club had met in the FA Cup gave the match an extra element of spice.

'There was a score to settle for us after the "Clive Thomas Derby" a few years earlier,' continues John, 'so that gave the match an extra dimension. The opportunity for us to get some payback was evident amongst Blues. Not that anyone gave us a hope in hell.'

The interest in the game was so widespread that demand for tickets massively exceeded supply. In response, officials from the two clubs joined together to ask the FA if Liverpool could set up a giant screen at Anfield. They'd done this before, back in 1967, when across the two stadiums, a combined total of nearly 105,000 fans had watched Everton win 1–0 at Goodison Park in the fifth round of the FA Cup.

On this occasion, the FA were in no mood to be accommodating. Not only was the plan knocked back, but so too was a request from both clubs to delay the kick-off until 7pm.

And so, on a cold, bright Saturday afternoon, on a pitch churned up and muddied by the elements and with the loathed Clive Thomas officiating once again, Everton started proceedings, kicking towards Gwladys Street.

As former Everton forward Imre Varadi recently told the *Liverpool Echo*, the lamentable Thomas was kept busy from the off:

'I've still got the video of the game and I watch it every now and again. Some of the tackles in the game were GBH – there was such passion and it was played at a great tempo.

'If the game had been played now, I reckon there'd have been five or six sendings off.'

Despite the Blues' poor form, they began the brighter of the two sides. 'The opening 20 minutes was all Everton,' remembers Phil Redmond. 'Varadi had a couple of chances and Liverpool barely got out of their half. It was one of those times when Everton looked like they were up for it. They weren't giving Liverpool space to breathe.'

On the 20-minute mark, Everton's pressure told. A lumped clearance from Cohen to the half-way line was headed back towards the box by Lyons, who outjumped Dalglish (the Scotsman visibly shitting out of the challenge). The ball reached Hartford, who brought it down neatly, watched for the run of Eastoe, and slid a defence-splitting pass into his path.

As Clemence rushed towards him, Eastoe clipped the ball towards goal with the outside of his foot. Although slowed by the keeper's advance, it trickled onwards. Phil Neal gave chase and, just as the ball crossed the line, slid to clear it. That might have been enough to keep the scores level but the clearance smacked into the onrushing Cohen anyway and the ball rebounded into the back of the net.

After consulting his linesman (quite probably in a desperate search to find some reason to disallow the effort), Thomas gave the goal, and Everton were ahead.

Despite having the lead, Everton were less dominant after the goal, and Liverpool began to creep back into the game. They enjoyed the better chances that came in the remainder of the half, notably when Dalglish made a smart turn in the Everton box and shot on goal, only to watch forlornly as the ball went through the keeper's legs, took a deflection and bobbled out for a corner.

'Although Everton were arguably worth the lead,' says Phil Redmond, 'there was a long time to go. And I doubt any Evertonian watching would have been confident at half-time of us going through.'

In the second period, Everton rediscovered some of their bite. Varadi forced a decent save out of Clemence, and O'Keefe had a half-chance that he put over the bar.

'I think one of my abiding memories of that day was how many Imre could've got,' recalls Everton's left-back that day, John Bailey. 'He ran himself ragged and seemed to be everywhere and with a bit more luck could probably have got himself a hat-trick.'

At the other end, Liverpool's only action of note was a sly challenge by Jimmy Case on Martin Hodge, which saw him slide in with a two-footed lunge after the keeper had gone down to collect the ball. It was a challenge that brought a strong reaction from the Everton players and ultimately led to Lyons and Souness being involved in a bit of 'handbags'.

As had been the case with the first half, Everton's pressure eventually yielded reward. Not long after that incident, Varadi, who had remained a persistent nuisance all afternoon, gave Evertonians what they had been asking for since Eastoe had opened the scoring.

'I think Trevor Ross won the ball for us and played it out to Eamonn O'Keefe on the left-hand side,' Varadi told the *Liverpool Daily Post*. 'Eamonn was about 20 yards out and crossed the ball in – it bounced and I managed to get to it on the way up and squeeze it into the corner of the goal.'

The Everton forward was so elated that he failed to give his celebrations enough thought. 'I ran around the back of the goal, not realising it was full of away supporters. I incurred the wrath of an angry Liverpool fan who chucked a meat and potato pie straight into my face – I can still taste it now!'

At 2–0, Liverpool should have been dead and buried. They had barely been in the Everton half, and, with 30 minutes left, the Blues ought to have killed the match off. But when do Everton ever make life easy?

The Blues sat back, inviting Liverpool on to them. As they probed, the visitors began to build up a head of steam. With 15 minutes left, Souness lumped a quick free kick out wide on the left to Cohen. The full-back headed the ball into the penalty area to Ray Kennedy, who turned and drove a pass into the Everton six-yard box. There, Case got to it first and was able to prod the ball into the net.

'Typical Everton,' mutters Phil Redmond. 'Never doing things the easy way.'

And yet, oddly, this wasn't the prelude to a sustained assault on the Everton box. There would be no catalogue of chances, no Red siege, no feeling of irresistible momentum.

'That's what you would expect from Liverpool,' continues Phil. 'Considering how good they were back then, and how much of a psychological hold they had on Everton, you would expect the Blues to be on the back foot. But that's not what happened.'

Ultimately, it was Everton who ended the stronger, and who came the closest to finding the net again when Varadi latched on to a through ball in the dying minutes, rounded Clemence and with the goal at his mercy, put it wide (perhaps put off by some residual meat pie).

'3–1 would have made life more bearable for supporters,' says Dave Kelly. 'But in the end, that extra goal wasn't needed. The whistle blew and they were out. It was perfect.'

The end brought with it a minor pitch invasion as happy Blues scaled the barriers to celebrate with their heroes.

'That was a great moment,' admits Phil Redmond, 'the kind of win we really needed back then. Wiping the smiles off their faces was pretty much all we had.'

After vanquishing Liverpool, Everton made it to the quarter-finals in the competition, where they were ultimately knocked out by Manchester City. In the league, they finished near the bottom, another disappointing campaign from the once-promising Lee.

'He might have been able to conjure up defeats of Liverpool,' says Phil, 'but as the season wound to a close it was obvious amongst the fans that the manager's days were numbered.'

v Oxford United 1–1

18 January 1984
Football League Cup Quarter-final
The Manor Ground. Attendance: 14,333

Everton: Southall, Stevens, Harper, Ratcliffe, Mountfield, Irvine, Reid, Sheedy, Heath, Johnson (Richardson), Sharp

Oxford United: Hardwick, Hinshelwood, McDonald, Train, Briggs, Shotton, Lawrence, Biggins, Vinter, Hebberd (Whatmore), Brock

Referee: J. Hunting

Kevin Brock Back-pass

AFTER Gordon Lee's sacking in May 1981, Howard Kendall had arrived at Goodison charged with reviving the fortunes of the struggling club. It was hoped that the new boss could arrest Everton's relative decline and restore some pride.

Kendall had been a player/manager at Blackburn Rovers since 1979 and pulled the Lancashire club out of the Third Division and into the Second. Having narrowly missed out on promotion to the top flight during the following campaign, he had caught the eye of the Goodison board.

But, despite the sense of expectation that always hangs over any Everton manager, there was no urgent pressure for instant success.

'I don't think anyone expected us to challenge for the title right away,' says John Black, 'and if they did then the quality of the players brought into the club would have left no doubt that it was going to be a rebuilding exercise. Personally, I thought we could maybe win the FA or League Cup and if we managed to get into the UEFA then that would be a bonus. But most of all you want to see progress on the pitch, tangible signs of a decent side being built.'

This lack of immediate expectation was probably just as well, because Kendall struggled to get his project off the ground. Despite some positive signs, periods of good form and the acquisition of a few decent players, the fans were underwhelmed. Kendall was only impressing sporadically, and the despondency that had settled over Goodison persisted.

'There had been hints that Kendall was on to something in his first few seasons, but we'd then started the 83/84 campaign really poorly,' says Phil Redmond. 'I'm not one to get into all that "sack the manager" stuff, but even I joined in with calls for him to go during an away game against Leicester in October when we'd just been shite. He'd had a few seasons and we were getting the sense as fans that he just didn't have what it would take to get Everton up to where we wanted them to be.'

By the New Year that season, patience seemed to be running out. At a particularly grim home match against Coventry City, just 13,000 had turned up to watch the side struggle their way through a 0–0 draw. Despite the meagre turnout, the shouts of 'Kendall Out', which had grown in prevalence during the course of the season, were deafening.

Unlike his two predecessors, Bingham and Lee, Kendall's arrival had not precipitated a dramatic turnaround and the sense of a club on the rise. Instead, he appeared to have replaced that part with mediocrity and then followed their template by heading towards disaster after a couple of seasons.

Matters looked bleak for the manager. And yet, with hindsight, it was evident that all the ingredients needed to create the greatness of what was to come were already there. Kendall just hadn't put them together yet. Or had he?

'A week earlier,' remembers former Everton captain Kevin Ratcliffe, 'before we had played Oxford in the League Cup, we'd played Stoke in the FA Cup in a game that I think first began to suggest we were getting our act together.'

Everton went mob-handed to Stoke's old Victoria Ground. 'There were about 7,000 Blues at that match,' says Dave Kelly. 'Considering how bad Everton had been playing, that's an amazing figure. Also, when you think about the problems affecting Liverpool back then, the unemployment and the poverty, it's a testament to the commitment of those fans that they still got behind the club on the road.'

Before kick-off, so the story goes, Howard Kendall enterprisingly turned the travelling army to his advantage. He opened the dressing room windows to allow the fans' singing to come through and said: 'That's your team talk today. Don't let those fans down.' Everton won the day 2–0.

'We played really well,' thinks former Everton midfielder Kevin Sheedy. 'It was a side that contained the likes of Reid, Gray, Southall and Sharp and which boasted the recently appointed Colin Harvey as assistant manager. And it was a side that clicked. It was like everything that Howard had been building was coming right.'

But fragility remained. This was still a side mired near the bottom of the table, a side low on confidence, a side packed with inexperienced young players.

'As good as Stoke had been,' remembers Dave Kelly, 'and as important as it was in hindsight, this remained an Everton team that didn't inspire confidence. If there *were* signs of promise, it could all still easily fall away. On the way down to the Manor Ground, I doubt anyone was filled with overwhelming confidence.'

Although a Third Division outfit, Oxford United were no pushovers. 'They had already put out Manchester United, Leeds and Newcastle in the League Cup, and the Manor Ground, with its sloping, winter-worn, bobbly pitch was a tricky place to visit,' says John Bailey.

Stylistically, the first half of the quarter-final revealed the gulf that existed between these two sides. Everton attempted, where possible, to pass the ball around. By contrast, Oxford were more dependent upon long balls and set pieces.

Both approaches yielded chances, with Everton going close through Irvine and Sheedy and Oxford causing the visitors all kinds of problems from corners, specifically via the presence of their statuesque centre-half Gary Briggs. But neither side could land a telling blow, and they went in at half-time level.

After the break, Oxford continued from where they had left off, while Everton appeared to shrink into themselves slightly. The pressure from the home side mounted, and the sense that they would score seemed to build.

And, midway through the second half, Oxford did just that. A free kick near the corner flag was pumped in from the left by Brock. At the far post, Briggs connected and headed the ball down into the six-yard box. There it was met by Bobby McDonald, who toe-poked the ball into the back of the net.

'They were so full of themselves after that goal, and the crowd so loud, that I thought we might have had it,' admits Kevin Ratcliffe.

And, for a time, it looked as though Ratcliffe might be right. With not long to go, Oxford appeared to be in control and cruising towards another big scalp in their glorious cup run.

But it wasn't to be.

With nine minutes left on the clock, Kevin Brock found himself caught in possession outside his own box, chased tenaciously by a terrier-like Peter Reid. As more Everton players swarmed in, Brock looked up and, believing he'd found salvation in his keeper, played a simple pass back. But he'd failed to see Adrian Heath hiding behind one of his own centre-halves. 'Inchy' latched on to the ball, took it around the keeper and clipped it into the back of the net.

'I knew that I was going to get the ball,' Heath explained to Simon Hart in *Here We Go*. 'But the hardest part was keeping my feet because if you look at it I am falling over virtually as I hit it. It was an important goal for the club but people forget it was a really good finish … it was one of the best finishes I've ever done. I don't think a lot of people appreciated that the bottom end of the field, kicking down the slope, was complete ice because the sun hadn't got across there in the day.'

It was only Everton's second chance of the half. But Heath took it with clinical efficiency. All the Blues had to do now was hang on.

As the match came to a close, Everton offered nothing of note except grim resilience, exemplified by the tireless duo of Reid and Richardson, both of whom tried valiantly to harry Oxford to their last breath. The home side, perhaps conscious of an opportunity being squandered, piled forward and came close to earning a deserved victory when Biggins got on the end of a looping cross from Lawrence. But the effort went narrowly wide.

When the final whistle went, every Evertonian there could breathe a sigh of relief. Against a better side, the Blues had earned an undeserved draw and escaped from the jaws of death.

'There's nothing like a late goal to win a game or level it in a cup tie,' says Dave Kelly. 'You just can't explain the sense of euphoria. I was one happy man leaving that ground.'

Oxford were dispatched 4–1 in the replay the following week, setting Everton on the path to the League Cup Final. But, perhaps more importantly, that match seemed to act as a catalyst.

'Even though form had been picking up slightly,' argues Simon Hart, author of *Here We Go*, 'particularly as illustrated in the Stoke game, before that momentous visit to the Manor Ground, Everton were languishing near the bottom of the league and finding wins and goals hard to come by (I recall at that point that we were the lowest-scoring team in the entire league pyramid). Our league season was pretty much over and so the cups offered salvation. If we had gone out against Oxford at their place, who knows how that would have affected confidence.'

After Oxford, the side went on a strong run of form, climbed up the table and also made it to the FA Cup Final.

'Without Kevin Brock's mistake,' laughs Dave Kelly, 'it's possible that what came later, the league titles, the European success, the years of glory, might also not have occurred. There's a reason why so many Evertonians know the name of an Oxford United midfielder. There's a case for him being our player of the season that year!'

v Liverpool 0–0

25 March 1984
League Cup Final
Wembley Stadium. Attendance: 100,000

Everton: Southall, Stevens, Bailey, Mountfield, Ratcliffe, Reid, Irvine, Heath, Sharp, Richardson, Sheedy (Harper)

Liverpool: Grobbelaar, Neal, Kennedy, Lawrenson, Whelan, Hansen, Dalglish, Lee, Rush, Johnston (Robinson), Souness

Referee: A. Robinson

Merseypride

IGNORE the fact that the match ended goalless, that chances were limited and that the trophy on offer was sponsored by the Milk Marketing Board (a commercial link-up to get the heart racing), the 1984 League Cup Final was an important game for Everton FC.

'Three months before Howard Kendall's men took to the Wembley turf on a rainy, Sunday afternoon,' argues Simon Hart, 'Everton had been in the doldrums. But whether you date the turnaround from the Stoke game in the FA Cup, the infamous "Kevin Brock back-pass" against Oxford, or any other of small moments referenced by Blues, something had changed at the club.'

After a few seasons of showing flashes of what could be, Everton under Kendall were starting to act on all that promise.

'We were winning games and reaching finals, which hadn't been the case for some time,' says George McKane. 'But, equally satisfying, the club was also playing some of the best football seen at Goodison Park for years. There was a sense amongst the fans that something magical was happening here.'

The factors that lay behind this turnaround will be debated by Evertonians for years to come. But the elements most frequently put forward usually include the appointment of Colin Harvey as first team coach midway through the season, the arrival of the talismanic Andy Gray and Peter Reid finally enjoying a period of injury-free football.

'All these factors played a role. But confidence played its part too,' argues Simon. 'The simple act of winning games and making headway in cup competitions let that side overcome its inhibitions and begin to play with freedom. Without the League Cup or the FA, even with the likes of Harvey, Gray and Reid, it's debatable whether Everton would have thrived and whether, by extension, Kendall would have kept his job.'

Everton's route to Wembley had not been a straightforward one, which was understandable for a club that had found the first half of the season such a struggle. In the second round back in October, a dire performance in a 2–2 home draw against Chesterfield had been greeted by a chorus of boos (from the 8,000 present), despite the Blues going through 3–2 on aggregate.

After that, there had been ties against Coventry City, West Ham United and Oxford United, during which there had been times when it seemed very unlikely that Everton would be gracing the Wembley turf any time soon.

'We were a side that was still finding its feet and trying to find a rhythm,' admits Kevin Ratcliffe. 'As good as we could be, it could still unravel now and then. We were a young side too, a little inexperienced and prone to making mistakes. There were plenty of times on the route to Wembley when the results could have gone against us.'

Despite their erratic form, Kendall's men kept progressing, and after dispatching Aston Villa in the semis they booked themselves a place at Wembley where they would face Liverpool. Improbably, considering how long these two clubs had been knocking around, this would be the first time that the Merseyside giants had met in a major final.

There once was a time, many years ago, when Liverpool were famous for winning stuff (rather than just being famous for the memory of winning stuff). This was the era when Liverpool were the side that others measured themselves against.

And the League Cup was one area where they'd been especially dominant. Liverpool had won the last three competitions and you had to go back to 1980 (some 38 matches) to find their last defeat, when they had exited at the hands of Nottingham Forest.

'Drawing them in the final would prove a stern test for our claims of revival,' says Kevin Sheedy. 'While another, easier team might have been a more welcome draw, if we ever had hopes of emulating our neighbours (which is what we wanted), then these were the sort of games that we had to win. We had to go up against Liverpool and illustrate that we had the measure of them.'

Along with the footballing importance of this clash for the people of Liverpool, there were wider social and cultural implications for the city too. In the early 1980s, Liverpool was suffering under the yoke of Thatcherism. Blighted by unemployment and facing a government indifferent to working-class suffering, football offered a rare source of pride to a city in desperate need of a boost to its self-esteem.

'Although playing the Shite was probably not what Evertonians necessarily wanted,' says Phil Redmond, 'considering how poor our record was against them, an all-Merseyside cup final did represent a chance to unify and celebrate a city that for too long had been attacked and maligned.'

And, in those days, both camps were strongly identified and connected to the city. This was the era before Liverpool gutted themselves in search of global appeal and that all-important corporate dollar. They might have had supporters' clubs in Norway, Ireland and Australia, but they remained, like Everton, primarily a local club, rooted in the community and connected to

Everton's victorious 1906 FA Cup winning side

Dixie Dean: The Colossus of Goodison

A victorious Everton parade the FA Cup through the streets of Liverpool in 1933

*Dave Hickson
– a bright light
through dark
times*

The Mersey Millionaires enjoy of a lap of honour after bringing home the title in 1963

Alex Young – The Golden Vision

*Taste of success: Everton's
1966 heroes drink from the
FA Cup*

*Harry Catterick
and his glorious
1970 title-winning
side*

*Bob Latchford celebrates
his 30th goal. A rare high
point in a difficult decade
for the Blues*

Everton parade the 1984 FA Cup through the streets of Liverpool (Jim Malone)

Trevor Steven scores the third against Bayern Munich to book Everton a place in the 1985 Cup Winners' Final (Jim Malone)

Fans pile into Goodison to see the team clinch the 1984/85 title (Jim Malone)

Andy Gray celebrates scoring the opening goal in the 1985 Cup Winners' Cup Final

Jubilant Blues celebrate on the pitch after Everton clinch the Title against Norwich in 1987

1991 FA Cup fifth round replay: the strangest of derbies

Everton fans watch Graham Stuart's vital penalty against Wimbledon from the demolished Park End (Jim Malone)

Joe Royle takes the helm for his first game in charge at Goodison

The 1995 FA Cup is paraded around Liverpool. A win that once seemed so unlikely (Jim Malone)

'A sombre day' Everton v Coventry 1998: the fight for survival (Jim Malone)

Remember the name! Rooney scores his wonder goal against Arsenal

Lescott, Rodwell, Cahill and Vaughan celebrate Everton's penalties victory in the 2009 FA Cup semi-final

Oviedo Baby! Bryan Oviedo fires past David de Gea to claim Everton's first win at Old Trafford in a generation

the city at an elemental level. This was not the hollowed-out shell that resides in Anfield today.

And so, on Sunday 25 March, the streets of the city emptied as coaches, trains, cars, all jammed with fans from both sides of the divide, converged on the capital.

But even those left behind joined in the celebrations, as Ken Rogers wrote in the *Liverpool Echo*:

'Back in Liverpool the ticketless Scousers organised special street parties, with the women playing their part. In Saxony Road, off Kensington, all the men had travelled to Wembley, but the wives threw a street party for over 100 kids. It was the same all over the city. When the special trains and buses finally arrived home and the cars poured off the motorways, the fans were still elated. They had been part of an historic occasion.'

Would the match live up to the hype? Would neutrals be delighted by the 'ding-dong' nature of a Merseyside derby, but on this occasion writ large? Could this be a game that would live long in the memories of those who watched?

Does that ever happen?

After all the build-up, a sense of anti-climax was probably always likely. On a rain-drenched pitch, neither side seemed able to take control of the game.

Everton were the more impressive in the first half. Sheedy and Richardson both came close, as the Blues restricted their opponents' ability to play their natural passing game. Although Liverpool could point to their midweek away match against Benfica in the European Cup in mitigation for their sloppiness, there was no doubt that Everton had been impressive.

They also, as John Bailey explains, should have been awarded a penalty. 'When Adrian Heath stole the ball from Grobbelaar and punted it towards the Liverpool goal, it looked like we might take the lead. But Alan Hansen, racing back to block the shot, had other ideas. The only way to stop us scoring was to handle the ball, so he did.'

As an infringement, it was blatant, obvious to all except one person. 'The referee, Alan Robinson, was perfectly positioned to see the offence and there was no excuse at all for not giving it,' wrote Kendall in *Only the Best Is Good Enough*.

Like Clive Thomas before him and Neil Midgley, Mark Clattenburg and Graham Poll after, Robinson joined the long list of referees crossed off Everton's Christmas card list.

Although the Blues were denied the chance to go in at half-time with a deserved lead, there was still much to admire in the team's performance.

'We had played well and had the better of the strongest side in the country,' feels former Everton centre-half Derek Mountfield. 'And that was something to take satisfaction in. Looking at that half, you wouldn't have known that

Liverpool were the more accomplished, more fancied side. We'd given them a game, and probably a bit of a fright.'

After the break, perhaps inevitably, the tide began to turn Liverpool's way as experience started to tell. Kendall's verdant fledglings were unused to playing at this level. Joe Fagan's men weren't. As Everton's initial energy and ingenuity began to dissipate, fading in potency as a goal refused to come, Liverpool started to take control of the game.

Ronnie Whelan and Alan Kennedy had goals disallowed for offside, while Neville Southall had to be at his best to foil Ian Rush on a couple of occasions. Uncharacteristically, Liverpool's talismanic forward also put the ball over from eight yards out, missing probably their best opportunity to take the lead during the whole afternoon.

'We rode our luck a bit in the second half,' admits Kevin Ratcliffe, 'but overall I think a draw was probably a fair result. We had the first half, they had the second.'

The draw was not a bad result for those watching at Wembley. The communal atmosphere and sense of unity could continue, with no set of fans facing that long, hard journey home, the bitter taste of defeat in their mouths.

After the end of the match, the players, both Red and Blue, saluted those who had come to watch, as John Bailey fondly remembers:

'At the end of the game I ran around Wembley with Alan Kennedy. We had a blue scarf and a red scarf tied together above our heads. I remember the fans singing "Merseyside, Merseyside, Merseyside", and it still brings a lump to my throat thinking about it now. It was an occasion that you just don't forget and which was a privilege to be part of.'

Although plastered all over the papers the next day, for some of those there, like Graham Ennis, the whole 'Merseyside' thing rang a little hollow.

'People travelled down together, and there was no division between the fans. But that's just what Liverpool is like. When it came to the game, I recall the Evertonians singing Everton songs because we were proud of what our team had done. I think the "Merseyside" stuff came from the Liverpool fans, largely because they knew they'd underperformed and probably wanted to extract a bit of pride from the game by jumping on the "Merseyside" bandwagon.'

The pride in what Everton had done was well founded. 'We had gone head-to-head against not just the best side in the country', says Kevin Sheedy, 'but also one that for over a decade had possessed a hold over us. And we had matched them. There was nothing in that performance to suggest that we didn't have what it took to challenge Liverpool. It was a confidence builder; a huge boost for that group of young players.'

Although a few days later the Blues would lose the replay at Maine Road 1–0, they had served notice on Liverpool. Everton were back.

v Watford 2–0

19 May 1984
FA Cup Final
Wembley Stadium. Attendance: 100,000

Everton: Southall, Stevens, Bailey, Ratcliffe Mountfield, Reid, Steven, Heath Gray, Sharp, Richardson

Watford: Sherwood, Bardsley, Price (Atkinson), Taylor, Terry, Sinnott, Callaghan, Johnston, Reilly, Jackett, Barnes

Referee: J. Hunting

Here We Go!

AFTER the near miss of the 1984 League Cup Final, when Everton had come tantalisingly close to claiming the club's first trophy in 14 years, Howard Kendall's men had given themselves a second bite at bringing some silverware back to Goodison by reaching that season's FA Cup Final.

Everton had got there after seeing off Southampton in the semi-finals, courtesy of Adrian Heath's extra-time goal.

'Talk about a great moment,' says John Daley. 'When "Inchy" headed that ball in, with just a few minutes of extra time left, every Blue in Highbury probably lost their heads for a bit. Getting to the League Cup Final was one thing, getting to the FA, that was something else.'

The last time Everton had made it to the final was 1968, so understandably there was a great hunger for the club to bring the cup home.

'It had been a generation since we'd won the trophy back in 1966,' remembers David France, 'and the disappointment of losing out to Liverpool in the League Cup only strengthened the desire for the day to go well. Amongst the tens of thousands who travelled down to Wembley, the need to bring that cup home, to end the season on a high point, was palpable.'

For those who couldn't make it that day, solace of a sort could be found by indulging in the BBC's seemingly endless build-up, hour upon hour of televisual padding before the main event. As was customary back then, the clubs were provided with a 'celebrity' fan. Everton got Freddie Starr, Watford, Michael Barrymore. Each was meant to provide light relief for the watching fans. Neither did. Although one (Barrymore) did provide a masterclass in racial insensitivity, when he blacked up to perform a nauseating 'Chalky'-style impression of John Barnes, which to this day represents a televisual low for the BBC.

Amongst the travelling Blue horde fortunate enough to swerve this particular car crash, the sense of desire for the club to win was undercut with genuine belief that, on this occasion, they might just do that.

'Watford were a good side,' says Rob Sawyer, 'but our form in the second half of the season had been great, the football we'd been playing a joy to watch, and we also had the valuable experience of having been to Wembley recently. It felt like we were the favourites.'

It was an air of confidence that, as Everton forward Andy Gray recalls, was shared by several of the players too. 'A lot of those who'd travelled down, like "Inchy", Trevor Steven and Gary Stevens, were very confident because they were so young. It was understandable. We'd been playing really well and were probably the more fancied of the two sides. But the old heads, like Reidy and I, we knew what the score was, we knew that few games are ever as easy as you think they might be, so it was our job to settle them down a bit.'

For the players heading out on to the pitch, the memory is one that will stay with them forever, as Derek Mountfield remembers:

'The old Wembley tunnel sloped. So, we couldn't see the stands or the terraces from the bottom. We could only see the sky to begin with. As Howard led us out, the tunnel began to level out and gradually we saw the top of the stands, then more, and then the whole stadium. When we reached that final point, and emerged out of the tunnel, it was like somebody had switched the volume on full blast. The roar as we emerged is something I will never forget.'

The neutral perspective that day would probably have favoured a Watford victory. That would have been the fairy-tale outcome.

Just a few years earlier, the Hornets had been languishing in the old Fourth Division. Under the helmsmanship of Graham Taylor, they had then enjoyed an improbable rise to the top flight in just five seasons. This outperforming minnow would have been the people's choice to win, and, early on, despite being the underdogs, it looked as though they might be in with a chance, when Barnes and Taylor had good opportunities to put them ahead.

'Had they scored then,' feels Andy Gray, 'it would have totally changed the match. We were still a young side, and going behind might have knocked our confidence. In the end, though, we rode our luck and gradually began to grow into the game.'

Despite their bright start, Watford were always likely to struggle because of the makeshift nature of their side. A long season had begun to take its toll injury-wise as the campaign came to a close (at one point, Taylor struggled to find a fit centre-half pairing). By contrast, Kendall had enjoyed the luxury of putting out a settled side for some time and was able to name his preferred starting eleven on the morning of the match.

'And, as a side, we were really starting to develop that understanding between players that is so important for successes,' says Kevin Ratcliffe. 'After a few years of chopping and changing, Howard now had the players he wanted and had them playing in the positions he wanted. We were getting used to each other and how Howard and Colin wanted us to play. And you could see it that day. The team was well organised in defence and attack and after the opening few minutes had no trouble dealing with Watford's long-ball game at the back, while constantly asking questions of them up front.'

Although Everton had been gradually growing more dominant, they had little to show for their efforts aside from a few half-chances. This changed as half-time approached:

'The ball fell to Gary Stevens outside of the box and he had a go on goal,' recalls Graeme Sharp, who had arrived at Goodison from Dumbarton a few years earlier. 'The shot was off target, but, luckily for me, the ball came my way about ten yards out. I was able to control it and put the ball past their keeper. I remember the Blue half of Wembley just exploding!'

Everton saw out the remaining minutes of the half comfortably, and so went in at the break with the upper hand and the sense that they had survived what Watford had to threaten them with.

'Howard never overdid things,' says Andy Gray. 'He wasn't one for the big speeches. He had a word with each of us, said what we needed to know. He just told us to keep on doing what we'd been doing. The first half had gone well, and we had the lead. It was man-management really, something he excelled at.'

Nobody, except probably Everton fans, would ever call that second half a memorable one. Limited goalmouth action and little incident was probably the best way to describe what occurred. And that's because the game was effectively killed off five minutes after the break, when Gray jumped to meet a looping cross from Steven and head Everton into a two-goal lead.

The goal was not without controversy, as Gray effectively headed the ball out of Steve Sherwood's hands. In the modern game it could probably not be given. But it wasn't the modern game.

'I say it was a fair challenge,' says Gray. 'He [Sherwood] says it wasn't. But either way, it stood and with that goal, Watford were done. The energy they had displayed in the first half just disappeared. It got to them and the rest of the game was very comfortable for us.'

Although always a bit of a long-ball outfit, Taylor's Watford were innovative in the way they pressed the opposition. But, after Gray's goal, their pressing dissipated and all that remained were long balls punted hopefully forward. Watford were aimless, a side going through the motions.

'The celebrations amongst the crowd started well before the end,' recalls David France. 'It's hard to put into words what it felt like. To see that side stroll to victory was one of my happiest moments as a Blue. Being an Evertonian had been so frustrating for years, that when the final whistle eventually went, it felt wonderful.'

It fell to Kevin Ratcliffe, a player who at the start of the season had not even worn the armband, to do what had eluded so many Everton captains for so long.

'Lifting that cup was like a dream come true; an absolute honour,' he recalled. 'Although, prior to going up those steps I was worried that I wouldn't be able to lift it! I'd done my shoulder in and it was killing me for most of the second half. I needn't have worried, though. I was so lost in the moment, so full of adrenaline, I could probably have lifted anything!'

For Howard Kendall, who as a player had tasted FA Cup Final defeat with Everton back in 1968, the victory was a sweet one, as he later wrote in *Love Affairs & Marriage: My Life in Football*:

'The first trophy is always the best. It's something no one can take away from you. You've made an indelible mark in the history of Everton Football Club, that you were manager when the FA Cup was lifted. Whatever else happened in my life and my career I was the manager when we won something. Joe Royle would feel the same way too. Nothing would ever feel as good as that first trophy.'

Everton had undergone a transformation that would have seemed barely believable just a few months earlier. Midway through the season, the side had a doomed air about them, as though every minute of football was a struggle. By the end of the campaign, they were joyous, a team playing with freedom and happiness.

'The side that played at Wembley almost bore no comparison to that which had started the season,' says Kevin Ratcliffe. 'But not just in terms of how they played. The personnel had changed a lot too.'

The likes of Andy King, David Johnson and Jim Arnold were no longer first choice. In their place came players such as Southall, Reid and Gray.

'It was taking shape to become the team that would etch itself into the minds of Evertonians for generations to come,' continues Ratcliffe. 'The team that would go on to achieve so much, one of the greatest Everton teams ever to play.'

v Liverpool 1–0

18 August 1984
FA Charity Shield
Wembley Stadium. Attendance: 100,000

Everton: Southall, Stevens, Bailey, Ratcliffe, Mountfield, Reid, Steven, Heath, Sharp, Bracewell, Richardson

Liverpool: Grobbelaar, Neal, Kennedy, Lawrenson, Whelan, Hansen, Dalglish, Lee (Walsh), Rush, Nicol, Wark

Referee: K. Hackett

Brucie Bonus

THE Community Shield is a curious head-to-head. A match that pitches the champions against the FA Cup holders should be a big deal. But, over the years, its appeal has diminished.

Part of this is attributable to the ever-growing allure of European trinkets. Always the less impressive sibling of the League Cup and FA Cup, as their appeal has withered in response to the expanding dominance of the Champions League and Europa League – inevitably the Community Shield has suffered, edging slowly into insignificance.

But it's also the case that as football has become more of a closed shop when it comes to silverware: the clubs that regularly feature in the Community Shield are so conditioned to winning things that they have inevitably begun to regard what's on offer to the victors in the season opener as hardly worth the effort.

Yet, for Everton, back in 1984, the Charity Shield (as it was known in those days) still held a degree of attraction. Not only was it still the era when domestic silverware still really mattered, but, for Everton, silverware of any kind was enough of a novelty to make its acquisition prized.

Added to this, desire was boosted by the identity of the opposition that day. The Blues were up against Liverpool. This alone would have given the match some added spice, as any local rivalry would. For Everton, though, there was also the issue of revenge for the previous season's League Cup defeat to take into consideration.

The fans were up for the occasion, and thousands (of both colours) headed down to Wembley, as Ken Rogers reported in the *Liverpool Echo*:

'A tenth of a million people flocked south to invade the pubs and clubs of London and pack out the giant stadium for the first ever sell out Charity Shield match.

'They came, as we knew they would, united on the long journey south. The scarves and favours of Everton and Liverpool flew side by side through the windows of a convoy of cars on the long trek south.'

And, once they were there, the sense of unity continued. 'Friends in Red and Blue strode side by side up Wembley way, beer cans, wine and whisky bottles in their hands,' continued Rogers. 'Good humour flowed as freely as the alcohol, as pensioners, babes in arms and every age group in between revelled in an atmosphere empty of fear and tension. Inside the ground the fans underwent a token separation to opposite ends of the pitch. But Red and Blue still mingled everywhere, singing their rival songs with partisan pride but not a hint of malice.'

No need for FanZones back then.

Over the course of the summer, both sides had undergone a degree of change, with the most notable alterations coming in the heart of midfield. For Everton, this meant the arrival of Paul Bracewell for £425,000 from Sunderland. This exquisite passer of the ball would go on to become an essential cog in Kendall's exemplary side that season.

For Liverpool, the biggest change was the loss of Graeme Souness, who took a lucrative move to Sampdoria. An unyielding, iron-willed wall of strength and shittiness, Souness had been a key part of Liverpool's success in the early 1980s, and his absence would initially prove a difficult factor to cope with.

'That absence,' says Graham Ennis, 'combined with Everton's growing confidence during the latter half of the previous season, meant that for the first time in a very long time, we went into that game (and that season) feeling confident that the Blue half of the city could possibly, at last, emerge from the Red shadow that had for so long clouded us.'

Before that game, Everton had toured Switzerland (taking part in the International Tournament de la Ville de Genève) and Greece. They had played well throughout pre-season and ended with a 3–0 battering of Olympiacos. It was hoped that the sense of momentum gathered during the excursions could be maintained.

'And from the minute the game kicked off in the sweltering heat of the capital,' remembers John Bailey, 'it looked as though those hopes would prove accurate. We felt good from the start. We had no fear of Liverpool and we also had a lot of confidence in ourselves. What Howard was looking to do at the club was really taking shape. We were playing good football and we had what it took to take on the best.'

Although Everton were vibrant, tough and certainly more than a match for Liverpool, it would be the league champions not the FA Cup holders who would enjoy the first clear-cut chance of the match.

After Reid uncharacteristically lost possession on the edge of the opposition box, Liverpool broke quickly. Following a few neat passes, Lee split the Everton back four with a perfectly weighted through ball to put Dalglish through on goal with just the keeper to beat. Southall advanced on the Scot and did what he could to close the angles as Stevens raced to try to intercept. Despite their efforts, Dalglish was still presented with a gap into which would normally have been a sure bet to clip the ball. But, for once, his poise deserted him, and, to the relief of those Blues in the ground, his effort glanced past the post and went wide.

Everton, roused by the effort, were not long in responding. After three Blue midfielders had harried Rush off the ball, Sharp latched on to a forward pass and clipped a through ball towards Heath, who had spun off his marker and surged into space. With Lawrenson in pursuit and the ball sitting nicely, Heath fancied his chances. From 30 yards out, his cleanly hit half-volley seemed to be heading for the top corner. In its way, though, was the acrobatic Grobbelaar, who leapt to palm the ball over the bar and out for a corner.

'I think before half-time they might have had one more chance', says Kevin Ratcliffe, 'when Nev did well to block another effort by Dalglish. But level by the break seemed fair. Both teams had played well and we'd certainly gone toe-to-toe with our neighbours.'

In the second half, Liverpool appeared to be afflicted by a growing sense of lethargy, as though the searing summer temperatures had depleted their energy levels. Everton, by contrast, seemed unaffected, busily swarming around the pitch as though their lives were dependent upon perpetual motion.

This buzzing intensity nearly paid dividends early on. After selling Dalglish a little dummy, Stevens lifted the ball towards the box, where Richardson nodded it towards Heath in the area. 'Inchy' took it on his chest and then passed it through to Sharp. Under pressure from Lawrenson and with the bounce against him, the Scot managed to get off a shot on the half-volley which Grobbelaar theatrically saved.

'We were creating everything of note and it felt like a goal was on its way,' says John Bailey.

With 15 minutes gone in the half, it arrived, as the Blues took the lead in comic circumstances:

'Graeme Sharp was in the clear,' reported Ken Rogers in the *Echo*, 'but saw his initial shot saved as Grobbelaar came out quickly. The ball broke loose, giving the striker a second bite and this time he saw defender Alan Hansen stick out a boot to clear off the line. The ball struck the luckless Grobbelaar as he tried to recover his ground and rebounded into the net.'

For every Evertonian watching, there was a sense of poetic justice that Hansen, of all people – the player who had got away with a deliberate handball to thwart an Everton goal last time the teams had met at Wembley – would be involved in the cock-up that put the Blues in the lead.

The goal seemed to visibly affect both sides. Everton were buoyed, their vibrancy enhanced. Liverpool, initially bewildered, appeared to further deflate. The lethargy that had crept into their play became more pronounced as the game progressed.

The songs of the Evertonians grew louder by the minute. In response, Liverpool and their fans seemed to have nothing to offer.

Although the Charity Shield might not have enjoyed the prestige of the league title, the FA Cup or the League Cup, when the final whistle went you could not have known that, if judged by the reaction of the Evertonians within Wembley.

'The atmosphere was fantastic,' recalls John Bailey. 'It was a great day for everyone that went down there, Red and Blue, but at the end all you could hear was our fans and you could tell how much it meant to them. It was the perfect start to the season, taking on the best in the league and controlling the game. Plus we'd got our own back too!'

During the mid-1980s, Everton reigned as the kings of the Charity Shield. The season opener featured the Blues four times on the trot and not once did the club endure defeat. Unquestionably, as time passed and the Goodison trophy cabinet was opened with more regularity, the value the fans placed on that particular piece of silverware diminished incrementally, an inevitable consequence of Everton's broadening horizons.

But the joy of that first win, the vanquishing of the 'mighty' Liverpool, the sense of a club that could be more than a one-season wonder, remained a cherished memory.

And also one that would have historical relevance. Everton have never beaten Liverpool at Wembley since, despite a few attempts. That sweltering August day has therefore become an important one for Blues. The goal might have been comical, the desire less pronounced and the trophy of marginal consequence, but Everton won. And that's what mattered. Proof that if it can be done once, then one day it can be done again.

v Liverpool 1–0

20 October 1984
Football League Division One
Anfield. Attendance: 45,545

Everton: Southall, Stevens, Van Den Hauwe, Ratcliffe, Mountfield, Reid, Steven, Heath, Sharp Bracewell, Harper

Liverpool: Grobbelaar, Neal, Kennedy, Lawrenson, Whelan, Hansen, Dalglish, Robinson, Rush, Wark, Molby

Referee: N. Midgley

Sharpy Silences the Kop

THE Anfield derby; do any other three words strike as much dread into an Evertonian's heart as those (except perhaps 'Koné's starting today')?

Back in 1984, when Everton travelled to Anfield in the early autumn, it had been 14 years since the Blues had last won there. On that occasion, it had been a 2–0 victory, the goals coming courtesy of Royle and Whittle.

Such a lengthy run without a win is obviously nothing new to modern Evertonians. At the time of writing, it's been 18 years since Everton last tasted victory across the Park. Back then, like today, the record seemed to warrant constant mention whenever the two sides met.

'We were all too aware of our record at Anfield before that game,' says Kevin Ratcliffe. 'The media were always bringing it up whenever a derby came around.'

'You try not to worry, and tell yourself that it's just another match, but in the back of your mind, when it's so constant it can have an effect.'

Because Liverpool were so successful in the 1970s and 1980s, it easy to assume that when the sides met that day, Everton would be facing the self-proclaimed 'Red Machine', the supposedly all-conquering juggernaut that Liverpudlians and those in the media so often eulogise.

But, in fact, Everton's opponents that day were well off form. A tricky start to the season had left the Reds struggling in the league. Prior to that October match, Liverpool had not won in six games and sat in the bottom eight, thoughts of title success being obscured by tongue-in-cheek local references to relegation.

By contrast, Everton were starting to find form. After a disappointing opening few games, when the FA Cup holders appeared half asleep, resulting in defeats against Spurs and West Brom, the Blues had started to pick up points and by mid-October sat sixth in the table.

Such a disparity in league position in favour of Everton before a derby had not been so great in years. The last time had been September 1964, when Everton had come to Anfield and won 4–0.

'This being Liverpool, though, form didn't really come into it for Evertonians,' says Dave Prentice. 'They always seemed to have a hold over us, a way of making us Blues think we were unlikely to beat them at their place. It was a bit like it is nowadays.'

Aside from the voodoo-esque hold that Anfield had over Everton, in typical Liverpool fashion, this would be supported by the return of Ian Rush from injury, a player who was already starting to be become a figure of fear and loathing amongst Evertonians.

Not only had his deadliness helped Liverpool in their continued quest for silverware, but Rush had also found the Merseyside derby to be fertile hunting ground for his goalscoring exploits. And it was his birthday too, just to make matters worse (he was 23, although looked to be in his mid-40s). It was just Everton's luck that Rush would choose this game to make his return.

But, despite the media attention, the history they had and the fact that you could never write Liverpool off in a derby – according to Kevin Ratcliffe, the visitors were quietly confident.

'Howard had tried a few things when we played Liverpool in the league. He'd played five in midfield, varied roles, shifted the personnel, things like that. Mostly it hadn't really worked. But he always told us that we were getting closer, and that we'd beat them in the league before too long. Despite our poor record at Anfield, we fancied our chances that day. We'd performed well in the League Cup and beaten them in the Charity Shield. We were less fearful of them than we had once been.'

Just over 45,000 crammed into Anfield that day, a sell-out. In contrast to modern derbies, there were Evertonians everywhere – even in the Kop, where hundreds had colonised their own corner.

'We were all in a little spec over by the Main Stand end,' says Phil Redmond. 'I got there a bit late and had to walk right across the length of the Kop. I was wearing my bobble hat when some arl-feller smacked it off my head (bear in mind I was only a young lad). Those lovable Kopites!'

The assembled Blues were huddled together against the swirling winds that were battering the ground. The conditions, as you'd expect in mid-October in the north-west, were difficult. To add to the winds, the pitch had been subjected to a deluge of rain prior to kick-off. The pass-and-move game of both sides would be trickier to implement than normal.

Along with the returning Rush, Liverpool also had Dalglish back in their ranks (after he had been dropped the week before). Everton, by contrast, were unchanged. The starting line-up that would come to be so recognisable to a generation of Evertonians was now becoming near ever-present.

'In contrast to the season before,' feels Graham Ennis, 'we had a relatively settled side from the start of the campaign, one that stayed that way pretty much to the end. You got the feeling as the season progressed that this was the team that Kendall had been searching for since he first arrived. It had taken him a while, and he'd gone through a few players, but finally he looked to be getting somewhere.'

It was evident almost from kick-off that this would be no ordinary Anfield derby. 'We just looked so much better than Liverpool that it was hard to believe that we wouldn't get something from the game,' remembers Phil Redmond.

Everton dominated the first half, carving out a succession of near-chances without ever finding one that could be easily put away (even with the assistance of the typically error-prone Grobbelaar, who appeared more fearful of crosses than Nosferatu).

The midfield trio of Heath, Reid and Bracewell were particularly impressive, utterly dominating their Liverpool counterparts. But throughout, the entire Everton side shone, paying no heed to recent history.

This being Liverpool, though, danger always lurked. Against the run of play, the two best opportunities of the half fell to the home side, and Rush. Although one was a tricky half-chance, when an awkward bounce gave Alan Harper enough time to intervene to prevent Rush from taking his shot, the other was the kind of opportunity that the Welshman usually lapped up.

As half-time approached, he played a perfect one-two with Dalglish and found himself one-on-one with the keeper. For once, his eye for goal let him down. Faced with the onrushing Southall, he hit a relatively tame shot towards the left-hand corner, which his Welsh compatriot was able to smother.

Despite their chances, after a rather lacklustre first half performance, you would imagine that Joe Fagan would have read his side the riot act during the break, and have them come out renewed and invigorated. But, if anything, Liverpool deteriorated.

Although it probably didn't help their cause when Everton took the lead three minutes into the half in a spectacular fashion.

'There was a perfect long ball played over the top by Gary Stevens,' recalls Graeme Sharp. 'My first touch was good, and I was aware that Mark Lawrenson was chasing, and in a race there was only going to be one winner and it wasn't me. So, with the ball bouncing nicely in front of me, I just thought, why not have a go? Fortunately for me, and the side, it flew in.'

A little corner of the Kop exploded in response. 'What a goal to witness,' says Phil Redmond, 'and what a way to go ahead in such a game. Our corner was rocking. It's the kind of goal you never forget. The moment it burst into the back of the net is seared into my memory.'

As much as the goal was attributable to Sharp's sublime technique, there was also a hint of Kendall's managerial acumen behind it too, as the goalscorer recalls:

'Liverpool used Adidas Tango balls in their games. So the week before, Howard had training with them. I think that little bit of practice gave me a feel for them and helped with the goal.'

There was a time when a 1–0 lead would be a dangerous thing for the Blues. The temptation would be to sit back and defend, inviting Liverpool on to the attack. But Everton were changing under Kendall, playing without fear. Over the remainder of the half, the away side played at the same tempo and with the same confidence as they had in the first.

Reid came close at one point, putting the ball narrowly wide after latching on to an error by Phil Neal. Then later, a defence-splitting ball by Bracewell put Harper through. The Everton utility man had time to put a low cross into the Liverpool box, which Heath, under pressure from Neal, wasn't able to properly connect with.

'Liverpool offered very little,' recalls Phil Redmond, 'and when the game ended they should've been grateful that the scoreline wasn't bigger. We could have easily won that 3–0. But any margin was fine with us. I remember feeling so happy when the final whistle went, joining in with taunts of "Going down, going down, going down".'

The sight of a handful of Blues dancing on the pitch, celebrating with their conquering heroes as they made their way to the tunnel, summed up what every Evertonian felt. As they jigged and danced joyfully, to the chants of 'Easy, easy, easy', there was a sense that something magical had happened, something momentous, a watershed moment that might finally suggest that the balance of power could be shifting on Merseyside.

v Manchester United 5–0

27 October 1984
Football League Division One
Goodison Park. Attendance: 40,769

Everton: Southall, Stevens, Van Den Hauwe, Ratcliffe, Mountfield, Reid, Steven, Heath, Sharp, Bracewell, Sheedy (Gray)

Manchester United: Bailey, McQueen, Albiston, Moses, Moran (Stapleton), Hogg, Robson, Strachan, Hughes, Brazil, Olsen

Referee: G. Tyson

Blues Fire off Title Warning

YOU wait years for some classic games and then what do Everton do? They only knock out two on the bounce! When Everton took on Manchester United at home towards the end of October 1984, few in the ground could have expected that they were about to witness a level of performance that is as close to perfect as you could ever hope for.

On the back of that morale-boosting win at Anfield, Everton had played a Cup Winners' Cup tie a few days later away against Inter Bratislava, in the old Czechoslovakia. The days of shifting fixtures to accommodate tired players were still some way off. Everton were expected to face title favourites Liverpool, deal with their Slovak opponents away from home and then head back to Goodison to face off against another title favourite, Manchester United, all in the space of seven days.

Although not the all-conquering, trophy-gobbling behemoth that would later emerge under Alex Ferguson, United were still a difficult side to play against. With Ron Atkinson at the helm (a manager who back then could be termed 'colourful' without it sounding ironic), they had finished in the top four in each of the past three seasons. And, with the likes of Gordon Strachan, Bryan Robson and Mark Hughes in the side, they were – along with Liverpool, Spurs and Arsenal – considered serious contenders for the title by bookies and pundits alike.

By contrast, despite having won the FA Cup and bested the champions in the Charity Shield, Everton were not thought to be capable of mounting a serious title challenge.

'I don't think we were fancied that much by anyone,' argues Dave Prentice. 'You sort of could understand why from one perspective – after all, Everton had been underperforming as a club for several years. But there was a sense of change about the place. For most of 1984, the side had been great, reaching two finals, winning one and beating Liverpool in the Charity Shield. I think people outside were slow to pick up on something the fans had known for a while, that under Kendall it felt like Everton were, finally, going places.'

This particular head-to-head pitted third against fourth in the league, and the form of both sides was good. Everton were coming into the game on the back of that encouraging victory against Liverpool; United had just dispatched Spurs. A tightly fought contest was predicted.

But that wasn't what transpired. Instead, as Howard Kendall later wrote in *Love Affairs & Marriage*, 'What followed that afternoon wasn't so much a win, but a rout.'

Everton started the game strongly and after a few minutes should have been 1–0 up when Mountfield shot over the bar after Sheedy had lofted a perfect free kick into the box.

'That was the season when I couldn't stop scoring,' remembers Mountfield, 'but even I missed the occasional chance!'

Not that it mattered. Just a few minutes later, Everton were ahead when Sheedy channelled his inner Andy Gray.

'I remember Gary Stevens put a cross into the box, just around the edge,' he recalled. 'If it had been a few inches lower I would have contemplated volleying it. But it was a bit high. Anyone who followed my career, knows that I'm not exactly a prolific header of the ball but the height was right so I gave it a go. The next thing I remember is being on the floor and the ball had flown into the back of the net. I later learned that Kevin Moran, who had jumped with me, had butted the back of my head, his way of putting me off as he couldn't reach the ball. In the end, it was the force of that which had made the header unstoppable. It still remains one of my favourite goals to this day.'

It was a tenacious leap by the Irishman, one that left him with a gash on his forehead so bad that he would eventually have to leave the field and be substituted. But not before he had put Everton 2–0 ahead.

'In the 23rd minute Everton went further in front … United lost possession in midfield and Bracewell transferred the ball rapidly to Heath on the left,' wrote Ian Hargreaves in the *Liverpool Echo*.

'Inchy' then dashed forward to the edge of the penalty area before he spied Sheedy's forward run. 'He put the perfect pass into my path. I ran on to it and smacked the ball into the opposite corner,' says the Irishman.

Just 12 minutes later, Heath then scored his eighth goal of the season when he was the first to react to a Trevor Steven cross amidst a bunch of United defenders and belted the ball past a hapless Bailey to put Everton 3–0 up and the game out of sight.

'We were 30-odd minutes in and controlling the game,' remembers Kevin Ratcliffe. 'Teams can come back from being 3–0 down, but nothing United had offered suggested they would. I can't remember them even having a chance. We were completely dominant and playing great football. It could have been five by that point!'

Shouts of 'Ole!' accompanied every Everton pass as the fans prepared themselves for a massacre. United were as poor as Everton were good, and any sense of these two teams being near peers (with United the senior partner) appeared to be wholly misguided.

'It was a perfect first half performance,' says Rob Sawyer. 'We had rolled them over. It was as simple as that. When you look back on Everton's history and think of all the outstanding performances that have taken place, those 45 minutes stick out. They were outstanding.'

For a side with title pretentions, United's response after the break was surprising. There was no attempt to use their abundant talents to match Everton, and instead there was merely an apparent acceptance that the game was done. It became an exercise in face saving.

'United were lucky that Everton took their foot off the gas slightly as the game went on,' thinks Graham Ennis. 'Inevitably, being so dominant, so in control and in turn facing nothing from United, the impetus that had been so evident in the first half dissipated a bit. Although, even playing at less than full throttle, chances still came.'

Heath had a header cleared off the line by Arthur Albiston as Everton continued to pour forward, the Gwladys Street eagerly expecting more goals to come. And they did, despite Everton only operating at 80 per cent. With ten minutes to go, Stevens picked up the ball from around 30 yards out, shimmied past an onrushing United defender and then struck a low, hard drive into the bottom-left corner.

'That was one of the great things about Kendall's side that season,' says Simon Hart, 'the goals were shared around. As good as the forward line was, the side was not reliant on them. Goals would pop up from all sorts of places. I think that was attributable to the quality of attacking football that the side played and the sense of confidence that coursed through the team.'

Four–nil was a scoreline that befitted such an imperious performance, although also one that slightly flattered Manchester United. Five–nil would have been better.

And, as full time inched nearer, 'the ball came in from the left and I managed to get a flick on it and steer it into the bottom-right corner,' remembers Graeme Sharp, whose goal represented his eighth in nine games. It was just reward for Sharp, who all afternoon had troubled the United defence, unselfishly put his team-mates into great positions and exemplified the quality and passion evident in Everton's performance.

'When Sharp had first come to the club from Dumbarton, he'd only per-formed well in snatches,' recalls Phil Redmond. 'Although he clearly had potential, his true quality had only made itself consistently apparent toward the latter half of the 83/84 season. He seemed to be growing in confidence and was perhaps surer of what he could contribute in a Blue shirt. Whatever the reason, it was evident by that point in the season that Everton had a centre-forward in Sharp who could make most defenders endure a miserable afternoon.'

When the 90 minutes were up, Evertonians could feel privileged at having been there when one of the truly great performances had taken place – one that the legendary Joe Mercer, who was sitting in the directors' box, described as the 'most complete' he had ever seen by the club.

It was also one, when taken into consideration with the vanquishing of Liverpool the week before, made the world outside Goodison sit up and take notice.

'It was around that time that people began to take Everton seriously,' remembers Graham Ennis. 'The idea of us winning the title began to be talked about in places other than Goodison. We had beaten Liverpool at their place and then murdered United. And that's what that latter performance was. We destroyed them. It was starting to become clear how good this side could be.'

For those who had played in the game, the result and the style of the victory had a profound impact, as Kevin Sheedy recalls:

'In the dressing room afterwards we felt that something momentous had happened. Personally, that was the moment I thought we had something special here, that the side was capable of going all the way. We had beaten our title rivals convincingly, and that gave us an enormous sense of self-belief. Confidence is so important in football, and that game proves it. The win gave us the belief that we could push on. I can honestly say it was one of the best performances I played in. But more than that, it was also probably the catalyst for what followed.'

v Bayern Munich 3–1

24 April 1985
European Cup Winners' Cup Semi-final, Second Leg
Goodison Park. Attendance: 49,476

Everton: Southall, Stevens, Van Den Hauwe, Ratcliffe, Mountfield, Reid, Steven, Gray, Sharp, Bracewell, Sheedy

Bayern Munich: Pfaff, Dremmler, Willmer (Beierlorzer), Eder (Rummenigge), Augenthaler, Lerby, Pflügler, Matthäus, Hoeneß, Kögl, Nachtweih

Referee: E. Fredricksson

Goodison's Greatest Night

PRIOR to the 1984/85 campaign, Everton's record in Europe had been patchy to say the least. In contrast to other big clubs, such as Manchester United, Spurs and Liverpool, all of whom had prospered on the European stage, success for Everton had never been remotely close.

'And that stung a little,' admits Simon Hart, 'specifically when set against Liverpool's record. There was a sense that to match them we not only had to succeed domestically but we also had to thrive in Europe too, just as they had been doing.'

As victors in the 1984 FA Cup, the club had been England's entry into the following season's European Cup Winners' Cup.

After an early scare against University College Dublin, when Everton had made a meal of getting past the Irish part-timers, progression to the semi-finals had been relatively formulaic, following straightforward victories against Inter Bratislava and Fortuna Sittard.

Between the Blues and the final now stood Bayern Munich: European football royalty at its finest.

Marshalled by Lothar Matthäus, and with a side packed with international quality, such as Belgian goalkeeper Jean-Marie Pfaff, the abundantly gifted Danish midfielder *Søren Lerby* and the talented German forward Dieter Hoeneß, the Bavarian giants were widely regarded as the strongest side in the competition and, as a testament to their strength, would go on to win the Bundesliga that season.

The first leg, played in the Olympiastadion München, was a tough game for the Blues. 'We went out there a bit of a patched-up side,' remembers Graeme Sharp, 'missing both Andy Gray and Kevin Sheedy, both of whom failed late fitness tests. I think I played alone up front as Howard really just tried to contain Bayern. The final score of 0–0 was regarded as a success.'

In between the first leg and the second, Everton were kept busy. Not only was a second consecutive FA Cup Final appearance booked (following a 2–1 win over Luton Town in the semis), but in the league the club also maintained that season's impressive run of form; and, as the Cup Winners' Cup showdown approached, Everton topped the division, ten points clear of nearest rivals Manchester United.

'We were on great form,' says Andy Gray, 'playing well and on course to win the title. But that didn't mean we were necessarily fancied in Europe. Nobody gave us a prayer and it was understandable why. This was the mighty Bayern Munich playing against a bunch of kids and a few old pros like me and Reidy. We were a bit of an unknown quantity I suppose, and so the question for those watching was probably whether we would rise to the occasion or buckle in the face of a more experienced opponent?'

On a balmy night in April, the moment of truth arrived. With Gray and Sheedy fit again, Kendall was able to put out his strongest side. He was also able to count on the rapturous support of the crowd, nearly 50,000 of whom were wedged inside Goodison.

'The atmosphere that night was incredible,' remembers Graham Ennis. 'Think of any other great Goodison occasion and then times it by ten. The place was heaving and the noise was breathtaking. You could hear the shouts in Bootle! You have to remember that there were only about 50 Bayern supporters there. We had 50,000 Blues, under the lights and completely behind the side. The crowd was like an animal, some threatening beast that was determined to get Everton through.'

In the first half, Everton were unquestionably the better side. But, despite their evident dominance, clear-cut chances were limited. Sheedy came close with a free kick, Sharp with a header, and there was also a decent penalty shout when the ball appeared to strike the arm of Dremmler in the box.

'I don't think Bayern knew what hit them,' says Andy Gray. 'Compared to other performances that season, we weren't playing with the same degree of fluidity. Instead, physicality seemed to have been given more emphasis. That was the game plan and it worked. Bayern looked rattled.'

The Germans, both during and after the match, were not happy with Everton's physical approach. At one point, Bayern's manager, Udo Lattek, protested to the Everton bench, shouting, 'Kendall, this is not football.' The response from the bench, according to Kendall in *Love Affairs & Marriages*, was a loud and unanimous 'F**k Off!'

In a later interview, Kendall outlined that this approach had been deliberate. 'We decided before the game to bomb them. I felt the best way to approach the tie was to put them under immediate pressure. The Germans were never able to settle, with the strikers challenging for everything. With the tackles flying in, Bayern were never going to be able to clear decisively around the box and the key factor was picking up the second ball.'

And yet, despite Everton's physically domineering approach, it would be the Bavarians who would take the lead. Against the run of play, Kögl played a neat one-two that caught Everton's high defensive line off guard. He charged through on goal and attempted to go around the onrushing Southall, but found his run checked by the keeper. Unfortunately for Everton, the ball bounced off Southall's chest to Hoeneß, who took his time and calmly put the ball past the two defenders who had got back to cover the line. The scoring of a vital away goal now meant that Everton would have to score twice (and concede no further) to progress.

'The moment that ball went in it was like someone had deflated a balloon,' recalls Andy Gray. 'Just for a second, all the life was sucked out of Goodison. But, to the credit of the fans, it didn't last long. Within moments, they were up again, willing us on to get an equaliser.'

Despite continued dominance, Everton went in at the break one behind. Kendall revealed his half-time thinking, with 45 minutes to save their European dreams, in *Only the Best Is Good Enough*:

'The tension in our dressing room at half-time was so palpable that you felt you could reach out and grasp it. I told my players not to worry but to carry on playing as they had been. One of the important things was that we would be attacking the Gwladys Street terracing in the second half, a section which is made up of supporters so fanatical that, at times, they seem to be almost capable of sucking the ball into the net.'

Within minutes of the start, figuratively, that's just what happened. Stevens launched a long throw into the box, which Gray was able to flick on into the six-yard box.

'I got in front of my marker,' recalls Graeme Sharp, 'and was able to get the deftest of touches on the ball, just enough for it to bobble into the bottom corner. I remember the noise from the crowd after that. It was like nothing I had experienced before.'

The atmosphere, which had been electric all night, appeared to become even more charged. According to Andy Gray, when added to Everton's physical approach, it tipped the balance in their favour.

'I'd not heard a noise like that crowd. And you could see that Bayern were suffering. It was intense. And they were also finding our physicality harder and harder to cope with. When you saw their players lying down on the pitch whingeing about a particularly tenacious tackle, then psychologically you knew we'd got the better of them. And that was a hugely important part of the battle.'

For the next 20 minutes, the Blues hustled and bustled, creating a few decent chances and barely letting the Bavarians get their foot on the ball. Even though at 1–1 Bayern were still in the stronger position, it only ever felt like one team would emerge victorious and that it was a case of when rather than if another Everton goal would come. When it did, with 15 minutes left, it came courtesy of Andy Gray:

'Another huge throw-in from Gary Stevens came into the box,' Gray recalls, 'where the Bayern keeper and a few defenders managed to miss the ball, which then fell perfectly for me to sweep it into the box. I remember the noise from the Gwladys Street almost hitting me when the ball crossed the line.'

For those watching on, the feeling was near indescribable. 'It's hard to put into words what it felt like,' says Graham Ennis. 'I think we all knew that Bayern were the best we would face and that this Everton side could beat what was left in the competition. So, not only had we come from behind against a giant of the game, we thought we were on our way to a final that we could win.'

And it was about to get better. 'With a few minutes left I found myself with the ball in the left-back position,' remembers Kevin Sheedy. 'I looked up and was waiting for Andy Gray to make a run, all the while having 50,000 Blues screaming "man-on". When he did, I pinged the ball through.'

Gray took the ball in his stride, controlled it and then threaded it past Nachtweih to Trevor Steven, who had surged forward in support. With the keeper and Nachtweih closing in on him, Steven took the ball a few paces and chipped an elegant finish into the back of the net – spinning off, right arm held aloft as the entire stadium ignited.

'It might have been the valium coursing through my body (given to me by a nurse in work to cope with the nerves),' says Phil Redmond, 'but what a night that was. Anyone who was there could never forget it. It was magical. A one-off! The greatest game to ever take place at Goodison and an atmosphere unmatched.'

Everton won that night because they wanted it more and were prepared to put aside the football that had worked so well in the league and adopt a more primitive, but no less effective, approach to the game. It proved what a shrewd tactician Kendall could be, and, more importantly, it had booked the Blues a place in the club's first-ever European final.

v QPR 2–0

6 May 1985
Football League Division One
Goodison Park. Attendance: 50,514

Everton: Southall, Stevens, Van Den Hauwe, Ratcliffe, Mountfield, Reid, Steven, Sharp, Gray, Bracewell, Sheedy

QPR: Hucker, Chivers, Dawes, Waddock, Wicks, Fenwick, Robinson, Fillery, Bannister, James, Gregory (McDonald)

Referee: J. Hough

Champions at Last!

I T was the season that the fans had been waiting for. After beating Leicester at home in early November, the Blues topped the table and never looked like letting go. As a parade of pretenders attempted to hang on to Everton's coat-tails, Kendall's men powered through the remaining games, dominating almost all who came before them.

'There was a sense of invincibility about that side,' recalls Kevin Ratcliffe. 'We never went out on the pitch thinking it was possible that we could lose.'

Kendall had created something magical, a side in perfect balance. In every position, Everton seemed to possess the man you would want in that role.

Southall – alert, impregnable and domineering – underpinned it all, the base upon which it was built. In front of him, the defence of Ratcliffe, Mountfield, Stevens and Van Den Hauwe was fast, strong and resolute. Within the centre of midfield, Reid's combative nature blended perfectly with Bracewell's exquisite passing. Out wide, Sheedy and Steven provided limitless ammunition for the front line and chipped in with important goals too. And up top, Sharp and Gray worked together to produce one of the most effective and difficult-to-play-against strike partnerships Goodison has ever seen.

And that was just the starting eleven. There were others, like Heath, Richardson and Harper, who contributed too, particularly 'Inchy' who scored 11 goals before suffering a serious knee injury in December.

But, more than just being perfectly balanced, this was clearly a side that worked for each other, as Graeme Sharp recalls:

'We got on with each other on and off the pitch. And that was important. There was a great camaraderie in the dressing room. So you had a group of players, (including those who didn't always feature in the starting eleven) who wanted to fight for each other and fight for the shirt. And when you have that, combined with quality, then you are always in with a chance.'

This sense of camaraderie, and the club's canny acquisition of cut-price gems such as Reid, Southall and Sheedy, dovetailed perfectly with what Derek Mountfield regards as the ideal coaching environment:

'Colin Harvey was a great coach, Kendall a fantastic man manager, and Mick Heaton kept us all laughing. It made going in fun and training something to look forward to. We worked hard, but we also had a laugh, and we improved as players and as a side too.'

After a breathtaking run of form from Boxing Day onwards, which saw Everton take 41 points from a possible 45, the title was within touching distance by early May. It was a run that was packed with performances that often exhausted superlatives.

Along the way, there were drubbings of Stoke City, Nottingham Forest and Newcastle United. There were games of near-perfect football, such as the 4–1 victory against Sunderland (that those who witnessed never forgot). And then there were hard matches against rivals, when Everton proved their mettle, grinding out the kind of tough wins that all champions must do now and then.

If one game within this run could be said to have made the idea of being champions concrete, it was a narrow 2–1 victory in April against rivals Spurs. In a tight match, where Everton were limited to a handful of chances, the Blues made their opportunities count and at the other end were thankful for yet another stellar performance from Southall in goal.

'After that game, I thought the title was ours,' admits Andy Gray. 'They are the kind of games you need to win to become champions.'

With six games left to go, Everton were riding high in the league. The only team that could still numerically catch them was Liverpool, who sat in fourth position (but with games in hand). But a win against QPR at home would put the matter mathematically to rest and bring the title home to Goodison for the first time since 1970.

'To win the league was one thing,' says Dave Kelly. 'That was a dream come true. But to take it off Liverpool – well, that was as good as it could get. It's like someone had written down your dream season and made it real.'

Unsurprisingly, on that fateful Saturday afternoon, demand to get into the game was high.

'I remember sitting at home watching *Footie Focus*,' recalls Dave Prentice, 'when I heard John Motson say, "And the gates are already locked at Goodison Park, where 50,000 fans are waiting to see Everton crowned champions." I never usually left ours until *Footie Focus* had finished. So, I got going sharpish, jumped train to Bank Hall with my mate, got to Goodison and sure enough, sold out.'

But this was a game not to be missed. 'I heard that Blues were getting into the away section by pretending they were from London. So I joined the queue, where the bizzies were taking names and addresses, and in the dodgiest cockney accent, I gave a false address and got in. But my mate didn't! Incredibly, his must have been worse. Once in, I told the bizzies I was in the wrong area and happily got put in the Everton section. I had to be there.'

The atmosphere in the ground was a carnival one. The whole place was filled with joy, a complete absence of the undercurrent of unease that often exists on matchdays at Goodison. Evertonians had waited a long time for this, and it was clear that they were determined to enjoy it. Even the rain that had been pouring down disappeared as the players emerged from the dressing room, with Goodison a cauldron of excitement and expectation.

'What a moment that was,' recalls Pat Van Den Hauwe. 'All that noise, all those fans, unforgettable.'

If anyone had expected QPR to roll over, they were sorely mistaken. The 'Hoops' (13th in the table) were not mathematically safe and were therefore in no mood to meekly surrender in front of the hugely partisan crowd. Under the guidance of their caretaker manager, Frank Sibley, QPR were determined to give Everton a game.

The Blues were unusually tentative in the early stages. 'Although it didn't help that QPR were so up for it,' admits Derek Mountfield, 'we weren't at our best either. It was a strange game, a lot of pressure, so perhaps that was inevitable.'

All season, Mountfield had not just provided Everton with strength at the back, he had also proven to be more than adept in front of goal, reaching double figures before the season's end.

'I think we all began to believe that scoring was just part of the job. The likes of Sharpy and Andy Gray might have led the line, but quite a few of us chipped in with goals during the campaign. It probably has something to do with the team ethic that characterised the side.'

After 25 minutes, Everton's moustachioed centre-half would strike again and, in doing so, ease some of those early jitters. A corner from the right was whipped into the box, and the ball was partially cleared before being headed to the far post by Gray. There, Van Den Hauwe managed to head it back across the six-yard box, where Mountfield met its flight with an impeccable volley that thundered off the underside of the crossbar, bounced out, hit the keeper and rebounded in.

'That was a special moment for me,' he recalls. 'In a season when there were so many, it definitely sticks out.'

Were it not for Peter Hucker in the QPR goal having one of those days, Everton would have sewn the game up before half-time. Acrobatic saves from Sheedy and Sharp meant that the Blues would have to wait until the second half before putting the match out of QPR's reach. And they left it late.

'With around ten minutes left,' remembers Graeme Sharp, 'a looping cross came in and I managed to meet it and direct it over the keeper into the top corner. That was the moment it was all over.' It was his 21st of the season.

Not long after, at 4.40pm, the referee blew his whistle and Everton were champions. In the *Liverpool Echo*, John Moores, a man who had done so much to restore Everton to the pinnacle of the game and who had seen so many false dawns at the club said:

'I never thought that I'd live to see another league championship come to Goodison. It's great to feel free of the domination of Liverpool.'

The sight of a delirious fan tying a scarf around Sir John's neck summed up the heady atmosphere shared by everyone present.

'I think any Evertonian who was around at that time will look back at that moment as something very special,' says Dave Kelly. 'After the 1970s, which had been so frustrating and dark for us, it felt like the sun had come out again. And it wasn't just like we'd narrowly won the league, we had stormed it.'

The transformation in Everton's fortunes had been complete. By the end of that season, a team of relative unknowns, one that nobody had tipped for the top, was one that had won the league at a canter and which boasted an array of internationals.

When Kendall had bought Gray in November 1983, only he, Ratcliffe and Southall had played for their country. By the campaign's end, almost every player in that side was a recognisable international, chosen by virtue of what they had done in a Blue shirt.

'The 84/85 side is probably the greatest Everton side to ever take to the pitch,' argues Graham Ennis. 'They were magnificent: a rare example of a group of stars who still played and fought like a team. And they were so wonderful to watch too: the kind of side that would live on in people's memories forever.'

v Rapid Vienna 3–1

36

15 May 1985
European Cup Winners' Cup Final
Stadion Feijenoord, Rotterdam. Attendance: 40,000

Everton: Southall, Stevens, Van Den Hauwe, Ratcliffe, Mountfield, Reid, Steven, Sharp, Gray, Bracewell, Sheedy

Rapid Vienna: Konsel, Kienast, Weber, Garger, Lainer, Hristic, Kranjᵡar, Weinhofer (Panenka), Brauneder, Pacult (Gröss), Krankl

Referee: P. Casarin

European Glory

FINALLY, Evertonians had what they had longed for: the chance to stake a claim on the European stage. The vanquishing of Bayern had booked the Blues a place in the Cup Winners' Cup Final in Rotterdam.

There they would meet the Austrian giants Rapid Vienna (who had won the previous season's ÖFB-Cup). Rapid had enjoyed a slightly easier semi-final against Dynamo Moscow, who they had beaten 4–2 on aggregate.

Although certainly no 'Bayern', any club that could make the final needed to be examined, and Kendall did just that:

'I went out to run the rule over them at the earliest opportunity,' he later wrote in *Only the Best Is Good Enough*. 'What I saw that night delighted me. They were nowhere near as good as Bayern and I knew we could beat them quite handsomely.'

Some of the players had come to the same conclusion after they too had watched Rapid play.

The Austrians' second round, second leg game against Celtic had been replayed after Rapid's defender Rudi Weinhofer had fallen to the ground and claimed to have been hit by a bottle thrown from the stands (later proven to be untrue). The replay took place at Old Trafford, which the Viennese team won 1–0 (going through 4–1 on aggregate).

'A few of us, Reidy, Inchy and Sharpy and I, went to watch the game in Manchester,' remembers Andy Gray. 'We all agreed that there had been nothing in that performance to give us any reason to fear them. We knew we were the better side.'

With the championship wrapped up against QPR earlier in the month, Everton had the luxury of heading out to the final in Rotterdam free from the prospect of a title run-in.

'Although we had the FA Cup Final a few days later,' says Kevin Ratcliffe, 'at least the league, the winning of which is always a gruelling slog, was out of our minds. We could concentrate on beating Rapid, which if I'm honest, we all thought we would. It wasn't just that they seemed weaker, we also felt invulnerable. We could have been playing anyone and that confidence would still have been there.'

The game itself would be taking place in the Stadion Feijenoord in Rotterdam, a ground that was two-thirds the size of the St. Jakob Stadium in Basel, which had hosted the previous season's final between Juventus and Porto.

This meant that only a fraction of those Blues who wanted to go were able to get tickets. For those that did, the build-up was memorable:

'It was a great experience,' recalls Phil Redmond. 'To be honest, it was more like a party. I'd gone over to Munich for the semi and that was tenser. I don't think anyone could see us losing against Rapid, considering just how good we were. So there was a happy atmosphere. None of the anxiety you usually get with the Blues. I think we'd used all that up against Bayern.'

For the players, the sight of the thousands who had travelled to lend their support was a welcome one, as Kevin Ratcliffe remembers:

'It felt as though the entire place was filled with Evertonians. That's how loud and present they were. They seemed to completely outnumber the Rapid fans. With that and the size of the place it was almost like we were playing at home. You look up at that when you come on to the pitch and just think how amazing it is. That level of support was worth a goal start.'

From the first kick, Kendall's predictions that Everton would be too much for the Austrians to handle proved prescient. As the *Liverpool Echo* reported:

'They [Vienna] appeared to be totally overawed by the prospect of meeting the English champions. Unsure at the back and reluctant to venture out of their own half they simply sat back attempting to weather a ferocious onslaught which was near ceaseless.'

Everton were dominant, specifically in the centre of the park, with Reid and Bracewell afforded so much time and space it must have felt like a training match.

'Sometimes when you think you're in for an easy game, it doesn't turn out like that,' recalls Pat Van Den Hauwe. 'Maybe complacency kicks in and you underperform, or perhaps the opposition are fired up and perform better than you imagined they could. But on that occasion, it was as straightforward as we hoped it would be.'

Southall, for all intents and purpose, was a mere spectator, and was not called on to make a save of any description until the half-hour mark (and that was from a wayward back-pass).

A goal for the Blues was on the cards from the off, and eventually, with five minutes to go until half-time, one appeared to arrive after Mountfield rose to meet Sheedy's 'training ground' free kick and head the ball to Gray, who managed to get a foot on it to steer the ball home.

'I remember getting up to celebrate and being stunned that it wasn't allowed,' says Gray. 'The linesman had flagged for offside on Degsy. It was a mistake, though. 'The goal should've stood. We should have gone in at the break one ahead.'

But it wasn't to be, and so, improbably, as half-time arrived, the scores were level.

'Exactly how these two poles apart sides found themselves walking from the field on level terms at half-time will remain a mystery for some time,' reported the *Echo*, continuing: 'Everton, who have adapted their bustling domestic style to suit the European game with admirable ease, had an embarrassingly high percentage of possession.'

Unsurprisingly, Rapid came out with a bit more venom after the break, and early on Everton found themselves defending for the first time that evening. The game could have been very different had Krankl's shot from the right, which took a wicked deflection off Pat Van Den Hauwe, crept under the crossbar rather than bouncing off it.

But the effect of whatever was said by Otto Baric to his players at half-time gradually dissipated, and as the game wore on, normal service resumed, with Everton continuing to press and dominate the Austrians.

The goal, which the Blues had threatened to produce since the first exchanges, did eventually arrive in the 57th minute, when Sharp latched on to a misplaced back-pass, rounded the keeper and chipped a pass through to Gray.

'I had an open goal', says Gray, 'and just volleyed the ball into the net. It was an incredible feeling. And it was the goal that killed the game in my opinion. Our opponents had shown little before that, and after we scored, you got the sense that they had nothing to offer.'

Everton were rampant from that point onwards, rarely giving Rapid any space to breathe. A second goal seemed inevitable, and it came when, as the *Echo* reported, 'Sheedy's corner from the right was flicked on by Sharp, Mountfield ducked and after the ball had eluded the outstretched legs of three defenders Steven arrived at the far post to volley home sweetly.'

At 2–0 up, Everton appeared to be in total control. 'It was as one-sided a final as you could imagine,' thinks Simon Hart. 'I think by this point, Everton were almost better than the competition. We were English champions, by some distance, and probably were better suited to the European Cup. We were possibly the best side in Europe.'

But – even when dominant, playing at their best, sweeping all before them – this was still Everton.

'Everything was going well,' recalls Kevin Ratcliffe, 'when, totally against the run of play, Rapid got back in the game.'

An innocuous through ball to Kranjčar on the edge of the box was deftly back-heeled by the Rapid midfielder past Ratcliffe into the path of Krankl (possibly in an offside position). The Austrian forward then took it around Southall and put the ball neatly away.

'It was a bit of a blow', says Pat Van Den Hauwe, 'to have been so dominant and with just five minutes left suddenly find ourselves with the prospect of defending a narrow lead. Luckily, it wasn't a prospect that lasted very long.'

If this had been the Everton of Mike Walker, Roberto Martinez or Walter Smith, then you would expect a capitulation to follow that goal (in the exceptionally unlikely event one of their sides would reach a European final). But this was the Everton of Kendall (Mark 1), and so what happened was exactly the kind of response a supporter would want.

'Undaunted Everton hit back straight away from the kick-off,' reported the *Echo*, 'tearing forward to expose a flat-footed defence which had charged forward to seek an equaliser. Sharp fed Sheedy out on the left and the Eire international made no mistake from 12 yards, firing high into the roof of the net to officially open the celebrations.'

'I think the Rapid fans were still celebrating when I put the ball away,' says Kevin Sheedy. 'Although, not for long, because at 3–1 that was the game over. It was the perfect response. And a scoreline that was no more than we deserved.'

To the delight of the thousands that had made the trip and the many more watching at home, the whistle blew shortly after, and Everton, for the first time in the club's history, had claimed a European trophy.

'It was a special feeling lifting that cup,' says Kevin Ratcliffe. 'It was an amazing moment for me. A real honour.'

The victory left Everton, as FA Cup finalists, tantalisingly close to the 'Treble'. Sadly, as most Blues recall, a knackered Everton side faced Manchester United a few days later and lost 1–0, the extra effort just being beyond them.

'It was disappointing,' admits Kevin Sheedy. 'But we still had so much to be proud of. To win the league and the Cup Winners' Cup marks that side out as a great. Rotterdam still stands as one of the club's most memorable moments and I was honoured to be part of that.'

v Norwich City 1–0

4 May 1987
Football League Division One
Carrow Road. Attendance: 23,489

Everton: Southall, Stevens, Van Den Hauwe, Watson, Ratcliffe, Reid, Steven, Heath, Sharp, Snodin, Power

Norwich City: Gunn, Brown, Spearing, Bruce, Phelan, Butterworth, Williams, Drinkell, Rosario, Biggins (Fox), Gordon

Referee: J. Bray

Make Do and Mend

THE 1985/86 season had been a tough one for Evertonians. Although filled with good games and good moments, it had ultimately been one characterised by misery and frustration as the club was pipped to both the title and the FA Cup by Liverpool. By the narrowest of margins, Everton had turned what could have been one of the greatest seasons in the club's history into one best forgotten.

It was a campaign that ended with both teams touring the city in open top buses: trophy-less Everton parading in advance of silverware-laden Liverpool. For the Blues who attended in an act of near-pathological loyalty, it was a dark moment.

The summer had then thrown up its own challenges. The club's top scorer, Gary Lineker, was sold to Barcelona, and there were rumours that Kendall might follow him to Spain too. Although this latter fear never materialised (at least that season), when the campaign kicked off, Everton seemed to lack the rhythm they had enjoyed during the previous year.

'Losing Lineker obviously took some adjusting to,' argues Kevin Sheedy. 'But, added to this, we also had an extensive injury list, which impacted on our form. Amongst others, Neville was out for a few months and Peter Reid and Paul Bracewell also had lengthy lay-offs. It's always hard to get going when your side is both disrupted and suffering from the absence of key players'.

Those who had been brought in to bolster the squad in the summer, such as the centre-half Dave Watson from Norwich City, the midfielder/defender Paul Power from Manchester City and midfielder Kevin Langley from Wigan Athletic, gamely (and with varying degrees of success) attempted to plug the gaps.

'Everton were OK as a side,' says Simon Hart, 'and still knocking around the top of the table, but that sense of fluidity and strength that had become the hallmark of a "Kendall" team seemed to go missing at times. There were reasons for it, but you got the feeling early on that maybe this wasn't to be our year.'

But any fear that the club might not have what it took to mount a concerted title challenge was partially allayed by Everton's form over Christmas and New Year.

'I have always regarded the Christmas and New Year programme', wrote Kendall in *Only the Best Is Good Enough*, 'as arguably the most important period of a league campaign and it was our inspired form between 20 December and 17 January – when we won six games in a row – which was ultimately to prove decisive.'

The title race was very far from over, but, as Kendall also wrote, 'by winning at places like Newcastle United and Aston Villa we had sounded a chilling warning to our closest rivals.'

Everton's main rival for the title was Liverpool (again), and despite that strong showing over the Christmas period, the Reds were setting the pace. Between Boxing Day and mid-March, Liverpool established a nine-point lead over Everton (albeit having played a few more games). But that's when everything changed.

'In my long years of following Everton I've never known anything like it,' says Phil Redmond. 'You expect Everton to fall apart, not Liverpool, especially not that version of Liverpool. But somehow, the wheels just came off their season and Everton kept going. It was wonderful.'

Suffering from a spate of injuries and a draining League Cup run, Liverpool faltered, and by early April Kendall's team had not only made up the distance but even managed to edge out in front.

'We then went on another strong run,' recalls Kevin Ratcliffe, 'which virtually guaranteed us our second title in three years.

'We got that sense of invincibility back, something that had been such a characteristic of the 1985 team. It was as though we just expected to win every game we played.'

It helped that, as the season wore on, some of Everton's stalwarts returned to the squad on a more settled basis – the kind of experienced and talented players that sides chasing the title needed. But equally handy were some of those additions that Kendall brought in, both in the summer and during the campaign.

Paul Power, bought with the intention of him being a cover player, ended up playing in all but two of Everton's league games that season, filling in at left-back and left midfield. Wayne Clarke, who arrived from Birmingham City towards the end of the campaign to provide cover up front, scored five goals in ten games during a vital period for the Blues. And last of all, Ian Snodin, signed from Leeds United in January, gave the Everton midfield a much-needed boost.

All in all that season, Kendall used 23 players. This was significant by the standards of the time. As a comparison, Liverpool only used an average of 17 in the course of winning their titles between 1972 and 1986.

'1984/85 had been a team performance when it came to winning the league,' argues Kevin Ratcliffe. 'We had a few players, like Kevin Richardson and Alan Harper, who covered and who were absolutely essential. But by and large the team was mostly unchanged for a significant chunk of the season. In 1986/87, everything was about the squad. What we did that year was, to a large part, dependent upon the support players that Howard was able to bring in who did such a magnificent job.'

It was also a squad that managed to rise to the challenge of losing a goalscorer like Lineker by sharing responsibility for finding the back of the net. In the league, Steven led the way with 14, followed by Sheedy with 13 and Heath with 11. Elsewhere, Clarke and Sharp hit five, Power got four, and Stevens, Watson and Mountfield got three apiece. Across the squad as a whole, theirs was a cumulative tally that enabled Everton to top the scoring charts.

With five games to go, this squad of all-talents had the opportunity to tie the title up at Anfield.

'It never happened, we lost,' remembers Dave Prentice. 'But how wonderful would that have been? Especially as it would have been payback for the misery of the season before. Sometimes you can't have it all, though, can you?'

A draw against Manchester City at home in the next game meant that Everton had to travel to Carrow Road to tie up the title, and a date with Norwich City.

The 5,000 Blues who had made the trip to East Anglia got an early boost when Everton took the lead not long after kick-off with a goal that came from an unlikely source:

'I have no idea how I ended up in the Norwich penalty area in the opening minutes,' recalls Pat Van Den Hauwe. 'But I did! I remember the ball coming across the six-yard box, I think after Norwich had failed to clear a corner and it just sat up nice for me, so I belted it. One Nil! It was the perfect start to the day.'

Despite Everton getting an early lead, Norwich were not cowed. Everton seem to have an unerring knack across the decades of facing opposition on title-winning occasions who seem intent on spoiling the party. The Canaries were chasing their highest-ever league position and before the game had outlined that they were determined to have a go at the Blues.

'We had 86 minutes to defend that lead, and at times it wasn't easy,' recalls Van Den Hauwe. 'I remember that their winger was giving me a tough game. Norwich were determined not to be rolled over. It was quickly obvious that this would not be a walk in the park.'

But, despite their intent, the home side didn't carve out too many clear openings. Drinkell and Rosario had two decent first-half headers, but that was the limit of their threat. And at the other end, Everton could have extended their lead on a few occasions, most notably when Bruce had to clear off the line from Steven.

Norwich's problem was the Everton defence, which according to Ken Rogers in the *Liverpool Echo*, was imperious:

'Dave Watson in particular was in commanding form, looking solid and confident against his old club. Skipper Kevin Ratcliffe was an inspiration throughout and both Van Den Hauwe and Gary Stevens showed their international class against lively wide men.'

'As the end of the match approached,' says Kevin Ratcliffe, 'Norwich had run out of ideas and it seemed clear that the title was coming back to Goodison. After the misery of the previous season, that was a glorious feeling.'

As champions that year, Everton became the first club to receive two title trophies: the Today League and the traditional league title trophy (the former being a crappy little trophy that would look more at home at regional sales awards in the stationery industry).

It might not have been as swashbuckling as 1984/85, but in some ways the 1986/87 title win was more impressive. Against the odds and often with a patched-up side, Everton had triumphed.

'A squad effort is harder to pull off,' argues Graeme Sharp. 'And so, the way that Howard brought players in and chopped and changed the side in response to adversity just showed what a great manager he was.'

Kendall was a 'great', arguably the greatest manager Everton have ever had. But he was also one with ambitions to compete at the highest level. With the European ban affecting English clubs (introduced after the Heysel Stadium disaster in 1985), staying with Everton would deny him that opportunity.

That title win in 1987 would be bittersweet for Evertonians. It might have been Kendall's greatest achievement at Goodison, but it would also be his last contribution for a while (and his last genuinely positive one). In the summer of 1987, Everton's manager departed for Spain, drawn by lure of European football. Although Colin Harvey, his replacement, tried gamely to carry on from where Kendall had left off, he and the club were never able to reach those heady heights again.

v Liverpool 4–4

20 February 1991
FA Cup Fifth Round Replay
Goodison Park. Attendance: 37,766

Everton: Southall, McDonald, Hinchcliffe, Watson, Keown, Ratcliffe, Atteveld (McCall), Newell, Sharp, Nevin (Cottee), Ebbrell
Liverpool: Grobbelaar, Hysen, Burrows, Nicol, Molby, Ablett, Beardsley, Staunton, Rush, Barnes, Venison
Referee: N. Midgley

Ta-ra, Kenny

I T was the match that nobody saw coming. On a cold winter's night in 1991, Everton hosted Liverpool in the fifth round of the FA Cup. The outcome was a derby that can claim to be one of the strangest to have ever taken place. It had been a difficult season for Everton. In the October of 1990, Colin Harvey, the man tasked with continuing the Kendall miracle, had been sacked. After three seasons of growing frustration, the wheels had completely come off his Everton project, and, by the time he was removed, the Blues were bottom of the league, plagued by poor form and riddled with internecine warfare.

'We were never a "team",' says former Everton winger Pat Nevin. 'That was the problem with Everton. We had really talented players and on our day could beat anyone. But those days were depressingly few. There was limited cohesion to the side, and at the root of this was an inability to reconcile the cliques that had developed.'

Roughly, these were divided between the 'old guard' that had thrived under Kendall and the more recent acquisitions brought in during Harvey's process of transition.

'I had no time for cliques and tried to get on with everyone,' continues Nevin, 'but I can remember how destructive they were to team morale. In short, you had the older players thinking that the new arrivals weren't as good as those they had replaced. And on the other hand, some of the new arrivals believed that a few of the older players were possibly past their best.'

Harvey's replacement ended up being his predecessor. After an indifferent time in Spain, Howard Kendall had returned to England and had taken up a manager's position with Manchester City. Following overtures from Everton, he quickly jumped ship and returned to Goodison, bringing unity to the warring factions, an improvement in form and entry into the promised land of mid-table security.

'I wasn't alone in thinking the good times were going to come back to Goodison,' says Stan Osborne. 'Although we were out of the League Cup and the title was well and truly out of reach, we still had the FA. I think every Blue hoped success in that could be the catalyst for the glory days to come back, just as had been the case back in 1984.'

But in the way stood Liverpool – a hurdle that Everton often found tough to overcome.

The game at Goodison was a replay, a second tussle following a scoreless first fixture at Anfield a few days earlier.

'The replay should never have taken place, though,' argues Graham Ennis. 'In the first game, Gary Ablett poleaxed Pat Nevin in the box. The referee, Neil Midgley, gave nothing. It was one of the worst decisions I've ever seen.'

In fact, Midgley went further than simply ignoring the foul. He pointed a finger in Nevin's face and made it clear that if the Everton winger went down like that again he would be sent off. In light of Midgley's apparent partisan sympathies, at the start of the second game, an Everton fan ran out on to the pitch and put a red scarf around his neck.

Prior to kick-off, Liverpool (under the guiding hand of Kenny Dalglish) sat second in the table. One point behind leaders Arsenal, they were looking to successfully defend their title. Everton, by contrast, were mid-table.

But, despite the table's suggestion of a Red victory, it was slightly deceiving. Liverpool were stuttering, and Everton were on good form. Chuck in the combustible nature of any derby tussle and the result was far from certain.

Although the game ebbed and flowed throughout, Liverpool would be first to draw blood. After Rush had dispossessed Ratcliffe out wide on the half-hour mark, he steamed in on goal, only to have his effort saved on the line by Andy Hinchcliffe. Unfortunately for Everton, the clearance fell to Peter Beardsley (via Rush's head), who drilled the ball home.

The goal proved what had been evident from the start, that Liverpool's attacking triumvirate of Barnes, Beardsley and Rush were capable of unlocking the Everton defence.

'Howard had opted for a back three, with me marking Beardsley,' remembers Kevin Ratcliffe. 'Man marking was never my strongest suit; that was probably better geared to Martin Keown. So defensively, specifically facing such a strong attacking side, I always felt it was going to be difficult.'

But hope for the home side was evident by the slackness of the Liverpool back four, who appeared to have taken a 'Mike Walker masterclass' in defending.

Two minutes after the break, as Hinchcliffe swung a telling cross into the box, Graeme Sharp peeled away from his markers:

'I was finding room all the time and felt a goal would come,' recalls Sharp. 'The Liverpool defenders lost me and I was able to connect with the ball and get us back into the game.'

After the goal, both sides continued to threaten, and it seemed less and less likely that the scoreline would remain unchanged.

'They were dangerous all night,' remembers Rob Sawyer, 'specifically Beardsley, and it came as no surprise when he put them 2–1 ahead. He put the ball beyond Southall with a wonderful shot from outside the box. It was a heartbreakingly good strike.'

But Everton showed a rare resilience that night. 'We just kept coming back at them, and we were level again soon after,' continues Rob.

The ball was played up to the edge of the area, where Nicol and Grobbelaar cocked things up between them. It then squirmed free and started rolling towards the line, where Sharp was on hand to run it in.

But, as is so often the case when it comes to Liverpool, the joy for Evertonians didn't last long. A few minutes later, Molby whipped an exquisite cross into the box. There, Rush reacted faster than the static defence and headed the visitors into a 3–2 lead.

'Despite the to-and-fro nature of the game,' recalls Phil Redmond, 'few Evertonians would have backed the Blues to come back yet again, such was Liverpool's psychological hold over the club.

'And so, with a few minutes to go and us apparently out of the game, I left. I needed to get off before that shower of shit started singing "Walk On". Nobody should have to suffer that. I think I was half-way down Diana Street when I heard the roar.'

Everton had been in need of a miracle. Luckily for the Blues, they had one sitting on the bench.

'Since Howard had come to the club, I hadn't really figured in his plans,' recalls Tony Cottee, who had arrived at Goodison from West Ham United a few years earlier for a then record fee of £2.3m.

'I wasn't exactly enjoying great form, but then I wasn't being given a run in the side. I don't think he fancied me much. I wasn't the kind of grafter that he liked.'

But, with Everton in dire need of a goal, Cottee was all Kendall had to turn to. 'I was on the touchline waiting to go on,' he continues, 'and Howard came over, put his arm around me and said, "get us a goal". I remember looking up at the old scoreboard and seeing that it read 84 minutes. I thought to myself "what the fuck do you expect me to do in six minutes?"'

Tasked by Kendall to work harder, drop deeper and assist other players, with the minutes ticking along Cottee opted to ignore that and do what he did best.

'I just went up top and waited for a chance to come, trusting in my ability to get a goal if an opportunity presented itself.'

Before full time, Cottee had two touches. First, an unremarkable lay-off, and second, one of the most memorable goals he ever scored for the club:

'It was the dying minutes of the game and the ball was flicked into the box where the Liverpool defence just appeared to switch off. Maybe being fresh on helped but I seemed to react faster than anyone else and just managed to slip in and slide the ball into the back of the net. It was an incredible feeling. I ran over to the corner of the Gwladys Street, where it was bedlam.'

The whistle went not long after, meaning extra time. When the game recommenced, unsurprisingly the goalscoring wasn't over.

The first arrived after ten minutes. John Barnes, the scorer, claims his 20-yard effort was deliberate. To less forgiving eyes, it was a cross/shot that caught Southall off guard.

'Either way,' recalls Rob Sawyer, 'Liverpool were once again in the lead and as the minutes ticked along it was a lead that they seemed set to keep. You just couldn't imagine Everton coming back again.'

Everton needed another miracle. And just like before, Tony Cottee was happy to oblige:

'One of their players hit a back-pass to their centre-half that sort of bobbled through into the box and I remember thinking "I'm in here". Everyone just seemed to watch the ball, but I knew I could get on to it. Grobbelaar was coming out, so the angle was a bit tight. I went for pace rather than precision, put my foot through the ball and in it went, straight through the keeper's legs. The noise from the Evertonians was incredible.'

The game ended 4–4, and in the replay the Blues beat Liverpool 1–0. In typical Everton style, after doing all the hard work, Kendall's men then went out of the competition at the hands of West Ham, effectively ending the club's season.

Despite the disappointment, though, the tie did have one other positive outcome. The draw was the final straw for Dalglish. The stress of dealing with the aftermath of Hillsborough combined with the ceaseless pressure of managing Liverpool had taken its toll. He was ready to quit the club.

Dalglish had tormented Everton as a player and a manager for much of the 1980s. He was a loathed figure amongst Evertonians and someone whose presence at the club seemed to suggest Liverpool's long era of success would continue. However small, that strange cup game still played a part in his decision to leave – even if it just acted as a catalyst. Evertonians could take satisfaction from the fact that not only had Liverpool been knocked out, but one of the chief causes of so much Blue anguish had finally been seen off too.

v Wimbledon 3–2

7 May 1994
Premier League
Goodison Park. Attendance: 31,297

Everton: Southall, Ablett, Unsworth, Watson, Snodin, Ebbrell (Barlow), Horne, Limpar, Stuart, Cottee, Rideout

Wimbledon: Segers, Barton, Elkins, Blackwell, Scales, Gayle, Earle, Fear (Blissett), Jones, Clarke, Holdsworth

Referee: R. Hart

The Great Escape I

RELEGATION: it's a dirty word. And one that strikes fear into the heart of any football fan. In the 1990s, Evertonians became worryingly familiar with it as the bottom three's gravitational pull exerted a powerful hold over the club.

The first time it was felt in earnest was during the 1993/94 season, when Everton came within minutes of going down.

It had been a challenging campaign for the Blues. In the December of that year, while mired in mid-table mediocrity, the club had parted company with the once talismanic Howard Kendall.

Despite promising so much, the second coming of Kendall had refused to take off. 'A lot of fans were waiting for a "Kevin Brock back-pass" moment,' believes Stan Osborne. 'But it was never going to happen. In truth, Everton were mediocre.'

Although unquestionably hampered by a lack of finance and a board that appeared rudderless, Kendall's managerial skills were also on the wane, and, as a result, his second spell in charge was more about mid-table consolidation than restoring Everton to the elite of the game.

His replacement was Norwich City manager Mike Walker, who arrived in January 1994. Despite his relative inexperience, Walker had impressed at Carrow Road, turning a club tipped for relegation into one that had nearly won the title.

Once installed in the Goodison hot-seat, Walker had initially enjoyed a bump in form, and for a few short weeks it looked as though he'd been the right choice. And then it all went wrong.

'I can't remember exactly when I realised we were in really deep trouble, but it was probably around the last month of the season,' says former Everton midfielder John Ebbrell. 'We couldn't score,' he continues, 'and we were sloppy at the back. We just seemed to slide down the table. With a few games left, I began to get the feeling that maybe everything wouldn't be alright and that the reality was we were in massive trouble here.'

He was right. By the time the final Saturday of the season rolled around, the Blues were second from bottom, facing a five-way fight to the death with Southampton, Sheffield United, Ipswich Town and Oldham Athletic. Damningly for Everton, a win against Wimbledon at home might not be enough to ensure survival. The club's future was in the hands of others.

Tantalisingly, should the club survive, the future *actually* looked bright. The club finally had a new chairman, Peter Johnson, a local hamper magnate who had recently arrived promising fresh investment and a savvier approach to running the club. It was hoped that Johnson would rescue the club from the torpor that had hung over Goodison during the dog days of the Moores regime, which had seen Everton plagued by boardroom inertia and financial malaise.

But for those at Goodison that day, the horizons did not stretch beyond 4.45pm. All that mattered was the upcoming 90 minutes. Thoughts of a brighter tomorrow could be placed on hold until the actual business of survival was put to rest.

'The stress involved with our predicament made for a strange atmosphere that day,' says Neil Roberts, author of *Blues and Beatles: Football, Family and the Fab Four – the Life of an Everton Supporter*. 'There was so much anxiety about the place that despite all the singing and shouting it felt unsettling. It's hard to describe just how odd Goodison felt.'

It probably didn't help that a quarter of the ground was missing. 'The Park End had been demolished earlier in the season,' Neil continues, 'so that changed the feel of Goodison. Although, to their credit, on the day itself there were actually a few fans down there making up the numbers – sat in the trees overlooking the building site.'

As the game started, it would be vital for Everton to assert dominance. The worst thing the team could do would be to gift the visitors an early advantage.

Five minutes in, Wimbledon got a corner on the left:

'I can still remember the ball coming over,' recalls former Everton midfielder Anders Limpar, 'and knowing that I'd misjudged the header. Instinctively, my hand went up and connected. It was one of those things that happens but you're not sure why. I was so disappointed.'

No question that it was a penalty. And the referee duly gave it. Goodison held its collective breath as Dean Holdsworth struck the spot kick. Absolute silence greeted its conversion. Everton had started in the worst way possible.

For the following quarter of an hour, the home side tried unsuccessfully to get back into the game. But, despite the toil, it would be the visitors who would claim the next goal. And it came in almost comic circumstances, when the Everton defence conspired to turn an innocuous long ball launched towards the box into a calamitous own goal, courtesy of Gary Ablett.

'I can remember a fella in his fifties sitting completely motionless for about two minutes,' recalls Kev Symm, who was sitting in the Family Enclosure, 'then, as play resumed, he just stood up and said he couldn't sit by and watch this happen and left without coming back.'

Everton needed a miracle. Not long after, Limpar was on hand to provide the possibility of one. Although he acknowledges that there was some contact, the Swede admits that he made the most of the collision that took place in the Wimbledon box. 'I dived, plain and simple. But in my defence, I think the situation called for it. We needed that penalty and we needed it converted.'

Enter Graham Stuart. 'I recall having a drink with Graham a few weeks earlier when he told me he was on pens for the club,' says Dave Prentice. 'I remember him saying that knowing his luck, Everton would get a pen that he'd have to take to keep the club up. It wasn't quite that but it was close enough.'

Most Evertonians were probably unaware that Stuart had missed the only other penalty he'd taken, while at his previous club, Chelsea. But, with supreme confidence, he stepped up and calmly slotted the ball into the bottom left-hand corner.

'The noise when that goal went in was incredible,' recalls Neil Roberts. 'It was such an important strike. We needed something positive to happen, and we had to get back into the game. For the first time in a while, you could feel a hint of belief return to the crowd. We watched the sides go in at half-time with some degree of hope restored.'

Everton emerged after the break with evident determination, putting the Wimbledon lines under greater pressure than had been the case in the first half. But the visitors retained their air of threat, and it was they who initially came closest to adding to their tally, when Holdsworth's goalbound header was cleared off the line by Stuart 15 minutes into the half.

Football is a game that is defined by moments: key points where a match, a career or a season can take a different turn due to a piece of luck, a dodgy refereeing decision or an instance of individual brilliance. For Everton, two moments that would greatly impact upon the club's future fortunes occurred in the space of mere minutes. The first was that goal-line clearance, the second, Barry Horne's howitzer of a goal.

Industrious, dependable and dogged, Horne was not the kind of figure you would expect to come to the rescue on a day like that – and certainly not one to produce a shot of such power and technique.

As the midfielder himself admits, the goal came at an important time: 'We were about 25 minutes in and there was a growing sense of frustration. Despite plenty of hustle and bustle, we'd only created one clear-cut chance, and that had to change. Something needed to happen or there was a danger that the game would slip away from us.'

According to Horne, so much of what happens in football occurs subconsciously – instinctive reactions to the game's numerous permutations and variables. And this was true of his wonder-goal.

'I never really thought about it until later. The ball was there in front of me, sitting invitingly and it just seemed instinctive to have a go.'

Horne caught it perfectly on the half-volley. The ball screamed past a helpless Segers and flew into the top-right corner of the net.

'The crowd exploded,' recalls Tony Murell, who was sitting in the Family Enclosure. 'People were hugging each other, jumping around, just losing their heads. I don't think I'd seen anything quite like it for a long time.'

Although drawing level had only really restored the parity that had existed at kick-off, proceedings felt different from the moment play resumed. Everton clicked in a way that had been totally absent an hour earlier and began to build a head of steam that pushed the visitors back.

They say that good things often come in threes. For Graham Stuart, that particular idiom was about to come true. First he had converted the penalty. Secondly, Stuart had cleared Holdsworth's goalbound header off the line. And then, to complete the trinity, he would secure his name in Everton folklore by scoring the team's third, final and most important goal. Not that he knew much about it, as he later confided to the *Liverpool Echo*.

'Anders played it across and I played a one-two with Tony Cottee. I sort of half-tackled the bloke, then I just heard the crowd roar. I didn't know how it went in.'

The roof came off Goodison as Stuart's bobbly shot crept over the line. 'That moment is one of Goodison's greatest,' thinks Tony Murrell. 'Sheer elation, uncomprehending joy, the relief; it all mixed together to produce something unforgettable.'

But Everton were not home and dry yet. With time added on, there was still around 15 minutes to go. It was going to be an anxious finish.

'Although Wimbledon might have had the wind taken out of them,' recalls Tony Cottee, 'they were still dangerous. It would have been sickening to have fought so hard only to throw it away at the end.'

To call the football of those dying minutes 'ugly' would be generous. Everton launched long balls aimlessly towards the opposition's corner flags, harried, chased and threw in some tenacious challenges. If an opportunity occurred to waste some time, then it was greedily embraced.

When the end finally came (and the network of Chinese whispers in the crowd had already confirmed other results had gone Everton's way), the pitch was flooded, the flanks of stewards unable (or more likely unwilling) to stem the tide of happy Blues that washed over them.

'It was a strange game, that Wimbledon one,' admits Stan Osborne. 'It's the kind of game that you never want to live through but are sort of glad that you were there. It was horrible and majestic at the same time. A great game, certainly. But also brutal in its own way too.'

v Liverpool 2–0

21 November 1994
Premier League
Goodison Park. Attendance: 39,866

Everton: Southall, Jackson (Rideout), Ablett, Watson, Unsworth, Horne, Parkinson, Ebbrell, Ferguson, Amokachi (Limpar), Hinchcliffe

Liverpool: James, Jones, Scales, Ruddock, Babb, Bjornebye (Redknapp), McManaman, Molby, Barnes, Fowler, Rush

Referee: D. Gallagher

Royle Resurrection

'I HADN'T really realised just how bad things were. And not just how far adrift the club was. I also found a squad that was devoid of morale and which had almost forgotten how to play as a team. It was a desperate situation at Everton.'

Such was Joe Royle's damning judgement on the side he had inherited from the outgoing manager Mike Walker. This was November 1994, a dark time for Evertonians.

Mike Walker, a name that will forever haunt fans of the club, had kept his job after the debacle of the previous season, the club initially laying culpability for Everton's death spiral at the door of others.

'But,' argues Graham Ennis, 'although there were issues, such as boardroom upheaval and a sense of inertia that had gripped the club, Walker's role was still integral. He was not right for the job and that was proven as the season started. Everton played as they had in the previous campaign under his management: which was terrible.'

Although benefitting from the financial support of Peter Johnson and bringing in both the players and the playing style he wanted, under Walker the Blues were a disaster. In the 1994/95 season, they took just three points from the first ten games. As Royle took over, Everton sat bottom of the league, a difficult fixture against high-flying Liverpool on the horizon. A change in approach was sorely needed.

'Everton were too easy to beat, I had to alter that,' says Royle. 'Willie Donachie and I watched some videos of the club's recent performances, and it was obvious that there was a soft underbelly to the side. There was no fight or grit. You need that, especially when you're fighting relegation. It was our job to bring in a new way of playing and, if needed, the kind of players who could provide that grit.'

When the teams ran out on that cold November night, a shift in personnel illustrated that a change was indeed in the air. The likes of Vinny Samways, Graham Stuart and Gary Rowett, skilful ball players but less likely to hunt down the opposition, were nowhere to be seen. Instead the midfield was staffed by more combative figures, such as Joe Parkinson, Andy Hinchcliffe and Barry Horne.

'We believed that these players,' says Royle, 'when combined to our new approach, which stressed pressing and a quicker tempo, would give us a new dimension. Then, when you add in the crowd, we thought we'd have a fighting chance against Liverpool.'

When this apparently tougher Everton took the pitch, they did so to a rapturous reception. Night games at Goodison always have the capacity to threaten. Chuck in the presence of our esteemed neighbours and you have a heady mix. But there was something else there that night: a sense of raw anger too.

'I think we were all just a bit pissed off,' says Mike Murphy, who was sitting in the Lower Gwladys Street. 'It had been a shit year, and everyone was talking up Liverpool. They were flying the league and we'd obviously been crap, so almost every pundit, and all their fans, just thought it would be a walk in the park. All of that just wound us up. You could feel that anger in the crowd. The atmosphere felt different to pretty much every game I'd been to since Kendall had walked / been pushed a year earlier.'

With the fans conditioned to watching Everton's anaemic performances under Walker, from kick-off it was evident that Royle had introduced a steelier approach.

'We worked much harder under Joe,' recalls Barry Horne, 'gave teams less chance to play and got the ball upfield quicker. We were a more tenacious side too, one that I doubt few teams would have relished playing. We chased teams, gave them less room to move. But in return, we could still work the ball too. It wasn't all about the "Dogs of War". We could play some lovely football.'

Liverpool, who had been dazzling in their attacking play since the season had begun, were suffocated by the Blues. Everton, under their new manager, were a different beast and the likes of McManaman, Molby and Barnes could barely get their feet on the ball, so effective were Royle's men in closing down space.

But Everton's new-found fortitude initially came at a cost. The team's front pairing of Daniel Amokachi and Duncan Ferguson were starved of service from a midfield grouping more defensively minded than most.

Not that much was expected from that duo by the fans. Since arriving from Club Brugge in the summer, Amokachi had disappointed, finding the net just the once. And Ferguson, on loan for three months from Rangers, had been an underwhelming presence, a man who gave no hint of the force he would soon become.

A possible solution to Everton's attacking impotency presented itself after the break, when an injury to Jackson necessitated a reshuffle. Horne deputised at right-back, Amokachi dropped slightly deeper and Rideout came on to partner Ferguson up front. It was a change that would transform the game and Everton's season.

'I was desperate to impress Joe,' recalls Rideout. 'What player isn't when a new manager comes along? To his credit, he'd given us a blank slate, so this was my chance to get out there and show him why I needed to be part of his plans.'

The injection of more attacking potency was dramatic. Amokachi, who always seemed to play better when positioned deeper, started to make driving runs at the Liverpool defence, shattering the composure that they had displayed during the first half.

Allied to this, with two target men to aim at, Hinchcliffe was beginning to whip crosses in with missile-like precision (something that would become a hallmark of Royle's sides that season).

With the front pairing of Rideout and Ferguson displaying a hitherto absent sense of understanding, this new attacking intent changed the momentum of the game. To add to the steel, which remained marked, Everton now possessed an air of threat. And this was exemplified in the transformation of Ferguson.

After being clattered from behind by Ruddock early in the second half, Everton's number nine underwent a marked change.

'Ruddock probably thought he'd done his job,' remembers Royle. 'But that nasty challenge brought something out in Duncan. You could almost see him turning green. From the moment he picked himself off the floor he was unplayable.'

Ferguson's transformation, combined with Everton's new attacking potency, meant that the goal, courtesy of the 'Big Man', had a sense of inevitability about it.

Stan Osborne takes up the story: 'Hinchcliffe's precision-guided corners had been causing Liverpool problems for a time, but without yielding anything for us. That was about to change. Around the 50-minute mark, Ferguson connected with one and put the ball narrowly over the bar. It was a warning to Liverpool, one that, to their cost, they failed to heed. When Ferguson met the next cross, he didn't head the ball, he butted it. There was a moment, just as the ball crossed the line but before it hit the back of the net, when Goodison was silent. Then, when we all realised what had happened there was just an explosion of noise.'

Even though the opposition was clearly cowed by the new, invigorated version of Everton, considering Liverpool's long-held propensity to inflict misery upon the Blues, and the relative distance between the two clubs in the league at the time, it would be natural to assume that a body of supporters as inclined towards the negative as Evertonians would still believe that defeat was inevitable, even after Ferguson had put the side ahead.

'But that never felt the case that night,' remembers Tony Murrell. 'It was strange. For once, in a derby, there was a feeling of inescapability about victory. When the second goal came toward the end of the match, it just made perfect sense.'

It was time for Everton's substitute to show his new manager just what he was capable of. 'I remember the ball coming in from the left, a high, looping cross from Andy [Hinchcliffe],' remembers Paul Rideout. 'Duncan [Ferguson] went up for it against David James, neither of them made a proper connection and the ball fell towards me. I had to reach for it but just about managed to get a poke of a shot at goal. It was strange when the ball went in. I recall the noise of the crowd almost hitting me.'

The reaction of the crowd was understandable. As this fixture had loomed in the calendar, it had carried with it a sense of dread. Everton under Walker would have most likely been decimated by this vibrantly creative Liverpool side, and the fans were acutely aware of how painful this would be, specifically as it would have further cemented Everton's position at the foot of the table.

In securing the win and shackling Liverpool so comprehensively, Everton had not only averted a long-foreseen disaster but also given the supporters hope. Hope that Royle was the right choice. Hope that the Walker nightmare was consigned to the past. Hope that relegation could be avoided.

In a decade largely characterised by disappointment and frustration, that night at Goodison was a rare high point – a night of genuine celebration.

'One of my favourite memories of that night', says Graham Ennis, 'was being on County Road after the match, waiting to get a bus into town and seeing Duncan Ferguson strutting down the road like he was the King of Liverpool. I think that moment sums up how we all felt. We all had the feeling that something had changed.'

It was a feeling that turned out to be spot on. Wins over Chelsea and Leeds followed, and, over the course of the next six months, Royle ushered in a turnaround in form that saw Everton shift from being the worst club in the division to one of the best. And in the process, survival, once thought unimaginable, was achieved.

'We earned Premier League safety with a game to spare that season,' says Royle, 'which, for me, still stands as my greatest managerial achievement. It was a run that had to start somewhere, and it started with that glorious night under the lights, a night when we first showed everyone just what that side could do.'

v Tottenham Hotspur 4–1

9 April 1995
FA Cup Semi-final
Elland Road. Attendance: 38,226

Everton: Southall, Jackson, Watson, Unsworth, Ablett, Limpar, Horne, Parkinson, Hinchcliffe, Stuart, Rideout (Amokachi)

Tottenham: Walker, Austin, Calderwood, Mabbutt, Nethercott (Rosenthal), Popescu, Howells, Anderton, Barmby, Sheringham, Klinsmann

Referee: R. Hart

Bollocks to Your Dream Final

IN November 1994, when Mike Walker was sacked and Everton sat bottom of the league, all Evertonians wanted from that season was survival. Any thoughts of silverware and trips to Wembley would have been considered a pointless distraction in the long, hard battle to avoid 'the drop'.

As such, Everton's FA Cup campaign started without much fanfare or enthusiasm. 'I was wary of the cup,' admits Joe Royle. 'I remember saying, half-seriously, that it was a bit of a hindrance. Our survival was so dependent upon us not getting injuries. For me, certainly early on, it just meant unnecessary games that I could do without.'

Expectation regarding progression and enthusiasm for the competition was hardly helped by Everton's poor performances in the early rounds, which saw narrow victories against Derby County and Bristol City.

'I don't know how we got through the round,' Joe Parkinson recently confided about the Bristol game on Radio City's *Match of My Life*. 'I remember playing the game and I think if we'd have been beat 10–1, then that would have been a fair result. But then Matt Jackson, with a volley from the edge of the box [which is unheard of], and then Junior Bent missed God knows how many chances and we managed to win 1–0. It was an amazing game and I think in the changing room, we sort of knew, because you need a little bit of luck and with our team-building and the way we stuck together ... afterwards we thought we had a chance of winning this cup.'

As Everton progressed and league form improved, slowly the competition began to engage the fans more too.

'We battered Norwich 5–0 in the cup,' says Simon Hart, 'then knocked out title-chasing Newcastle and suddenly found ourselves in a semi-final. At the same time, although we were still embroiled in a relegation dogfight, we were the form team. Everton were down in the lower reaches of the division because of our horrific start under Walker. Royle's side was a different beast; one that we felt had what it took to get out of the mire. Because of that, the excitement surrounding the cup built and built.'

Everton's opponents in the semi-final at Elland Road were Spurs. Boasting an impressive array of attacking talent, including Nick Barmby, Teddy Sheringham and the Football Writers' Association Player of the Year, Jürgen Klinsmann (a player who scored 30 goals in all competitions that season), they were viewed by the media and by most neutrals almost as the 'Anti-Everton'. Where the Blues were seen as dogged, determined and difficult to break down, Spurs were by contrast regarded as stylish, cavalier and filled to the brim with attacking brio.

Before the game, newspapers and pundits were united in their hope and belief that Spurs would progress to the final. And there they would meet Manchester United rather than Crystal Palace, the other two clubs fighting it out for a place at Wembley. It was the media's 'dream final', an early indicator of the 'big club' fixation that was just beginning in earnest within English football.

'We were meant to be fodder for Spurs,' says Royle, 'at least according to the press. We were totally written off, seen as a team that couldn't match them at all. Of course, we knew better.'

Elland Road, the semi-final's host stadium, had not been the happiest of hunting grounds for Everton over the years, with only two wins there since the war. But, on this occasion, as Neil Roberts recalls, despite the stadium's long-standing curse, for once the ground actually seemed intent on giving the Blues a natural advantage.

'It was a joy to behold entering Elland Road to see three sides of the stadium bedecked in blue and white. Three sides of the ground rammed with Evertonians and a far from full Main Stand with Spurs fans in it. It felt like we were at home.'

In a season filled with its fair share of highs and lows, that game sticks out. It's fair to say that it ranks as one of Everton's best performances of the past 25 years. As the pundits and sports writers had correctly predicted, one of the sides present would outclass and dominate the other. The only problem was that they backed the wrong horse.

Even without the influential Duncan Ferguson, who was out suspended, Everton were rampant. The Blues started the game like a rocket, harrying Spurs, refusing to let them 'play' or create anything of meaning, while at the same time constantly threatening.

'Although we did outfight them, we also outplayed them,' argues Barry Horne. 'We were sensational from the first kick that day, passing and moving in a way that Spurs could not cope with. That side often gets dismissed as one that simply tackled its way to get results. But we were creative too. You don't play like a top-six club without having that.'

So dominant were Everton that when Jackson converted Hinchcliffe's corner around the half-hour mark, there was no surprise that the Blues had taken the lead.

'We had already missed a few decent chances and you got the sense that a goal was coming,' says Anders Limpar. 'Our opponents had been riding their luck and were fortunate not to be about a couple down before we scored.'

Everton continued in the same vein after the goal, and, as the sides went in at the break, Spurs must have wondered what had just hit them.

When play resumed, the expectation was that Spurs, only a goal behind, would take the game to Everton, and finally utilise their much-heralded attacking potency. But little altered in the early stages as the Blues continued from where they had left off: squeezing the life out of their opponents, while building momentum for a second goal.

Ten minutes in, it arrived as Everton went 2–0 up courtesy of Graham Stuart, who found himself with an open goal after Walker had parried Rideout's effort into his path.

With half an hour left to save their Wembley dreams, Spurs then got a huge slice of luck when the referee awarded them a penalty (following a 'foul' by Watson on Sheringham).

'It was a terrible decision,' says Joe Royle. 'We hadn't conceded a single goal in the competition until that point and it seemed wrong that the first we let in, after Klinsmann converted, should have been so undeserved.'

After the goal, there followed a nervy time for the Blues. 'Inevitably Spurs had a moment in the game where they tried to bomb on and unsettle us,' recalls Limpar. 'And for a time they looked threatening. But then everything changed.'

With the minutes ticking along and an anxious ending appearing more and more probable, an unlikely hero entered the fray.

'Although Amokachi was a bit of a hit with the fans, he hadn't done much since he arrived,' remembers Simon Hart. 'Ferguson and Rideout had become the first-choice pairing up top, and "Amo" had largely been confined to the bench. When he came on, I doubt anyone expected much.'

The strange thing was, as the man himself recently told the *Liverpool Echo*, he wasn't really meant to come on in the first place.

'I'd been sat there listening to the physio, Les Helm, telling Joe that Paul Rideout was injured and needed to come off. The gaffer kept saying he wanted to give him five minutes, but he wasn't getting any better so I decided to bring myself on.

'Klinsmann was on fire and really piling on the pressure, and I felt I could help change the game. I just thought "hope this works", and thank God it did, or it could have been my last game for Everton.'

It was the best substitution that Royle never made, and Amokachi secured himself a place in Everton folklore when, with eight minutes of normal time remaining, he met a cross at the far post and headed Everton into a 3–1 lead.

'I think both the players and the crowd knew it was all over then,' remembers Paul Rideout. 'Spurs weren't getting back into the game after that. You could sense it in the stands, and, as players, we had that realisation that we were going to Wembley. It was such a magical moment.'

But the man from Nigeria wasn't done. With the match nearly over and Spurs throwing everything forward, Limpar broke. He played the ball forward to a marauding Gary Ablett, who, with a degree of precision usually absent from his attacking game, put in a perfect cross, which Amokachi met on the half-volley to grab his second and Everton's fourth.

'Elland Road erupted,' recalls Simon Hart. 'It was a special moment after what we had all been through. Six months earlier we looked doomed to be relegated, and yet here we all were nearly safe in the league and a place booked at Wembley. I remember that, as I was leaving that afternoon, "Brown Eyed Girl" by Van Morrison was playing over the tannoy system. I felt like I was walking on air. I can honestly say that it was my happiest single moment as a Blue. Why? Because of how bad we'd been and how utterly unexpected it all was.'

Unvalued, marginalised, written off before a ball had even been kicked, the Blues had not just reached the club's first final that decade – they had also upset the pundits' predictions in the most unforgettable of ways.

'I came out to meet the press,' says Royle, 'and said, "Sorry about the dream final, lads – but bollocks to you. And that's with a double 'L'." It felt good to say that. We had earned our place in that final by destroying Spurs despite nobody giving us a chance. We always knew how good we were, how no team provoked fear in us but now it was time for others to realise it too.'

v Manchester United 1–0

20 May 1995
FA Cup Final
Wembley Stadium. Attendance: 79,592

Everton: Southall, Jackson, Watson, Unsworth, Ablett, Limpar (Amokachi), Parkinson, Horne, Hinchcliffe, Stuart, Rideout (Ferguson)

Manchester United: Schmeichel, Neville, Bruce (Giggs), Pallister, Irwin, Butt, Ince, Keane, Sharpe (Scholes), Hughes, McClair

Referee: G. Ashby

The Underdogs of War

IF Everton had been viewed as underdogs in the semi-final, that was nothing compared with how little they were fancied for the main event. The Blues, a club who had slid from mediocrity to relegation dogfighting in the past few years, were lining up against Manchester United, then the dominant force in the domestic game. Few gave Everton a hope in hell.

'Once again we were cast as underdogs,' says Joe Royle, 'despite our impressive league form since I had arrived. But I turned this lack of expectation into a plus for us. I simply told the players that nobody thought they'd win, so they should go out there and prove the lot of them wrong.'

It was an approach to the game that the players welcomed, as Barry Horne recalls:

'Joe always gave us the belief that we could beat anyone. Although we were the underdogs, we felt that there was no reason why we couldn't win. We'd beaten United in the league and we'd destroyed Spurs in the semi-final. There was no sense of fear in that dressing room. We knew United were good, but we felt we were too and had enough quality to beat anyone on our day.'

Evertonians flocked in their thousands to Wembley, savouring the Blues' first trip to the 'Home of Football' since the twilight of the club's 1980s heyday (if you discounted pointless shite like the Zenith Data Systems Cup).

For those who had been lucky enough to get a ticket (in typical Everton style, there had been a cock-up with the allocation, leading to thousands queuing overnight, many of whom ended up being turned away), there was a feeling that Evertonians seemed more dominant than the United fans that day.

'We were louder and more prominent than them,' remembers Neil Roberts. 'Maybe it was because it was a bigger deal for us. It had been a while since we had won something and we'd had a torrid couple of years. United, by contrast, were getting used to picking up silverware.

'Whatever the reason, it felt like Wembley had been colonised by Evertonians.'

Amongst those who had come, there was an unusual sense of optimism. The dark outlook that so often characterises the Blue perspective was less common than was traditionally the case.

Although part of that was attributable to the unpredictable nature of cup football (Everton might have been facing one of the best sides in the country, but anything was possible in the FA Cup), lifelong Blue Paul Gielbert thinks there were other factors influencing this most un-Everton of outlooks.

'Being honest, it felt inevitable that we would win. We'd been lucky against Bristol, then powered past everyone to the semis, battered Spurs and ruined the so-called "dream final" – I think our name was just on the trophy that year.'

There was also a feeling that Royle, unlike many managers of the day, had the measure of Alex Ferguson.

'Fergie always had a knack of getting under the skin of managers,' thinks Stan Osborne. 'But that was never the case with Joe. There's a great interview of the two of them from before the game, and on every occasion Ferguson tries to needle Royle, he has a smart answer back. Watching the two side by side, you never got the sense that Joe was remotely bothered by Ferguson's reputation, his mind games or the fact that United were the favourites.'

This sense of confidence was less apparent amongst those who were following Everton's opponents that day.

'We might have been more confident had we not just blown the title the week before,' argues Barney Chilton, editor of the Manchester United fanzine *Red News*.

The final game of the 1994/95 season had seen United and Blackburn Rovers locked in a desperate fight for the title. United had travelled to West Ham and Blackburn to Anfield, with the latter just two points ahead in the table.

'Liverpool beat them (to our surprise) but we blew it,' Barney recalls, 'squandering chance after chance to end up drawing. We were so low after that, I struggled to see how even Fergie could lift the side.'

Yet despite that gut-wrenching loss of the title, United displayed no sense of despondency early on. They unquestionably enjoyed greater possession and appeared to be the more threatening of the two sides. Despite this, from the very first kick, it was evident that Everton had the capability of hurting their opponents on the break. Royle appeared to have regarded counter-attacking as United's Achilles heel.

'And that's exactly how the goal came about,' says Paul Rideout.

On the half-hour mark, from a United attack, Everton broke fast through Limpar, catching the opposition napping and finding themselves four-on-two. The ball was played wide to Jackson on the right, who cut inside and played a pass across the box to Stuart.

'Everything after that seemed to happen in slow motion,' continues Rideout, who was also part of the breaking Everton horde. 'Graham hit the bar with his strike and the ball looped out into the six-yard box. It was hanging high and I had to work hard to jump and get enough power on the header. I can still remember the second it hit the back of the net. That moment is not something you easily forget.'

The Blue half of Wembley ignited. 'The atmosphere had been breathtaking all afternoon from the Evertonians,' says Neil Roberts, 'but the place rocked when that goal went in. The Blues in the ground probably shook that old stadium to its foundations.'

The goal seemed to lift Everton, and for the remainder of the first half Royle's men looked dangerous. Although United had more possession, Everton pressed, were resolute in defence and remained a threat on the counter. At half-time, the Everton players and fans could be satisfied with how the game had gone. Not only did the side possess the lead, but it had also ensured that the favourites had remained largely frustrated.

But, as most Blues recall, matters can change very quickly in such games. Back in 1986, when Everton had faced Liverpool in the first all-Merseyside FA Cup Final, a half-time lead (and dominant first-half performance) had been reversed during the second period as Liverpool rampaged home to a 3–1 victory. And that was when Everton boasted one of the best sides in the country.

'We knew a time would come when United would get their chances,' remembers Barry Horne, 'they were too good a side not to. But we knew that we were defensively solid and could likely weather whatever they threw at us. We also, importantly, had the lead, so the pressure was more on them than us.'

The introduction of the always-dangerous Giggs for the injured Bruce didn't bode well, and during the second half United were much more of a threat going forward. Despite Ferguson (who'd been recovering from an injury) entering the fray not long after the break, Everton had lost much of the attacking potency that characterised their first-half performance.

United's dominance grew bit by bit as they edged closer to that equaliser. Luckily for Everton, they still had Southall in goal.

There had been times during the previous few seasons when the fans, the press and more than one manager had questioned whether Everton's legendary goalkeeper might no longer be up to the job. But if ever a performance rebutted the critics, it was that one. Southall was superb, pulling out a succession of saves that kept Everton in the game and without which the side would surely have forfeited the cup.

'It wasn't necessarily my best performance,' remembers Southall modestly, 'but a decent one. There were good saves, and the one that gets mentioned the most, a double save from Paul Scholes. But that's what I was there to do, make sure nothing got past me.'

With Big Nev's help, Everton hung on to that lead. 'What a moment that was when it was all over,' says Dave Kelly. 'It was the perfect end to the season.

Six months earlier we Evertonians had been staring into the abyss. Few of us could see anything other than relegation. Then Joe, using pretty much the same group of players that had been there under Walker, had come in and transformed us. We had risen, phoenix-like, and turned what could have been the worst season in the modern era into one of the greatest. Although the FA Cup was really only the icing on the cake (after all, survival was more important), it was icing that Royle and the fans deserved.'

When Dave Watson lifted the trophy, the sight provided everyone watching with a timely reminder that the Blues still had what it took to succeed at the highest level.

'That was a great moment for every player in that side,' thinks Anders Limpar. 'We'd all been through a lot in a very short time, and been written off on more than one occasion. But we'd fought hard and ended the season on a high note. From a personal perspective, that was probably my sweetest moment in football. I'd been an Evertonian since I was about ten, so to win a trophy with the club I loved was an unbelievable experience.'

Everton later got to parade that cup through the city, the streets lined with Blues. As Duncan Ferguson later told the *Liverpool Echo*, it was a sight to behold:

'We had the open-top bus tour in the city the next day. To come down Queens Drive by the megastore, which was still being built, and see the fans hanging off it was unbelievable. They were sitting on the scaffolding. Then all the multi-storeys when you're going down Everton Valley and on Scotland Road, they were everywhere. How they climbed up there God knows but it was incredible. What a sight to see all that blue.'

v Coventry 1–1

10 May 1998
Premier League
Goodison Park. Attendance: 40,109

Everton: Myhre, O'Kane, Short, Ball, Watson, Tiler, Farrelly (McCann), Hutchison, Barmby, Madar (Cadamarteri), Ferguson
Coventry: Hedman, Shaw, Burrows, Breen (Williams), Huckerby (Haworth), Whelan, Dublin, Telfer (Hall), Soltvedt, Boateng, Nilsson
Referee: P. Alcock

The Great Escape II

'**W**IMBLEDON in '94 was supposed to be a one-off,' says Graham Ennis, 'a brush with death that was never meant to be repeated. We were promised that it would never happen again and yet, four years on, Evertonians were being put through that horror once more.'

On the final Sunday of the 1997/98 season, Everton squared off against Coventry City at home. The Blues were third from bottom. One place above them in the table sat Bolton. Of these two, one would face 'the drop'. Devastatingly for Everton, the mathematics of survival favoured their rivals. In short, victory against Coventry might not be enough to escape the bottom three. 'The whole season had been terrible and we were relegation candidates almost from the start,' continues Graham. 'Unlike in 1994, when mediocrity had morphed into a death spiral, in 1997/98 we started badly and continued in that vein for the remainder of the campaign.'

Everton had ended the previous season managerless, after Joe Royle had left his post (effectively pushed out by Peter Johnson). The 'good times', when Johnson's money and Royle's managerial acumen had provided silverware and a top-seven finish, had been disappointingly brief.

'Results had gone against Joe while he was enduring a spate of injuries,' argues Phil Redmond. 'That, and a hostile relationship with the local press, made Johnson panic, and he got rid of the manager. It was one of the moments that you look back on, taking into account what followed, and think how different, and better, life as a Blue could have been had that never happened.'

After Johnson promised the arrival of a 'world-class' manager, the club had been linked with a variety of high-profile appointments. When nobody 'world-class' wanted the job, Howard Kendall had bailed him out and taken the role for the third time.

Starved of cash and with his managerial talents on the wane, Kendall put together a side that many regard as one of Everton's worst.

'Although there were some good players in there,' argues Simon Hart, 'like Ferguson, Nick Barmby and Don Hutchison, they were too few to compensate for the mediocrity that filled the ranks elsewhere. The team had been weakened by the loss of Gary Speed during the season and in many ways looked like a second-tier side seemingly fixed on finding its level. That side is probably the worst I've ever seen in all my years of supporting the club. They were poor enough to go down and possibly even deserved it.'

In contrast with 1994, when the novelty of a relegation dogfight combined with the arrival of fresh investment from Peter Johnson gave Evertonians hope, in 1998 the mood was more despondent.

James Cleary, who was sitting in the Lower Gwladys Street that day, recalls: 'At the Wimbledon game, there was a sense that we were on the verge of something, if only we could stay up. The sun was shining, the takeover had been completed, Mike Walker had been installed and some money spent. In contrast, the wet, humid gloom of that Sunday was an accurate assessment of my pre-match Coventry mood, and the nervousness felt all round. It was grim.'

Despite the despondency that hung over the club, the sell-out crowd gave Everton the support they needed. As 'Z Cars' rang out, Goodison roared in unison, the crowd letting the players know that they would do their part (whatever reservations they felt).

For those coming out on to the pitch, the response was a welcome one. 'The atmosphere was incredible,' says former Everton defender Michael Ball, 'a huge roar of noise that kept going for most of the afternoon. And we needed that. We needed Goodison at its most intimidating. It was a lot to ask of the fans after the season we had delivered, but they came through for us nonetheless.'

In stark contrast to what had occurred four years earlier, when Everton had started the game exceptionally poorly, the Blues were lively from the off, and after seven minutes it was an approach that bore fruit.

'You hit lots of shots that you're convinced will go in but they never do. That one luckily did,' recalls Gareth Farrelly, a Kendall acquisition from Aston Villa in the summer. The young midfielder was perhaps symptomatic of that side: willing and handy, but not exactly the kind of player to drive Everton forward.

'I remember,' he continues, 'catching it with my right foot and watching as it spun off. The keeper didn't get near it, and the ball flew into the back of the net. Over time [largely because Everton haven't been in that position since] that goal has probably grown in significance in people's minds. But back then, for me, it was just great to score.'

Goodison shook when the ball smacked into the back of the net. In a rare similarity with 1994, a strike of genuine class from a most unlikely of sources had given Evertonians hope.

The goal was a statement of intent, a marker that had illustrated the home side's desire to take command of the game. For the next 40 minutes, hard running and hard working, Everton outfought and outplayed Coventry in every department and were unfortunate not to go in at half-time further ahead.

'There was urgency to our play that had been lacking for some time,' admits Everton's tenacious midfielder Don Hutchison. 'Every player there was up for the occasion, and for once we were showing what this side could do. The atmosphere, which was incredible, helped. You can't fail to be motivated by that. But we also seemed focused in a way that we hadn't been for a while. I imagine Coventry didn't know what had hit them.'

The side came out from the break to another rapturous reception. The atmosphere hadn't ebbed all afternoon, and with the club facing 45 vital minutes, each Evertonian in Goodison seemed determined to give everything they had for the cause.

But something had changed. Before the break, Everton had been quick, aggressive and bubbling with creativity. In the second half, the side was timid, ponderous and devoid of any creative ideas except launching the ball forward for Ferguson to head or Cadamarteri (who had come on for Madar just after half-time) to chase.

'Although Coventry were much better in the second half, it was mainly because we stopped playing,' thinks former Everton centre-half Craig Short.

For him, the cause of this was a growing nervousness that crept into Everton's play. 'We could probably have done with not having half-time, because up until that point we were on top. I think the break helped them and hindered us. It was like the importance of the game, and the fragility of our lead, suddenly became more real and we lost the momentum to our play that had been there in the first half.'

Although Everton were on the back foot and it looked like the precarious lead could slip away at any minute, around the 70-minute mark a cheer went up, erupting in pockets around the ground. News had filtered through via the network of transistor radios that Gianluca Vialli, the Chelsea player-manager, had scored against Bolton.

Not long after, lady luck gave the Blues another boost. 'I remember the ball breaking kindly for me,' says Danny Cadamarteri, the young Everton forward who had hustled and bustled tirelessly since he'd come on.

Uncharacteristically, Everton had strung together a coherent attack. The ball had ricocheted across to Barmby in the middle of the Coventry half. He then threaded a headed pass that split the visitors' centre-backs in half and fell kindly into the path of Cadamarteri:

'I was through on goal, trying to control the ball while jostling with the Coventry defender. The next thing I know, I'm on my arse and the ref had signalled for a penalty.'

Barmby stood over the ball, in front him the goal and behind that 10,000 Evertonians standing in anticipation, the entire Gwladys Street waiting to erupt in celebration. He ran up and struck it to the keeper's right. It was too close to Hedman, too easy to push behind for a corner. Everton's chance to finish this game had been and gone.

'A miss like that hurts a team,' says Michael Ball. 'You go from thinking you're home and dry to suddenly being aware of just what an amazing chance you have squandered. It deflates a side.'

If ever you wanted to illustrate to someone what it's like to be an Evertonian, show them the closing moments of the Coventry game. In those final minutes, the nature of Evertonianism is perfectly captured. The highs, the lows, the way in which the club refuses to give its fans an easy ride.

A few minutes after the penalty miss, with collective nerves still on edge, Coventry did what they had been threatening to do for some time. Burrows swung in a left-wing cross, which Dublin connected with and headed towards goal. The ball slipped through the hands of Myhre and suddenly the complexion of the game had changed. It was 1–1, a scoreline that transformed Goodison into a mass of anxiety for the closing minutes.

'I couldn't believe the ball had gone in to be honest,' says Michael Ball. 'I remember watching it slip through the keeper's hands and just thinking, "How has that happened?" In the space of a few minutes we had potentially thrown away our survival. And it was nothing to do with Coventry. It was all us.'

Thank God then for Chelsea. At some point in those dying minutes, word spread through the crowd that they had made it 2–0. Bolton were finished. If Everton could hold on (still a big if), then safety was assured, as the Blues would be level on points but with a superior goal difference.

'When that whistle went, I was drowned with relief,' says James Cleary. 'I couldn't believe that we'd managed to survive when it looked like it could go against us so easily. We hadn't won and yet still survived. It didn't seem real.'

Survival would always have engendered a rapturous response, but you got the sense that noise had been accentuated a few decibels because of the way in which Everton had secured safety.

As had been the case after the Wimbledon game, the pitch was instantly flooded, invaded by Blues from all directions, everyone eager to get near the players and be part of the congregating mass.

But the mood amongst them was different to four years earlier. Back then, the outpouring of relief and joy was underpinned with optimism about the future: a new owner, more money, the sense of renewal.

'It was different in '98 though,' says Mark Godfrey, editor of the *Football Pink*. 'We'd been through the renewal and we were back at square one. There was a feeling that Johnson was dragging the club down. He'd sacked Joe, brought in a non-"world-class" manager and starved him of funds. It was of no surprise to me that cries of "Johnson out" filled the air. Evertonians, despite the relief of survival, were angry, really angry.'

v Liverpool 1–0

27 September 1999
Premier League
Anfield. Attendance: 44,802

Everton: Gerrard, Dunne, Weir, Gough, Ball, Xavier, Hutchison, Collins, Barmby, Jeffers, Campbell

Liverpool: Westerveld, Heggem, Hyypia, Carragher, Staunton, Smicer (Camara), Hamann (Meijer), Redknapp, Berger, Fowler (Gerrard), Owen

Referee: M. Riley

Super Kev Sinks the Reds

THE late 1990s was a dark time for Evertonians. The brief flirtation with hope in the middle part of the decade now seemed like a distant memory.

After Kendall's miserable third stint in charge was brought to a sad end, Johnson had gone north of the border and brought the Rangers manager, Walter Smith, to Goodison. A debt-fuelled transfer splurge had accompanied his arrival as Johnson sought to gamble everything on European riches. It hadn't worked. Smith found the English top flight a more difficult environment than the Scottish Football League, and Everton had only just escaped relegation during his first season in charge.

In the summer of 1999, with Johnson looking for a buyer, the cash tap turned off and Everton facing debts of £18m (largely attributable to that transfer splurge), Smith had taken a machete to his squad, selling the likes of Marco Materazzi, Olivier Dacourt and Craig Short simply to make ends meet.

'It was a worrying time for Evertonians,' admits Graham Ennis. 'The club was riddled with debt, we had sold key players and nobody wanted to buy us, which left us saddled with a hated chairman and no money. We had been embroiled in a relegation dogfight during the previous campaign and there was every reason to believe that we would be again.'

And yet, on the pitch, despite the boardroom issues, the shrunken squad and Smith's inability to act freely in the transfer market, Everton started surprisingly brightly.

'Luckily,' says Lyndon Lloyd, the man behind ToffeeWeb, 'we'd bought Kevin Campbell, who had come to us on loan at the end of the previous season and played a huge role in our survival. That gave us a valuable outlet up front. It meant that we had a point to our play, something that had been lacking for much of the previous campaign. It enabled Everton to actually get goals and win matches.'

Eight games in, Everton sat seventh. The side was playing some good football, particularly the forward line of Campbell and Francis Jeffers, who were helping turn a team once incapable of finding the net into one that put four past both Southampton and Wimbledon in successive fixtures.

'Because the late '90s was a difficult time for Everton,' thinks Don Hutchison, 'people seem to forget that there were occasions when we were pretty good. That season, when Walter was beginning to find his feet in England, we had the foundations of a decent side. I'm not saying we could have won the league, obviously, but who knows what the manager could have done if he'd had a few more quid in the kitty?'

In late September, Everton went to Anfield. 'As a Blue, you're not meant to be confident playing there,' says Mark Godfrey. 'But back then, there wasn't the sense of dread that perhaps there is today. We seemed able to take the game to them. In that decade, we'd had the measure of Liverpool to such an extent that not only had we held them a few times at their place, we'd also beaten them there a few years earlier when Kanchelskis had torn them apart.'

Everton started aggressively, and with just four minutes gone and the game barely in its rhythm, they got off to a flyer. Campbell and Jeffers combined to split the Liverpool back four, providing the former with a clear chance which he just about put away.

'Playing in a Merseyside derby is a unique experience,' says Campbell, 'simply because the game splits families down the middle: dad Blue, mum Red, daughter Blue, son Red. It's not logical, yet it works and makes for a fantastic spectacle and atmosphere mixed in with all the usual bragging rights, showmanship and nervous energy the derbies bring. As for scoring in a derby – it is very special! These are moments that will live with me for life.'

The goal set the tone for what was to come. As many Blues can attest, it is one thing for Everton to go to Anfield and outmuscle Liverpool, quite another to go there and outplay them. Yet, that is exactly what happened.

Coming on the back of three home defeats and some iffy form in general, Liverpool were there for the taking. And for once, Everton took them.

'Every time a Liverpool player found himself in a position to launch an attack,' reported the *Liverpool Echo*, 'so first one Blue shirt and then a second, sometimes a third, surrounded him. Those tactics offered were no real surprise, and maybe neither anymore should the football that followed it. Swift and incisive, controlled and thoughtful.'

During the remainder of the half, Everton continued to dominate, and on a couple of occasions, first from Jeffers and later from Campbell, Liverpool had to thank Westerveld for keeping them in the match.

According to the *Echo*, in comparison to the magnificent Blues, 'Liverpool were sloppy, never keeping hold of the ball long enough to properly test Paul Gerrard and their frustration was evident in the 26th minute when Michael Owen was guilty of an awful tackle on David Weir which could so easily have been the first of the glut of dismissals which were to follow.'

Derbies have a tendency to be bad-tempered affairs. But even contextualised, this derby was particularly nasty.

'Tackles flew in. Players were jostled and pushed, it was a real blood-and-guts sort of game,' remembers Don Hutchison.

Surprisingly, though, Liverpool were the worst transgressors. Evidently feeling the pressure when their natural game failed to trouble Everton, they started getting stuck in.

Not that it had much impact. For most of the game, Everton were in control, and they should have gone further ahead early in the second period, if only Jeffers had been on better form, as 'Mickey Blue Eyes' reported for ToffeeWeb.

'All he had to do was square it to unmarked Nicky [Barmby] and it was game shot. Instead, he did what all instinctive strikers do – try to score ... but got caught in two minds and the ball went harmlessly across the goal area with thousands of Blue Bellies trying to suck it in.'

And then, five minutes later, continued Mickey, 'he [Jeffers] got completely clear on their left and had only the Cheesehead to beat. And then screwed it maddeningly, infuriatingly WIDE.'

As the second half progressed, Liverpool did begin to settle slightly after Houllier replaced Hamann, Fowler and Smicer with Gerrard, Meijer and Camara.

The home side began to see more of the ball, but in response Everton defended resolutely.

With 15 minutes left to go, and Liverpool growing increasingly frustrated, the complexion of the game then altered completely when Jeffers and Westerveld, who had clashed in the first half, were red-carded.

'The pair traded half-hearted blows inside the penalty area after Jeffers, who was flagged offside by a linesman, had collided with the keeper chasing a throughball,' reported the *Echo*.

With all substitutes used, Staunton took over in goal and didn't do too bad a job. Frustratingly, the Liverpool defender even managed to execute an excellent save, tipping over from Abel Xavier to thwart Everton's attempts to capitalise on his inexperience.

That chance aside, the sendings-off seemed to sap some of the energy out of the game. With the seconds ticking along and neither side looking particularly creative, the likelihood of an Everton victory began to look more and more certain.

But the game still had one more talking point to throw up.

In the dying minutes, Steven Gerrard received a straight red after a horrific tackle on Campbell, which saw him attempt to cut the Everton forward in half with his boots. Gerrard later admitted that he had come on with the expressed intention of taking out an Everton player, a revealing vignette that was excluded from the many articles that pored over his career when he left

Liverpool (which largely painted him as a professional of exemplary character and intent).

Gerrard's red was pretty much the last action of the game, and when the whistle sounded soon after, Evertonians could savour a well-earned and rare victory. 'It doesn't get much better than this, people,' wrote 'Mickey Blue Eyes'. 'Savour it. Relish it. Take the piss out of 'em mercilessly. You've earned it after the last three seasons.'

'Over the years, our club has played its part in many memorable Merseyside derbies,' says Lyndon Lloyd, 'but more often than not ended up on the losing side. It made a nice change for us fans to be part of a memorable game that for once saw Liverpool take on the role of the vanquished. It was a time to celebrate.'

But, if Evertonians were hoping that the victory could be a springboard for the remainder of the season, they were to be disappointed. Despite the sense of euphoria that followed the Anfield victory, Everton were unable to maintain momentum. Over the following months, Smith's men became draw specialists, enduring stalemates in half of the club's ten fixtures, and sliding down the table in the process.

'That was a frustrating time,' remembers Phil Redmond. 'You got the feeling that there was a better side hiding in there somewhere, one that could have turned those draws into wins with a bit more quality or a slightly more attack-minded approach. But at least we weren't near the bottom, and at least we could look back on that campaign and say that we beat the Shite in their own backyard. And that really mattered.'

At the time of writing, that game represents the last time that Everton have enjoyed victory at Anfield. The spell of near two decades without a win has ensured that the match has taken on an extra significance. For many Blues, it is depressing that it has. A club of Everton's stature should be able to do at Anfield what lesser clubs have managed over the past 20 years. The 'Kevin Campbell derby' was a great game. But there's not a Blue alive who doesn't wish that it was no longer held in quite the same high regard.

v Arsenal 2–1

19 October 2002
Premier League
Goodison Park. Attendance: 39,038

Everton: Wright, Hibbert, Weir, Yobo, Unsworth, Carsley (Stubbs), Li Tie (Linderoth), Gravesen, Pembridge, Campbell, Radzinski (Rooney)
Arsenal: Seaman, Lauren, Campbell, Cygan, Cole, Toure (Wiltord), Gilberto Silva, Vieira, Ljungberg (Edu), Henry, Kanu (Jeffers)
Referee: U. Rennie

Remember the Name!

LIFE as an Evertonian had been tough in the late 1990s and early 2000s, an era characterised by debt, penury and the near-constant threat of relegation.

As the four-year reign of Walter Smith ground to an end, an outcome that Evertonians willed with an almost palpable sense of desire, the Blue half of the city was in desperate need for change.

'By the end of the Smith era, things were a mess,' argues Lyndon Lloyd. 'We had ageing players, nobody seemed to give a shit and our form was awful. And, once again, we were facing a fight for survival in the league. The new manager, David Moyes, had a huge challenge on his hands.'

Moyes arrived in March 2002 after four years with Preston North End, during which he had dramatically turned around the fortunes of the Lancashire club, taking them from the nether regions of the third tier to within a whisker of the Premier League.

Inexperienced but with a reputation of being an 'Alex Ferguson in the making', the Scot quickly earned respect from the Goodison faithful by steering the club to safety after his arrival. He also appeared to 'get' Everton, buying into the history and ethos of the club, and did himself no harm after uttering this near-immortal phrase to the local press:

'I am joining the people's football club. The majority of the people you meet on the street are Everton fans.'

During his first full season in charge, Moyes made few changes. Some of the deadwood, like Paul Gascoigne and David Ginola, was cleared out and a few new acquisitions brought in, like the young Nigerian centre-half Joseph Yobo, the Chinese midfielder Li Tie and the English goalkeeper Richard Wright.

'But, perhaps more important than the limited personnel changes, was the fact that he brought with him a new approach,' argues former Everton centre-half David Weir.

'He was a tracksuit manager,' continues David, 'always out on the pitch with us. He also brought a deeper tactical awareness to our game. We drilled to a greater extent, we were better organised, more of a unit than had perhaps previously been the case. It might not necessarily have been as enjoyable to play under as the previous regime, but it was certainly more effective for a side like Everton at that time.'

Hamstrung by debt and with pretty much the same group of players he had inherited, Moyes's Everton were a much more formidable proposition than Smith's. They worked hard, kept their shape well and yet in Kevin Campbell and Tomasz Radzinski had enough threat going forward to worry teams.

'The impact he had was pretty immediate,' says Lyndon Lloyd. 'We seemed to have a new trajectory, new energy, and Everton looked like they knew what they were doing, which hadn't been the case for such a long time. And, contrary to the "knife to a gunfight" mentality that seemed to define his later years, early on we could really play against anyone [specifically at home]. It was an interesting time to be a Blue.'

Moyes had given Evertonians confidence again, something that had been in short supply at Goodison. But, as important as that was, the fans also needed a bit of excitement, and for this they looked elsewhere.

'Wayne Rooney had been causing a buzz around Goodison for some time,' recalls Mark Godfrey. 'We'd all endured false dawns before, of course, times when supposed "wonder kids" came through and amounted to very little. And we had also watched with jealousy as Liverpool's kids, like Fowler, Owen and McManaman, lived up to their promise. But this one seemed to be different. This time everyone believed he was the real deal.'

Rooney had been with Everton since the age of nine, and his record was impeccable. He'd scored freely at youth level, played above his age group with ease and made no secret of the fact that all he wanted to do was play for Everton.

'He was one of our own, and after years of misery and frustration it was great that we had somebody so exciting coming through the ranks,' says Lyndon Lloyd.

Aware that he had a potentially exceptional talent on his hands, Moyes was cautious with the youngster. Although included as part of the 2002/03 squad, by the middle of October the 16-year-old had made only a handful of starts and a few substitute appearances.

'When he'd appeared, he had looked the part, though,' argues Simon Hart. 'I remember he came on away against Manchester United in the October. He picked up the ball at one point and just ran at them, bursting past their players like they were nothing.

'It was exciting, the kind of thing you hadn't really seen Everton players do for ages. And even though he was only 16, it looked like the age difference meant nothing. He was ready.'

In mid-October, Arsenal rolled into town. Champions, FA Cup holders and on the back of a long unbeaten run in the league (over two seasons), there was talk that the Gunners could go the whole campaign without being defeated.

Despite Everton's improvement, which had been tangible under Moyes, few Evertonians expected a win or even a draw against such an accomplished team. And, not long after the sides had kicked off, it was a prediction that seemed prescient.

'It had all looked so bleak and predictable,' wrote Jonathan McEvoy in the *Liverpool Daily Post*, 'when Freddie Ljungberg delivered the inevitable Gunners goal by preying on Everton's defensive frailties to take to 49 the number of consecutive games Wenger's men have now scored in. David Weir slipped as he tried to defuse Thierry Henry's deep cross and the ball squirted around the area before falling invitingly to Ljungberg, who swept home from six yards.'

Had this been a Smith side, Evertonians would have been justified in expecting a capitulation following that opening goal.

'But Moyes brought something different to Everton,' says Lyndon Lloyd, 'certainly in those early days: if not quite fearlessness, then possibly a sense of determination. The side was certainly willing to have a go at teams, and you never really saw heads drop. As time passed, you stopped expecting us to just give in when losing and instead started to believe that we could fight back.'

In response to going one down, Everton came back strongly. Arsenal were snapped at and chased. This was a physical Everton, one more redolent of the old 'Dogs of War', a sight that had been disappointingly absent from Goodison for too long. But there was more than just bite and snarl to this dog. There was intelligence too, intelligence that brought threat with it. Within minutes, the Blues were level:

'The equaliser came from a powerful and positive run by Gravesen which took him across the edge of the Arsenal penalty area,' wrote Dave Prentice in the *Liverpool Echo*. 'He looked to have run out of runway when he looked up and slipped a pass to Carsley. His drive cannoned back off the post but was collected by Radzinski on the edge of the area and he drifted inside before clipping a rising shot into the Gwladys Street net.'

Chances were limited after that, and the sides went in at half-time level. In the second period, although Arsenal continued to have their rhythm unsettled, opportunities still arrived for the visitors. Ljungberg came close twice, and Henry uncharacteristically scuffed a shot wide. The away side's wayward finishing and a dissipating amount of guile on Everton's part suggested a draw was the most likely of outcomes.

And then, on came Rooney. 'Looking back now on the career of David Moyes,' says Simon Magner, chair of the Everton Supporters Trust, 'this was an uncharacteristically bold substitution, considering the age and relative inexperience of Rooney, and the fact that we were holding the best team in England at bay and they didn't really look like breaking through. Secretly we all wished for something special to happen, but I don't think anyone in their wildest dreams could have predicted how the game ended up.'

Rooney's ten-minute cameo would ultimately be the only thing anyone talked about after that game. There might have been big performances throughout the Everton team, specifically the full-backs, Hibbert and Unsworth, and the front line of Campbell and Radzinski, but it was the teenager who would be making all the headlines the next day.

There was barely any time left when Wright launched a goal kick downfield. Campbell headed it back to the half-way line. A touch from Stubbs gave the ball to Gravesen, who punted it forward.

Forty yards out, Rooney killed it and turned, his back to goal. 'The Arsenal centre-halves dropped back,' continues Simon. 'In response, Rooney pushed the ball forward. We all knew what was coming. He exquisitely wrapped his foot around the ball and hit it from 25–30 yards to beat a flailing David Seaman. We were on our feet celebrating almost before it had hit the back of the net. I've heard some loud noises at Goodison before in my time, but that was easily one of the loudest.'

The teenager, still a few days shy of his 17th birthday, still on £75 per week, had announced himself to the world. As Everton took the 2–1 victory, it felt as though those present had witnessed something monumental.

'For so long we as Blues had suffered the feeling that we were becoming increasingly irrelevant in the Premier League era,' says Simon Hart. 'I recall a woman I worked with saying that she hated Everton because we were so boring. And she had a point (even if "hated" was a bit strong). Yet, from 2002 onwards, we became relevant again, reborn almost. And Rooney was part of that. He was young and exciting, and, perhaps more importantly, he was something other clubs did not have. For the first time in a long time, other fans were looking at us with envy.'

v Newcastle United 2–0

7 May 2005
Premier League
Goodison Park. Attendance: 40,438

Everton: Martyn, Hibbert, Weir, Yobo, Watson, Carsley, Cahill (Stubbs), Arteta, Kilbane, Ferguson (Beattie), Bent (McFadden)

Newcastle: Given, Carr (Ramage), Bramble, Boumsong, Babayaro, Jenas, Ambrose, N'Zogbia, Milner (Shearer), Kluivert, Ameobi

Referee: B. Knight

Breaking the Glass Ceiling

EVERTONIANS entered the 2004/05 season low on confidence. After a decent, top-seven finish in his first full season in charge, in his second, Moyes's Everton had stuttered. A collapse in form near the end of the campaign had traded mid-table safety (tolerable if not desired) for fourth from bottom.

They had ended a miserable run with a 5–1 tonking away to Manchester City and a performance as abject as the scoreline suggests.

'It was obvious at the time, and Moyes made no secret of it, that the squad lacked quality and depth,' says Lyndon Lloyd. 'The need for investment was evident. But it wasn't forthcoming. In fact, the summer was marred by boardroom disharmony, minimal transfer activity and the feeling that the club was in for another difficult season.'

The sense of a club in crisis was compounded not long into the campaign, when Wayne Rooney, who had been the subject of near-ceaseless transfer rumours (and who had agitated for a move himself) was sold to Manchester United for around £27m.

'Losing Rooney really hurt,' says Adam Partington of the GrandOldTeam fan forum. 'Deep down I understood it because he wanted to go and win things, but I did think it was too early. He was only young. At the time I was with my first girlfriend and she broke up with me in the same week, but I couldn't work out which I was more upset about.'

With the transfer coming just four hours before the window closed, and Moyes sagely unwilling to panic-buy, Everton faced months before any of the Rooney cash could be spent. This meant that the side that had performed so poorly towards the end of the previous season (albeit with the summer additions of attacking midfielder Tim Cahill from Millwall and Ipswich Town striker Marcus Bent) would be the one taking to the pitch week-in-week-out until the New Year.

'It was a worry,' admits Mark Godfrey. 'All summer we had been told that what Everton needed most was investment. But here we were, months on, and all that had really happened was that we'd bought a few players from the lower leagues and sold our brightest and best talent.'

Yet, regardless of the gloom that had settled over Goodison, Everton defied the pundits' predictions. Despite losing the opening game of the season 4–1 to Arsenal, the Blues went on a strong run.

The magical '40-point mark', which for most of the previous decade had disappointingly become something that mattered during the course of an average Everton season, and which some believed the club might not hit at all, was reached by Boxing Day. Everton were threatening to turn a season when relegation was predicted into one where Champions League football might be clinched.

'We never really played teams off the park,' remembers former Everton right-back Tony Hibbert, 'but we worked hard, we were organised and we got lucky with having a settled team. We also brought in some really good players, like Tim Cahill in the summer and Mikel Arteta later in the season, and just got some momentum behind us. I think the season before, we had just underperformed. We had the talent and the players, but it hadn't gone right. In 2004/05, everything went right.'

Everton made it into the top four in September and stayed in contention from then on. But, after Christmas, a place in the top four became a trickier proposition.

'In the second half of the season we were awful,' feels Peter Mcpartland of Toffee TV. 'The loss of Thomas Gravesen to Real Madrid in January played its part. But equally, a threadbare squad, not always blessed with the highest-quality fringe players, was perhaps always likely to find a top-four push difficult to sustain.

'Also, I think so much effort had been put into the first half of the season that we sort of ran out of energy at the end.'

Between the beginning of January and the end of the season, Everton only managed to collect a further 21 points. The Blues were hanging on.

Luckily, their rivals for fourth place, Liverpool and Bolton Wanderers, were unable to consistently make up the ground, and after a decent April, which saw Everton pick up victories against Crystal Palace and Manchester United, Moyes's men were poised to virtually guarantee Champions League football if they could beat Newcastle United at home.

Prior to the game, Everton were given a huge boost when it was announced that the football authorities had confirmed that the top four teams would enter the Champions League the following season. There had been some doubt over the issue, as Liverpool had made it to the Champions League final in Istanbul. There were some who felt that if Liverpool won, the fourth place should go to them.

'Oh God! Us Blues are decent at a bit of fume, so I imagine someone would have set fire to the Kop if that had happened!' laughs Adam Partington.

Everton's opponents that day, Graeme Souness's Newcastle, had struggled during the season and coming into the game were in poor form, their campaign effectively over. Everton might not have been firing on all cylinders, but Newcastle were there for the taking.

Before the match, there had been a misguided attempt by the club to try to create some 'atmosphere' by encouraging the supporters to indulge in a bit of 'Sky-Fan' bullshit by wearing loads of blue, getting out the flags and having their faces painted. Not only do such efforts go against the Everton grain, there was no real need to bother. Just as they had at the Manchester United match a few weeks earlier, the supporters 'turned up' that day.

'There was a great atmosphere,' remembers David Weir. 'The kind you want. There was a lot of pressure on our shoulders, and it helped to have such a big noise behind us.'

From kick-off, the Blues displayed all the hallmarks of Moyes's Everton at their best: combative, organised and resolute. They were physical, trying to disrupt Newcastle's attempts to settle on the ball.

But it wasn't entirely successful. For the opening half-hour, Newcastle remained dangerous and did occasionally break through the Blue armour. On a number of occasions, Evertonians were grateful that Nigel Martyn was yet again proving what a canny signing he had been in goal.

As half-time approached, Everton began to come back into the game. At the heart of this was Cahill, a player who best exemplified the strength of the side that season.

'Tim Cahill is a pure footballer,' wrote Scott McLeod in the *Liverpool Echo*. 'He would be as committed and wholehearted playing for a Sunday league side … He epitomises what this side is all about. He was pushing forward to panic defenders, he was winning possession simply by thinking faster than his rivals in the midfield, and he was on hand to batten down the hatches at the back.'

Everton's growing presence reaped reward just before the interval when an Arteta free kick was floated into the box, where David Weir met it with his head to power the Blues into the lead.

'That was my first goal for quite some time,' says Weir. 'Although it was the perfect time to get one. It was the kind of goal to really settle the nerves of the crowd.'

At the break, despite not playing particularly well, Everton were half-way to success. The Blues now just had to hang on for a further 45 minutes to secure an outcome that would have seemed improbable ten months earlier.

When play resumed, the home side received a huge boost as Newcastle were soon reduced to ten men, after Ameobi lashed out at Cahill and got himself a straight red. From that point on, the visitors were finished as a force. Everton began to push forward with more and more threat, both crowd and the players clearly up for the game.

Almost instantly, it was an approach that yielded reward. Fittingly, the opportunity fell to the club's driving force. Arteta's shot from outside the box went straight to Cahill, who had all the time in the world to rifle his 11th goal of the season into the roof of the Gwladys Street net.

'That Cahill goal is one of my favourites,' says Adam Partington. 'I think Sky Sports News used his celebration on their intros over the next season. Maybe they don't hate us?'

For the remaining half-hour, the game was a formality. Two up and against ten men, Everton had the comfort to kill the match off, frustrating the 'Toon' with extended periods of keep-ball. When the end came, Goodison roared its approval.

'Although, in typical Everton style, our celebrations were slightly tempered,' says Peter Mcpartland. 'Liverpool could still, technically, overtake us if we lost our last two games and they won theirs. So, we had to wait until the next day, after they had lost to Arsenal, to really relax.'

What Moyes had achieved that season was nothing short of a football miracle. Shorn of his one stellar talent, the Scot had turned a team languishing in the doldrums and tipped for 'the drop' into one that had qualified for the Champions League.

'When we were in fourth back in September, I obviously wanted us to stay there but I knew that Liverpool and Bolton would be pushing us hard,' Moyes told the *Post*. 'We lost Thomas Gravesen in January, who was massively important to us and we had to find another way of playing and that took us a while but we settled down in the end. We have kept at it and we've never said we were the best. We've kept our talking in the dressing room, had a lot of belief and we've delivered the goods.'

In the context of football back then, when the top four was effectively a closed shop, Everton's achievement must be ranked as one of its greatest. With a threadbare squad, largely bereft of cash and with the loss of his sole world-class player, Moyes broke through the glass ceiling. No cup might have been won, no title celebrated, but that should not detract from the achievement. In the face of doubt (and at times ridicule), Everton defied the form book in one of the sweetest ways possible.

When Skies Are Grey probably put it best when its editorial wrote: 'All season we've heard and read how the lack of star names and the style of football we play means that we will eventually deservedly fall away from the European places and allow more moneyed types to take over from us. It hasn't happened that way, though, and an awful lot of smart-a***s have been made to eat their words. And that, friends, is what Everton are all about.'

v Liverpool 3–0

9 September 2006
Premier League
Goodison Park. Attendance: 40,004

Everton: Howard, Hibbert, Yobo, Lescott, Naysmith, Neville, Carsley, Osman (Beattie), Cahill, Arteta (Valente), Johnson

Liverpool: Reina, Finnan, Carragher, Hyypia, Aurelio, Gerrard, Alonso, Sissoko (Pennant), Garcia, Fowler (Riise), Crouch (Kuyt)

Referee: G. Poll

Der, Der, Der, Der, Andy Johnson

EVERTON victories on derby day have become a rare thing in recent years. Times when Liverpool have been beaten and outplayed rarer still. To see the last time that they were sent packing with their tails between their collective legs, Blues have to travel back in time to 2006.

By the mid-2000s, the lengthy 15-year spell, which had spanned the mid-1980s to the late 1990s, during which Liverpool appeared to hold less fear for Evertonians, was on the wane and a creeping sense of Red menace over derby day was beginning to slowly reassert itself.

Since that victory at Anfield under Walter Smith in 1999, Everton had won just the once.

'Like a lot of Blues, I'm never confident playing them, and I don't remember being confident about this one,' recalls Adam Partington. 'I'd just started dating a girl who was a Red, and I remember her texting me the morning of the match giving me a bit of stick. The usual stuff about how they were better. She was tapping into the insecurity that has only grown since amongst Blues. And so, I was expecting the worst (me and that girl didn't last long, by the way. Dating a Red is tough).'

As is so often the case, the season was being tipped as 'Liverpool's Year'. But for once this wasn't just attributable to the slavish devotion of pundits to the Red cause, a media so enthralled by the idea of Liverpool claiming the title that they dispense with any sense of critical reasoning or the jaundiced perspective of their own fans, who seem to be forever frozen mentally in the early 1980s. No: for once, there might have been an element of truth to those assertions.

Under Rafa Benitez, Liverpool had once again become one of the division's stronger sides. Not only had they recently won the Champions League and the FA Cup, they'd also finished third during the previous season.

That said, back in September 2006, for all Liverpool's apparent strength, Blues could take some comfort from how Everton had started the campaign, which had seen the club take seven from nine in the opening three games, including an impressive away win at White Hart Lane.

'It might rarely be a predictor of the season to come, but Everton had at least started well, and were playing some good football,' says Mark Godfrey. 'We were also reaching that point in the Moyes era when we seemed, at Goodison at least, capable of making life difficult for the bigger clubs. We've certainly been in worse positions going into a derby. Even if it wouldn't count for that much once the game started.'

Although Moyes had reinvigorated Everton, they were still a side better regarded for their strong organisation than their attacking verve. The Blues needed an effective outlet.

'It had been a long time since Everton had fielded a prolific finisher,' remembers Simon Hart, 'and despite having the likes of Rooney, Ferguson and Campbell over the years, the best our top scorers tended to reach was the early teens.'

The latest name to be added to those upon whom the attacking hopes of the club were placed was the former Crystal Palace forward Andy Johnson. After Palace had failed to gain promotion to the Premier League, several clubs had begun to circle around their leading goalscorer.

With deeper pockets than rivals in the hunt, Everton had the edge, and, in May 2006, Johnson was sold to the Blues for £8.6m.

On his arrival, David Moyes (who had been after the striker for over a year) told the *Liverpool Echo* that:

'His record over the last four seasons is one goal in two games. That's right up there with the best. If he came here and produced one goal every two games for Everton, I think it would be a signing the supporters would see as positive. I think the fans will accept him because they know he has got goals in him. He'll work hard for the team … we are getting him in his prime years and we hope we are going to benefit.'

Johnson's early form suggested that Moyes's pursuit had been well worth it. Despite not finding the net in pre-season, the new arrival scored on his debut (against Watford) and then again a week later as Everton beat Spurs 2–0.

'He was fast and had a decent pedigree (albeit partly in the second tier),' continues Simon. 'I think we all hoped that he would provide that bit of class in the final third.'

On a sun-drenched afternoon, the Goodison derby started frenetically. Tackles flew in, players raced around and the ball sometimes appeared a secondary consideration.

'Amongst it all, Liverpool didn't look comfortable at the back,' recalls Tony Hibbert. 'After about ten minutes I just had a feeling that it was going to be our day. And the reason for this was Andy Johnson. It was obvious that the Liverpool centre-halves just had no idea how to handle him. His pace and his strength looked unmanageable.'

Although not the eventual scorer, Everton's new forward would have a hand in the opening goal, which arrived 25 minutes in. Some smart interplay between Johnson and Arteta put the Spaniard free on the right-hand side of the Liverpool box. The ball was then clipped into Lee Carsley, who flicked it on into the path of the unmarked Cahill. The Australian made no mistake with his effort, drilling it powerfully under the body of Reina.

'Cahill is the sort of player that we've really missed in modern derbies,' argues Peter Mcpartland. 'He understood what it meant to win one and also what it took. He was great at needling Liverpool players, getting under their skin. We don't have anyone close to that in the team today.'

Liverpool, unsurprisingly, upped their tempo in response. Gerrard hit the side netting from 25 yards out, and Garcia, cutting in from the right wing unleashed a vicious shot that Howard palmed out and Gerrard, stretching at the back post, was only able to steer on to the woodwork.

But, just as the Blues in the ground felt that Liverpool might get back into the game, the club's new man made a name for himself. A seemingly innocuous ball lumped forward into the box from Carsley fell between Hyypia and Carragher. With Johnson steaming past the Finn on the outside, Carragher came to cover but failed in his attempt to clear the ball, which instead fell kindly for Johnson, who then slotted it past the onrushing Reina with ease.

'Although we were two up, I don't think I was relaxed at that point,' says Peter. 'This was Liverpool after all, and a version of Liverpool that was still living off all that Istanbul stuff, and their ability to turn around games that looked unwinnable.'

In the second half, Liverpool began brightly. Half-chances fell to Fowler, Alonso and Gerrard, as they attempted to force their way back into the game.

'But, whatever they tried to throw at us, we coped with,' says Tony Hibbert. 'We were defending well, sitting back and soaking up what they had to offer, always with an eye to a counter-attack. We had the lead and were comfortable. The pressure was on them to change the game, not us.'

And those 'counters' did come. On a few occasions, Everton caught Liverpool cold, and both Johnson and Osman had chances to extend the Blues' lead. As it was, the Evertonians in Goodison would have to wait until the dying minutes to see a scoreline with a winning margin greater than any Blue had seen for a generation.

By that point, Liverpool were down to ten men. Despite dangerous tackles and yellow cards flying around, this wasn't because anyone had been sent off. With around ten minutes left, Riise had clipped Arteta as he raced clear and in the process earned himself some torn ankle ligaments. With Liverpool's three permitted subs on the pitch, the visitors had to play out the remainder of the game at a numerical disadvantage.

Although this contributed to Everton's dominance of possession, it can't explain the third and final goal. With the final whistle approaching, Gary Naysmith fed Carsley in space 25 yards out. The Everton midfielder had time to unleash a blistering drive that Reina parried into the air.

'He punched the shot away upwards, but the ball was still heading back to goal,' says Mark Godfrey. 'So then, Reina ran back and sort of caught the ball on the line. But, realising that his momentum would carry it over, he opted to sort of toss it into the air. Johnson was following up, and he was presented with the simple task of heading it into the roof of the net. It was a strange goal. Reina really ballsed things up. But then, they all count, don't they?'

Everton had not just won, they had won convincingly. Such a rarity in the modern era was savoured by all involved, not least the man who had masterminded it, as Dave Prentice recalls:

'At the end of that game, David Moyes was interviewed. After doing the normal Sunday newspapers press conference, he was ushered on to the staircase to do the presser for the Monday papers, directly above the main entrance. The fans were congregating outside the Winslow and singing the Andy Johnson song. Moyes was in his element. He opened the window and smugly told those there, most of whom were Reds, "Ah, listen to that." We spent the remainder of the interview with that as the backdrop while Moyes took the piss out of the Liverpool-supporting journalists. It was a very sweet and unprofessional way to finish the afternoon.'

v Fiorentina 2–0

(2–2 on aggregate (Fiorentina win 4–2 on penalties)
12 March 2008
UEFA Cup Round of 16, Second Leg
Goodison Park. Attendance: 38,026

Everton: Howard, Neville, Yobo, Jagielka, Lescott, Arteta, Osman, Carsley, Pienaar (Anichebe) Yakubu, Johnson (Gravesen)

Fiorentina: Frey, Ujfalusi, Dainelli, Gamberini, Pasqual, Kuzmanovic (Gobbi), Donadel, Montolivo, Jorgensen (Santana), Osvaldo, Vieri (Pazzini)

Referee: E. Braamhaar

Purple Pain

DESPITE Everton's Herculean effort to finish in fourth place in 2005, their quest for Champions League glory had fallen at the first hurdle, after the side was knocked out in the qualifying rounds by Villareal. This was then followed by a swift exit from the UEFA Cup at the hands of Dinamo București.

Everton's next opportunity for European glory came two seasons later, when a sixth-placed finish booked entry into the 2007/08 UEFA Cup. Such adventures were important for the club.

'Financially, Europe began to matter more and more in the 1990s and 2000s,' says Rob Wilson, football finance expert at Sheffield Hallam University. 'The money involved, and the impact on "brand value", specifically in the Champions League could often make the difference between a club being able to compete and it failing to keep up with the pace.'

After dispatching Metalist Kharkiv over two legs in the first round, Everton entered the group stage to face Nürnberg, Zenit St. Petersburg, AZ Alkmaar and Larissa. These games coincided with an upturn in the form of the Blues in the league, which was carried over into Europe. Everton swept all before them, winning each game and topping the group.

An 8–1 aggregate win over Norwegian side SK Brann in the round of 32 set up a tantalising tie against Fiorentina in the last 16.

Despite finishing only sixth in Serie A during the previous season, La Viola had done so while enduring a 15-point deduction, incurred because of the club's participation in the Calciopoli scandal (which saw major clubs, including Fiorentina, Juventus and AC Milan, involved in match-fixing). In reality, Fiorentina had finished just a couple of points behind second-positioned Roma. This was a Champions League-quality team in all but name.

'We were looking forward to going out there, playing against one of the best sides in Europe,' recalls former Everton forward Yakubu Aiyegbeni. 'Both sides were on good form, so we thought that the tie was neatly balanced.

Although I enjoyed the wonderful atmosphere of their stadium, in the end, we just didn't play to our best, so it was very disappointing.'

In the Stadio Artemio Franchi, Everton put in one of their worst performances of the season. Second best throughout, the Blues failed to register a single shot on target and were lucky that, despite their complete dominance, Fiorentina were only able to emerge 2–0 victors, with goals from Kuzmanovic and Montolivo.

'We just weren't good enough,' a shell-shocked David Moyes told the *Liverpool Echo*. 'Some did not play to their potential – in fact the majority did not … The best team won. It is a big job because Fiorentina are a good team. On that performance we need to be a lot better!'

The return leg took place a week later, on a cold Wednesday night. Progression would be a challenge, but one that, should it happen, would put Everton into the final eight of a European competition – a rarity for the Blues.

'Sometimes the Goodison crowd works best when it is in harmony with the players,' remembers Dave Prentice. 'On that night, that was the case. Both elements of what makes Goodison so special and such a hard ground to come to were in unison. The players were up for the game and so was the crowd. The noise was incredible; the place was absolutely rocking.'

What Everton needed more than anything was a good start, and, for once, that's what they got. Just past the quarter-hour mark, a cross from Pienaar on the left should have been routine for Frey, the Fiorentina keeper. But, rather than gather it safely, he misjudged its flight and palmed the ball across his goal, where it fortuitously hit the onrushing Andy Johnson.

At 2–1 on aggregate, the tie was on. The crowd sensed it, and Everton's performance levels could not have been more different compared with the game that had taken place a week earlier.

'From the goal onwards, there was only one team in it for most of that match,' says Dave Prentice. 'Everton were magnificent, carving open the Italians and constantly threatening at goal. It was almost a mirror image of the away tie.'

That Fiorentina remained in the game at all was entirely attributable to their goalkeeper, as Ian Doyle reported in the *Liverpool Daily Post*:

'Frey in particular seemed intent on making amends for his earlier blunder with a string of fine saves. His first, repelling a 25-yard Arteta free-kick, was more for the benefit of the cameras than anything else. But the keeper was alert to parry Osman's powerful drive in the 26th minute.'

Frey was at it again ten minutes later, when Yakubu bamboozled the Fiorentina centre-half Gamberini and smacked a low shot that was blocked by the keeper. In contrast to the ever-busy Frey, Tim Howard was called into action just the once, a routine save from Jorgensen's side-footed volley.

'When the side went in at half-time,' recalls Simon Hart, 'short of getting that second goal they had done everything we could have asked of them. It was a magnificent display, a Moyes Everton at its best: strong, organised and threatening in all the right ways.'

As the second half started, Everton maintained their pressure. Early on, Fiorentina had two fortunate escapes, first when Pasqual cleared a deflected Arteta corner off the line, and later when Ujfalusi was lucky to avoid conceding a penalty after the ball struck his hand inside the area.

As the minutes ticked along, it was all Everton. But, in the face of a dogged defence and a keeper in inspired form, there was a sense that it would take something special to level the tie. Around the 70th-minute mark, Arteta took a pass and drove forward towards the Fiorentina 18-yard box. With their defence uncharacteristically switched off and backing away, from around 25 yards out he unleashed an angled shot that fizzed into Frey's bottom right-hand corner.

'I remember that it felt as though the whole ground had taken in an intake of breath', says Peter Mcpartland, 'as the ball left Arteta's boot and then it seemed to take ages for it to hit the back of the net. When it did, the noise was incredible.'

Sensing the game was there for the taking, Everton piled forward. But once again Frey was there to thwart the side's dreams. First, he saved point-blank from Yakubu, when the Everton forward had toe-poked an effort towards goal from an Arteta corner. He then thwarted the Nigerian again not long after when he palmed away his headed goalbound effort.

'We played some great football that night and had some great chances,' feels Yakubu. 'Sometimes the luck doesn't go your way, and, on that occasion, their keeper was amazing. On another day, we would have taken those chances and gone through with ease.'

As the game became more stretched, both in normal and in extra time, Fiorentina began to find some space, and before the 120 minutes were up either side could have taken the honours. Pazzini came close on a few occasions, and at the other end Frey continued to frustrate Everton. But, ultimately, the score would remain unaltered, making it 2–2 on aggregate. The tie would be decided by penalties.

'It was a great shame that we hadn't gone through,' says Peter Mcpartland. 'We deserved to. We had battered Fiorentina, and it was frustrating that it was going to be decided in that way.'

Everton started proceedings with Thomas Gravesen calmly converting to make it 1–0. Pazzini levelled before Yakubu stroked a delicate strike against the post (the fear surging within the hearts of Evertonians watching).

Montolivo put La Viola ahead, Arteta scored for the Blues and then Osvaldo made it 2–3.

Next came Phil Jagielka. With almost no run-up, he belted the ball down the middle of the goal, where (perhaps unsurprisingly) Frey got a hand to the strike and palmed the ball away.

Against a chorus of boos, Santana then ran up and placed Fiorentina's final penalty into the bottom-right corner, making it 2–4 to the visitors and ensuring that, once again, Everton's European dreams had come to nothing.

'It was a heartbreaking moment,' admits Dave Prentice. 'To have come so close and fallen at the final hurdle. You could feel the sense of disappointment all around Goodison.'

Everton had fought valiantly yet fallen short. But, as Phil Neville outlined to the *Echo*, the Blues could take heart from what they had done:

'After a monumental performance the word which springs to mind after that is proud – I'm proud to play with this set of players. I thought we were fantastic. We should have won the game by four or five goals. There's a lot of fighting qualities in our dressing room, but more importantly there's a lot of quality. We took on the fourth best team in Italy tonight; I've watched videos of them and I've never seen them have that many chances created against them in four videos, never mind one. We can be proud of the way we've played.'

Despite the defeat, the atmosphere that night, combined with the stirring performance, helped weave Everton v Fiorentina into the tapestry of great games that the club and the fans have enjoyed over the years.

'In some ways, you can look at that as such an "Everton" night,' says Simon Hart. 'If that had been Liverpool, they would probably have pushed for that third goal and got it in a flukey manner, maybe bouncing in off a defender's arse. But we have a magical European night and it ends with us not just exiting but exiting by losing a penalty shoot-out. And yet, we still look back on it fondly. Whether for good or ill, that's such an "Everton" thing to do.'

v Manchester United 0–0

(Everton win 4-2 on penalties)
19 April 2009
FA Cup Semi-final
Wembley Stadium. Attendance: 88,141

Everton: Howard, Hibbert, Jagielka, Lescott, Baines, Osman, Neville, Fellaini (Vaughan), Pienaar, Cahill, Saha (Rodwell)

Manchester United: Foster, R. Da Silva, Ferdinand, Vidic, F. Da Silva (Evra), Welbeck, Gibson, Anderson, Park (Scholes), Tevez, Macheda (Berbatov)

Referee: M. Riley

Penalty Kings II

SINCE taking charge at Everton, David Moyes had effected a transformation at Goodison Park. The days of struggle that had characterised the late Royle era, Kendall's swansong and the grim Smith years, times when Blue eyes were near constantly fixed on what was happening at the bottom of the table, seemed to have passed.

Top-six finishes, European football and a squad filled with genuine talent, such as Leighton Baines, Tim Cahill and Tim Howard, had produced a club that the fans could have faith in – one that suggested brighter times to come, and which had slowly banished the dark memories of the recent past.

But, for all the improvement, tangible reward had proven elusive. The trophy cabinet remained resolutely locked, silverware hard to come by. For many supporters, Everton could not truly claim to be 'back' until the club captain held something shiny aloft.

In the 2008/09 campaign, there were with four avenues to silverware open to the club: the league, the League Cup, the UEFA Cup and the FA Cup. As is customary for Everton, the League Cup fell by the wayside early on as the Blues exited in the third round at the hands of Blackburn Rovers. In the UEFA, Everton fared no better, going out in the first round to Standard Liege.

In the league, always a very long shot, Everton had performed well, but, as the title run-in approached, the club was unsurprisingly off the pace. So, for those hoping that Moyes could cement Everton's revival with some silverware, all that remained was the FA Cup.

'At that point,' says Lyndon Lloyd, 'it had been over a decade since Everton had last visited the "Home of Football". Under Moyes, despite our revival, the FA Cup had not been a particularly happy hunting ground. We seemed to be developing a habit of being knocked out early on, so I doubt many Blues invested much faith in that particular competition to begin with.'

For once, though, Moyes put together a good cup run, as Macclesfield Town, Aston Villa and Middlesbrough were dispatched. There was even a win against Liverpool in the fourth round – rare enough at the best of times (rarer still in the cup).

'We'd vanquished a title-chasing Liverpool in a replay,' remembers Simon Hart, 'an outcome that most of us would never see coming. As we progressed, that was a result that lent credence to the belief that our name could be on the cup.'

The defeat of Middlesbrough in the quarter-finals booked Everton a tip to Wembley to face Manchester United, at that point chasing an historic quadruple. FA Cup semi-finalists, top of the table, League Cup winners and semi-finalists in the Champions League, Alex Ferguson's side, which boasted the likes of Cristiano Ronaldo, Wayne Rooney and Paul Scholes, were on the cusp of achieving something truly remarkable (if they could hold their nerve).

Despite facing such a formidable opponent, there remained confidence in the Everton camp.

'We've acquitted ourselves well over the two games against United so far this season,' Leighton Baines told the *Liverpool Echo*. 'We drew at Goodison and we were beaten by one goal at Old Trafford. We always feel we are capable of nicking a goal, and if we keep it close then by making sure that we stay tight at the back we definitely have a chance.'

Allied to the squad's confidence, there was also a touch of good fortune. United's chasing of the quadruple meant that their attention was spread. With important fixtures either side of the semi-final, Alex Ferguson was compelled to think carefully about selection.

In the end, he chose to prioritise the league and Europe. As the lesser of the three competitions (along with the fact that Everton were thought beatable by a weakened United side), the FA Cup was given second billing.

When the teams were announced for the game, Ferguson had made several changes from the side that had played (and won) against Porto in the Champions League a few days earlier, dropping the likes of Rooney, Ronaldo and Van der Sar. By contrast, David Moyes picked his strongest starting eleven.

'The team selection gave us a helping hand,' argues Mark Godfrey, 'but don't forget we were still facing a United side that was blessed with international quality. Everton remained the underdogs.'

As the respective team sheets illustrated, each club viewed the competition differently. But so too did the supporters, thinks Dave Prentice:

'While many of United's fans strolled in shortly before kick-off, the Everton section was awash with colour, noise and song long before the beginning of the game: almost every fan in the West Stand decked in royal blue. It was evident from what you could see and hear that the Evertonians wanted this more. This was what we had been waiting for. Starved of success and silverware, the Evertonians were making the most of their day.'

And as the teams kicked off, this divergent attitude, this desire, this hunger for meaningful silverware was evident in the two teams, as though each were feeding off their supporters' complacency/yearning. Everton raced out of the blocks, playing the semi-final like a Goodison derby, all flying tackles, heavy challenges, crunching intent. United, by contrast, were lethargic, almost treating the day like a training exercise.

But, irrespective of the approach taken by each side, they both shared something in common, namely an absence of quality. Poor control, wayward passes and lapses of concentration suggested two sides that appeared unable to find their rhythm.

Despite this, inevitably, there were some moments of drama. Everton had some half-chances early on, Phil Neville sent a shot harmlessly over and Saha almost embarrassed Foster when the goalkeeper dawdled on a back-pass. And then, as the break approached, United began to threaten. Tevez struck wide under pressure before Welbeck hit a volley that deflected narrowly wide off Lescott from Rafael's cross.

'It was a poor first half, though,' says Mark Godfrey. 'It's possible that a stronger United would have found us wanting. But 0–0 at half-time against the league leaders wasn't bad.'

The second half pretty much aped the first. Everton came out of the blocks, buoyed by the crowd and bristling with energy. Cahill smacked an early 25-yard stinger that forced a fine save from Foster, and Saha had a half-chance that went wide.

And then, once again, the game turned cagey before United began to assert a degree of menace. Park Ji-Sung dragged a shot just wide, and Gibson belted one in from long range that Howard palmed away.

In a half largely devoid of excitement, one moment of contention did occur with 20 minutes to go.

'Sensing hesitation in the Everton defence,' reported the *Liverpool Daily Post*, 'Welbeck reached a loose ball ahead of Howard only to go tumbling inside the area under pressure from Jagielka. Mike Riley waved play on, Ferguson fumed, and even the defender later admitted Moyes's side had enjoyed something of a lucky escape.'

Full time arrived, and with it, extra time. United now boasted Scholes and Berbatov on for Park Ji-Sung and Macheda, while Moyes had thrown on Rodwell and Vaughan for Saha and Fellaini.

Not that any of it made much difference. Chances remained limited, and when the referee blew to signal the end of 120 minutes, it merely confirmed what most watching had known for some time, that one of these sides was exiting the cup in the cruellest way possible.

'First up on penalties was Tim Cahill,' wrote Luke O'Farrell in *Everton Tales and Other Tall Stories*, 'but the Australian blazed his spot kick into the red sea of United supporters behind the goal. First blood to the opposition, my pessimistic nature took over; we were doomed, or so I thought. Fortunately, for those of the Blue persuasion, Dimitar Berbatov attempted a penalty draped in his languid style. Tim Howard saved easily courtesy of his trailing leg. Game on!'

Baines then blasted Everton ahead, before Howard rose to the occasion once again by saving Ferdinand's fine effort. Advantage Everton!

Neville calmly sent Foster the wrong way, Vidic and Vaughan traded penalties, before Anderson coolly bamboozled Howard to keep United in the game.

And so it fell (again) to Phil Jagielka. Understandably nervous, a few wise words from Moyes enabled Everton's defensive stalwart to find the strength for one last push.

'Before the penalty shoot-out, the manager knew we were a bit fragile,' he told the *Echo*. 'So he told us that he was as proud as punch and we had nothing to lose. We were still underdogs and he could see there were nerves but he settled us down.'

Betraying not an ounce of nerves, 'Jags' calmly strode up. This being a centre-half, and not one particularly known for his deftness of touch, most would have expected him to belt his effort (much as had been the case against Fiorentina). But he didn't. Instead, Jagielka stroked the ball into the bottom-right corner.

Cue pandemonium amongst the Everton supporters. 'I remember turning to my son as Jag scored,' remembers Dave Prentice. 'But he was gone. He was around three or four rows in front, lost in the magic of it all. It was that kind of moment.'

After an announcement regarding the final, 'Z Cars' rang out over the PA. 'I must admit there was a tear or two,' wrote Luke O'Farrell. 'Thousands singing along, hundreds dancing on their seats, strangers hugging each other, it is a struggle to serve justice to those scenes. Nevertheless, to paraphrase Alan Harper, when 'Z Cars' rang out over the PA and the fans joined in, it was a moment I wanted to bottle and keep forever.'

v Manchester United 1–0

4 December 2013
Premier League
Old Trafford. Attendance: 75,210

Everton: Howard, Coleman, Distin, Jagielka, Oviedo, McCarthy, Barry, Pienaar (Osman), Barkley (Deulofeu), Mirallas (Naismith), Lukaku

Manchester United: De Gea, Da Silva (Januzaj), Vidic, Smalling, Evra, Fellaini, Giggs, Valencia, Kagawa (Nani), Welbeck (Hernandez), Rooney

Referee: M. Atkinson

Oviedo Baby!

DESPITE the rivalry that exists between the two cities, head-to-heads between Manchester United and Everton contain none of the toxicity that is conjured up when the Red halves of each city meet.

But although far from toxic, back in 2013 there was a frisson of resentment directed towards United from the Blue half of Liverpool. When David Moyes had left Everton to take the manager's job at Old Trafford in the summer, he had gone while largely still appreciated by the supporters. At his final home game in charge, a 2–0 victory over West Ham United, Moyes had been given a guard of honour by the players and a standing ovation from the crowd.

'By the end of his tenure,' says Lyndon Lloyd, 'there might have been the sense that perhaps he was installing a self-imposed glass ceiling at Goodison. But, despite this, I think most fans appreciated what he had done for us, certainly enough for us to feel slightly disappointed that we were being ditched in favour of United, however understandable that decision was.'

Over the course of the summer, though, a slight hardening of attitude occurred towards the Scot. Behind it lay his attempts to lure Leighton Baines and Marouane Fellaini to Old Trafford for as little as possible. A cumulative bid of £28m was tabled for two of the club's best players, which was dismissed as 'derisory and insulting' by the Everton board. Considering it valued Fellaini at £16m (just £1m more than Everton had paid for him), there was some validity to that assertion.

'I remain a fan of Moyes, but it felt like a shitty way to treat us,' argues Phil Redmond. 'It definitely caused some bad blood. If you were a fan who didn't like the way he left, then it hardened your attitude against him. If you were a fan who accepted why he left, it cast him in a slightly different, more unsavoury light. From either perspective, he didn't emerge well from the episode.'

In the end, only Fellaini left, for a very generous £27.5m (a late-summer panic buy by United). Everton's new manager, Roberto Martinez, used some of this largesse to bring additions to the squad: loanees Romelu Lukaku,

Gareth Barry and Gerard Deulofeu, and permanent signings Arouna Koné, Joel Robles and James McCarthy.

It was a flurry of transfer activity that perfectly illustrates that sometimes it really is advisable to try before you buy.

Although not all of these were successes, the addition of new talent and a more free-spirited, attack-minded approach to the game worked well for Everton as the campaign kicked off. Prior to the trip to Old Trafford, Martinez's men sat seventh in the table.

'We had started the season well,' says Martinez. 'The style of play I had in mind and the process of renewal I was attempting to introduce was going to take time. But, with the addition of some new players and new ideas, I was pleased with how we had begun. The players were being creative, looking to get on the ball and playing some great attacking football. And, at the same time, we were defending well and making Everton a tough team to play against. I was very pleased with how we were progressing.'

But, although form suggested that Everton were in with a shout, history did not. At that point it had been over 20 years since the Blues had beaten United at the 'Theatre of Dreams': a 3–0 drubbing masterminded by Howard Kendall's tactical nous and Robert Warzycha's silky skills back in 1992. The bookies had United as overwhelming favourites, as they and pundits alike expected another red victory.

'Like most Blues,' says Simon Hart, 'you looked at the away game at Old Trafford in the same way that you viewed going away to the Emirates or Anfield, as simply a write-off. Although we were playing well, I don't imagine there were many of us whose outlook differed to those held by the wider football world.'

Riding high on the momentum of a 4–0 drubbing handed out to Stoke City a few days earlier, Everton started the game brightly. The front three of Lukaku, Barkley and Mirallas were fizzing with energy. Mirallas was unlucky not to score early on with a rasping 20-yard shot that forced a smart save from de Gea in the United goal.

But, from the quarter-of-an-hour mark, United began to grow into the game. First, Rooney, from eight yards out, forced a decent save from Howard. Then Giggs glanced a header wide from Valencia's right-wing cross. Everton next really rode their luck when Rooney's shot deflected off Distin and struck the base of the post. Fortunately for the Blues, the wrong-footed Howard was able to clear with his foot before Kagawa could pounce on the rebound.

As the break approached, Everton came back into the game and both sides indulged in a period of frenzied attacking football, Barkley wasted a great chance when, with United outnumbered on the counter-attack, he overhit a pass to Lukaku. At the other end, Rooney was gifted a second bite after misreading Kagawa's cross, but his improvised flick was held.

'The first half was very encouraging,' says Martinez. 'We were playing Manchester United at Old Trafford, so obviously we expected them to have chances. But we had defended well, had plenty of possession and caused them problems too. Before the game, my players had looked focused and confident, so that was exactly the kind of performance I had expected.'

For much of the early part of the second half, the Blues spent large spells attempting to contain United. Despite pleas from the home crowd for United to 'attack, attack, attack', their efforts were frustrated by a resolute Everton.

Lyndon Lloyd wrote on ToffeeWeb: 'With James McCarthy and Gareth Barry in invincible mood as the holding pair in midfield – the former seemingly covering every blade of grass as he hunted United's midfielders down, the latter breaking things up defensively and controlling the tempo when the Blues were in possession – and both Oviedo and Coleman now tenaciously keeping things as tight as they could on United's flanks, Moyes cut an increasingly frustrated figure in front of his dugout.'

With half an hour left, both benches turned to youth. United brought on their Belgian youngster Adnan Januzaj, and Everton withdrew Barkley for Barcelona loanee Gerard Deulofeu. Both had an instant impact, Deulofeu firing a decent chance straight at de Gea and Januzaj forcing a smart stop from Howard.

With the end approaching, United must have then thought the game was theirs when Welbeck was presented with a gilt-edged opportunity after Howard had saved Evra's point-blank header. But, with the goal at his mercy, the United forward could only head the rebound at the bar, and for the second time that night the woodwork came to Everton's rescue.

Perhaps sensing that the footballing gods were on their side, Everton began to push and unquestionably finished the game stronger. With four minutes of normal time remaining, their efforts yielded an unforgettable reward.

On the attack and with Blue shirts filling the United box, the ball fell to Jagielka 25 yards out. A precision pass was played into Lukaku, who held Fellaini off, turned and hit a speculative shot/cross low and hard across the United six-yard box.

Since arrival, Martinez had been encouraging his full-backs to get up the pitch, and often you could see the likes of Coleman and Baines playing as high as the front men. It was an approach that paid off handsomely that night. With three United defenders caught ball-watching, Bryan Oviedo (in at left-back for the injured Baines) stole in at the far post and drove the ball past a helpless de Gea.

According to Lyndon Lloyd, the enormity of what was happening was not confined to the Blues in the crowd, who had exploded in response:

'As the ball went in, I remember Coleman stood in disbelief, unsure what to do with himself. Oviedo skidded to his knees was mobbed by his team-mates. And even Lukaku, a player that the media, even back then, portrayed as some kind of mercenary, stopping off on his way to better things, fell to his knees before punching the turf in delight. Those players knew what that goal meant.'

When the final whistle sounded a few minutes later, the 3,000 Evertonians that had made the trip partied like it was 1992. But amidst the untrammelled joy there remained a slight undercurrent of sharpness directed to the club's former boss. 'Oh David Moyes is full of shit!' rang out from the crowd. Memories of that final game against West Ham, when Moyes had been applauded by the Goodison faithful, were seemingly confined to the past.

While Everton's former manager might have cut a dejected and forlorn figure, for the club's new boss, it was a much happier occasion.

'That was more than a football game for us,' says Martinez. 'It was about mentality. Before the game, someone told me that it was 20 years since Everton had won at Old Trafford. To try and start challenging the better teams we had to believe we could meet them at their level and win. So that day was about making sure that we pushed each other mentally to do that. And I was really proud in that respect. It wasn't our best performance that season. I think we played a lot better in other games but at Old Trafford we had a real mentality. And I think it gave us a huge boost during the rest of the season.'

Everton, playing wonderful attacking football, would go on to finish that season in fifth place, collecting 72 points, the highest number the club has ever achieved in the Premier League era.

'Results like the one against United gave a huge amount of confidence to that side,' says Mark Godfrey. 'They were wonderful to watch, and for a time there we thought that Martinez might be the man to take us to the next level. Sadly, in the end, that turned out not to be the case. But, despite his later failings, he did give us a fantastic season and some days and nights that, as Blues, we will never, ever forget.'

Epilogue

SO that's your lot, 50 gems from Everton's past. To be honest, I was hoping to include one from the Koeman era too, a final chapter that would have ended on a truly high point. But it wasn't to be. Despite the improvement, the sense of a club that has turned a corner, the feeling that better times are on the horizon, Everton still ended Koeman's first campaign without silverware, without victory over Liverpool and without a game that could really be defined as a 'great' (even if that 4–0 win over Manchester City gave me cause for reflection).

It would be comforting to think that if I wrote this book in another few years, with the Koeman era in full swing, with the Moshiri money behind the club and with the possibility of Everton ensconced within a brand new stadium, then later chapters would be populated with new memories to rival those from the club's past.

At the time of writing, though, this is a mere hope. It could very well be that those memories don't come true, that Everton continue on the same path, that tangible success remains tantalisingly out of reach.

This latter perspective would be familiar to most Evertonians. As a group, we are often weighed down by our pessimism. The years of 'nearly' and the sense of a club that has consistently thrown opportunities away have coloured our perspective.

But, if this book proves anything, it's that Everton have only had so many 'nearlys' because we have been amongst the best for so long (an achievement in itself) and that there have always been times when we have tapped into our potential and risen to the top.

And, more often than not, the times when we have done this have been preceded by eras of misery and disappointment. Dixieland came after the barren post-war years, the time of Catterick and Moores followed on from the grim 1940s and 1950s, and the glory of the first Kendall era came on the heels of the frustrating 1970s. Everton have made a habit of turning a corner just when such a turn seemed at its most unlikely.

But, until that happens, we will have to make do with our past. When the parishioners of St Domingo's first began kicking a ball around the local park, nobody could have foreseen what their endeavours would become. The media might paint it otherwise, but Everton are something unique in English football. Other clubs might have had more success, might have more money, might have a greater global reach, but none have our history. We've been around for a very long time, and, for most of that, we've been at the top.

Everton really are a Grand Old Team to play for and a Grand Old Team to support.

Acknowledgments

WITH regard to the book, I would like to say a big thanks to everyone who agreed to be interviewed. Each person featured has been exceptionally generous with their time, and I hope that they're satisfied with the outcome.

Special thanks need to go to my dad (Brian Keoghan) and mum (Lin Keoghan) for invaluable research assistance, and to Darren Griffiths and Pat Labone for helping me secure important interviewees (and putting up with my countless emails).

Several newspapers have been kind enough to allow me to reproduce their work, for which I would like to say thanks. These are the *Liverpool Echo*, the *Liverpool Daily Post* and the *Lancashire Evening Post*. Special thanks to Trinity Mirror for their assistance in this area.

Some online publications have been kind enough to reproduce elements of their work, including the *Football Pink*, Sporting Intelligence and *The Blizzard*.

And I have also used quotes from a number of books: *Only the Best Is Good Enough: The Howard Kendall Story*; *The Cannonball Kid*; Howard Kendall's *Love Affairs & Marriage: My Life in Football*; *Harry Catterick: The Untold Story of a Football Great*; *When the Cheering Stopped*; *Three Sides of the Mersey: Oral History of Everton, Liverpool and Tranmere Rovers*; and *A Different Road*.

I am thankful for the permission provided by authors/publishers.

At Pitch Publishing, I'm grateful to Paul for giving me this opportunity and would like to thank everyone else there who's been involved with the creation of the book.

On a personal level, Emma and Jamie have continued to provide a welcome and much-needed distraction. The former (a girl with no interest in football) is kind enough to feign interest in what I do, and the latter (a boy who loves football) is also kind enough to feign interest in what I do.

But I save my biggest thanks, as always, for Nicky, without whom there would be no book. You have no interest in Everton (there's a theme here) and yet put up with me talking about the club, its history and the book. And, what's worse, I make you read about it all too, as you patiently correct my appalling grasp of spelling and grammar while proofreading.

Although the cups of tea have actually diminished in number (something once thought numerically impossible) I am forever grateful for the support you give me.

Bibliography

Books

Clegg, Barbara. *The Man Who Made Littlewoods: The Story of John Moores* (Hodder & Stoughton 1993).

Corbett, James. *Everton: The School of Science* (deCoubertin Books 2010).

Cottee, Tony. *My Autobiography: Claret & Blues* (Independent UK Sports Publications 1995).

Galvin, Robert; & the National Football Museum. *The Football Hall of Fame: The Ultimate Guide to the Greatest Footballing Legends of All Time* (Portico 2011).

Groom, Andy. *The Illustrated Everton Story* (Apex Publishing 2014).

Harvey, Colin. *Colin Harvey's Everton Secrets: 40 Years at Goodison from Catterick to Moyes* (Trinity Mirror Sport Media 2006).

Hickson, Dave. *The Cannonball Kid* (deCoubertin Books 2014).

Keith, John. *Dixie Dean: The Inside Story of a Football Icon* (Robson Books 2001).

Kendall, Howard. *Love Affairs & Marriage: My Life in Football* (deCoubertin Books 2013).

Kendall, Howard; & Ross, Ian. *Only the Best Is Good Enough: The Howard Kendall Story* (Mainstream Publishing 1991).

Keoghan, Jim. *Highs, Lows and Bakayokos* (Pitch Publishing 2016).

Keoghan, Jim. *Punk Football: The Rise of Fan Ownership in English Football* (Pitch Publishing 2014).

Labone, Brian. *Defence at the Top* (Pelham, 1968).

Latchford, Bob. *A Different Road* (deCoubertin Books 2015).

Lawton, Tommy. *When the Cheering Stopped* (Golden Eagle 1973).

Metcalf, Mark. *Everton FC 1890/91: The First Kings of Anfield* (Amberley Publishing 2013).

NSNO.co.uk. *Cup Final Blues* (lulu.com 2009).

Pattullo, Alan. *In Search of Duncan Ferguson: The Life and Crimes of a Footballing Enigma* (Mainstream Publishing 2015).

Prentice, Dave. *Ten Years Blues* (Bluecoat Press 2003).

Rogers, Ken. *Goodison Glory: The Official History Hardcover* (Breedon 1998).

Royle, Joe. *The Autobiography* (BBC Books 2005).

Sawyer, Rob. *Harry Catterick: The Untold Story of a Football Great* (deCoubertin Books 2014).

Everton Greatest Games: The Toffees Fifty Finest Matches

Southall, Neville. *The Binman Chronicles* (deCoubertin Books 2015).

Tallentire, Becky. *Still Talking Blue: A Collection of Candid Interviews with Everton Heroes* (Mainstream Publishing 2002).

Taylor, Rogan P.; Williams, John; & Ward, Andrew. *Three Sides of the Mersey: Oral History of Everton, Liverpool and Tranmere Rovers* (Robson Books 1993).

Newspapers

Accrington Observer 1888
Cricket and Football Field 1892
Football Express 1928
Lancashire Evening Post 1888
Liverpool Courier / Daily Courier 1890–1925
Liverpool Daily Post 1887–2013
Liverpool Echo 1906–2014
Liverpool Football Echo 1906–1953
Liverpool Evening Express 1915–1937
Liverpool Mercury 1887–1893
Liverpool Post and Mercury 1915–1932
North Wales Chronicle 1894
Sunderland Daily Echo and Shipping Gazette 1935

Magazine Articles

James Corbett, 'Namesakes' (*The Blizzard* – The Football Quarterly: Issue Seventeen, 2015 p43)

Online Articles

ToffeeWeb: Tony Onslow, 'In Search of John Houlding'
https://www.toffeeweb.com/season/15-16/comment/history/32552.html

When Saturday Comes: Roger Titford, 'Football League, 1888–89'
http://www.wsc.co.uk/the-archive/23-Season-in-brief/1498-football-league-1888-89

The Daisy Cutter: Steven S, 'This Weekend in Football History: 13 October 1894 – The First Merseyside Derby'

http://www.thedaisycutter.co.uk/2012/10/this-weekend-in-football-history-13-october-1894-the-first-merseyside-derby/

Sporting Intelligence: John Roberts, 'Dixie Dean'

http://www.sportingintelligence.com/2010/03/09/dixie-dean-i-never-had-any-lessons-at-school-no-maths-no-english-nothing-except-football/

The Guardian: Frank Keating, 'The Incomparable Dixie Dean'

https://www.theguardian.com/football/2014/nov/24/dixie-dean-everton-interview-frank-keating-archive-1977

The Guardian, Tom Donnelly, 'From the vault: Everton, Liverpool, Tottenham and Arsenal in top four'

https://www.theguardian.com/sport/blog/2013/oct/04/from-vault-everton-tottenham-liverpool-arsenal

The Guardian: Jason Rodrigues, '"The Battle of Goodison" at 50: 1964, Everton and Leeds lose their manners and tempers'

https://www.theguardian.com/football/from-the-archive-blog/2014/nov/07/everton-leeds-football-goodison-1964-archive

The Guardian: James Corbett, 'Bob Latchford'

https://www.theguardian.com/sport/2006/mar/05/features.sport12

The Guardian: Scott Murray, 'The Joy of Six: Merseyside Derby Moments'

https://www.theguardian.com/football/blog/2011/sep/30/joy-of-six-merseyside-derby

The Guardian: Lawrence Ostlere, 'Golden Goal: Wayne Rooney for Everton v Arsenal (2002)'

https://www.theguardian.com/football/blog/2016/jan/08/golden-goal-wayne-rooney-everton-arsenal-2002

The Guardian: David Lacey, 'Everton's league winners in 1986–87 were worthy of "unstinted praise"'

https://www.theguardian.com/football/blog/2013/oct/04/everton-1987-first-division-winners-unstinted-praise

Those Magical Nights: Sam Carney, 'Dixie Dean: goal machine'

https://thosemagicalnights.wordpress.com/2014/11/03/dixie-dean-goal-machine/

These Football Times: Brian Benjamin, 'Dixie Dean: Football's first great number 9'

http://thesefootballtimes.co/2015/07/06/dixie-dean-footballs-first-great-number-9/

Everton Greatest Games: The Toffees Fifty Finest Matches

The Mighty, Mighty Whites: Dave Tomlinson, '7 November 1964 – Everton 0 Leeds United 1'

http://www.mightyleeds.co.uk/matches/19641107.htm

Dixies60: Ed Bottomley, '60 Games That Shook Goodison: #7 Everton vs Leeds "The Battle of Goodison"'

http://www.dixies60.com/2011/05/22/60-games-that-shook-goodison-7-everton-vs-leeds-the-battle-of-goodison/

GotNotGot: thefoxfanzine, 'The 1977 League Cup Final – The One Month Final'

https://gotnotgot.wordpress.com/2013/04/15/the-1977-league-cup-final-the-one-month-final/

The *Football Pink*: Steve Mitchell, 'Bob Latchford'

https://footballpink.net/2015/11/18/everton-legend-bob-latchford-speaks-to-the-football-pink/

Sporting Intelligence: Andreas Selliaas, 'Bob Latchford and Me: a Boy's Own Tale'

http://www.sportingintelligence.com/2016/04/28/bob-latchford-and-me-a-boys-own-tale-280401/

That 1980s Sports Blog: Steven Pye, '1981 FA Cup Fourth Round: Everton v Liverpool'

http://that1980ssportsblog.blogspot.co.uk/2016/01/1981-fa-cup-fourth-round-everton-v-liverpool.html

Everton Viral: Luke O'Farrell, 'Road To Wembley'

http://evertonviral.com/road-to-wembley/

Information Sites

11 v 11
http://www.11v11.com
BBC Sport
http://www.bbc.co.uk/sport
Blue Correspondent
http://www.bluecorrespondent.co.uk
The Everton Collection
http://www.evertoncollection.org.uk/home
Everton FC
http://www.evertonfc.com

Everton Results
http://www.evertonresults.com
Everton Seasons
https://en.wikipedia.org/wiki/List_of_Everton_F.C._seasons
Historical Kits
http://www.historicalkits.co.uk
Liverpool FC
http://www.liverpoolfc.com
Stats Football
http://stats.football.co.uk
ToffeeWeb
http://toffeeweb.com

Visual and Audio

FA Cup Final, Everton v Manchester City, 29 April 1933 (1)
https://www.youtube.com/watch?v=k1BTYQSa8WA
FA Cup Final, Everton v Manchester City, 29 April 1933 (2)
https://www.youtube.com/watch?v=PkgLWaXKn4Y
Everton Former Players' Foundation interview: 1966 FA Cup Final hero, Mike Trebilcock
https://www.youtube.com/watch?v=y-SpVTfnFBw&t=2160s
European Cup second round, second leg, Everton v Borussia Mönchengladbach, 4 November 1970
https://www.youtube.com/watch?v=o-9NVX6Csq0
League Cup Final second replay, Everton v Aston Villa, 13 April 1977
https://www.youtube.com/watch?v=Ci30iFaU-6s
Bob Latchford interview, Toffee TV
https://www.youtube.com/watch?v=ankvknRTShQ
Everton v Liverpool, 28 October 1978
https://www.youtube.com/watch?v=nwzflFV3wyA&t=641s
TalkSport: Andy King remembers his famous goal for Everton in the Merseyside derby at Goodison Park in October 1978
http://talksport.com/radio/richard-keys-and-andy-gray/121026/andy-king-remembers-his-merseyside-derby-stunner-1978-183915
FA Cup fourth round, Everton v Liverpool, 24 January 1981

https://www.youtube.com/watch?v=Jn3duscRVgo

League Cup quarter-final, Oxford United v Everton, 18 January 1984

https://www.youtube.com/watch?v=GTgDZLaDNek

FA Cup semi-final, Everton v Southampton, 14 April 1984

https://www.youtube.com/watch?v=UlYeLDFiGrA

Liverpool v Everton, 20 October 1984

https://www.youtube.com/watch?v=abt9B8DWgWA&t=3s

Everton v Manchester United, 27 October 1984

https://www.youtube.com/watch?v=1B2keCsMM3g

Everton v QPR, 6 May 1985

https://www.youtube.com/watch?v=avY3oBQOof4

Cup Winners' Cup semi-final, second leg, Everton v Bayern Munich, 24 April 1985

https://www.youtube.com/watch?v=UtZyEvdDhMU

Cup Winners' Cup Final, Everton v Rapid Vienna, 15 May 1985

https://www.youtube.com/watch?v=1oBKT7v1-lQ

FA Cup semi-final, Everton v Tottenham, 9 April 1995

https://www.youtube.com/watch?v=515QJhovCvw

FA Cup Final, Everton v Manchester United, 20 May 1995

https://www.youtube.com/watch?v=Hz8iYjI25So

Everton v Coventry City, 10 May 1998

https://www.youtube.com/watch?v=TKUFQ7NSdNA

Everton v Arsenal, 19 October 2002

https://www.youtube.com/watch?v=E4dBWUjuCU0&t=16s

UEFA Cup, round of 16, Everton v Fiorentina, 12 March 2008

https://www.youtube.com/watch?v=yghfGTKNYdE

Everton v Manchester United, 4 December 2013

https://www.youtube.com/watch?v=hi1hs4MTyJM